THE REFORMATION OF MORALS

Yaḥyā ibn ʿAdī

The Reformation of Morals

A parallel Arabic-English text
translated and introduced by
Sidney H. Griffith

Brigham Young University Press • Provo, Utah • 2002

LIBRARY OF CONGRESS CATALOGING-IN-PUBLICATION DATA

Yaḥyā ibn ʿAdī, ca. 893–974.
[Tahdhīb al-akhlāq. English & Arabic]
The reformation of morals : a parallel English-Arabic text / Yaḥyā ibn ʿAdī ; translated and introduced by Sidney H. Griffith.
p. cm.—(Eastern Christian texts ; 1)
Includes bibliographical references and index.
ISBN 0–934893–69–1 (alk. paper)
1. Christian ethics—Jacobite authors. I. Griffith, Sidney Harrison. II. Title. III. Eastern Christian texts (Provo, Utah) ; 1.
BJ1250.5.Y34 2002
241′.04163—dc21 2002013257

PRINTED IN THE UNITED STATES OF AMERICA

02 03 04 05 06 07 08 9 8 7 6 5 4 3 2 1

First Edition

Contents

The Reformation of Morals

Abbreviations

AHDL	*Archives d'histoire doctrinale et littéraire du moyen-âge*
AJSL	*American Journal of Semitic Languages and Literature*
BACh	*Bulletin d'arabe chrétien*
BEO	*Bulletin d'études orientales de l'Institut Français de Damas*
BJRL	*Bulletin of the John Rylands University Library of Manchester*
BMus	Bibliothèque du Muséon
BPhL	Bibliothèque philosophique de Louvain
BSPh	Bochumer Studien zur Philosophie
CSCO	Corpus scriptorum christianorum orientalium
CStS	Variorum Reprints Collected Studies Series
EI²	*The Encyclopaedia of Islam: New Edition* (ed. H. A. R. Gibb)
EtMu	Études musulmanes
JRAS	*Journal of the Royal Asiatic Society*
JSS	*Journal of Semitic Studies*
MIDEO	*Mélanges de l'Institut Dominicain d'Études Orientales du Caire*
Mus	*Muséon*
OCA	Orientalia christiana analecta
OLA	Orientalia lovaniensia analecta
OrChr	*Oriens christianus*
OrSyr	*L'Orient syrien*
PAC	Patrimoine arabe chrétien
POC	*Proche-Orient chrétien*
QSA	*Quaderni di studi arabi*
RMet	*Review of Metaphysics*
ROC	*Revue de l'Orient chrétien*
SHR	Studies in the History of Religions
SOC.C	*Studia orientalia christiana. Collectanea*
StOC	Studies in Oriental Culture
StT	Studi e testi
UCOP	University of Cambridge Oriental Publications
VivPen	*Vivre et penser*
ZDMG	*Zeitschrift der deutschen morgenländischen Gesellschaft*
ZGAIW	*Zeitschrift für Geschichte der arabisch-islamischen Wissenschaften*

Foreword

The Institute for the Study and Preservation of Ancient Religious Texts at Brigham Young University is pleased to present the first volume of its EASTERN CHRISTIAN TEXTS series. It is a double delight to present such an important translation by so qualified a translator. Professor Sidney Griffith has distinguished himself as one of the foremost scholars of Arabic and Syriac Christianity. His generosity in contributing the opening volume to this series is just one instance of his continual solicitude for EASTERN CHRISTIAN TEXTS and its editors. His choice of author and work for translation could not be more suitable or timely, for Yaḥyā ibn ʿAdī and *The Reformation of Morals* speak to some of the most pressing modern religious needs. In Yaḥyā's integrated society, Christians and Muslims engaged in a vigorous intellectual and cultural exchange that fostered understanding and growth. While he wrote passionately in defense of his Christian faith, Yaḥyā was also eager to promote universal truth in the interfaith idiom of philosophy and ethics. He accomplished this most admirably in *The Reformation of Morals,* a work of such high and broad regard that it has been misattributed to both Christian and Muslim authors. Perhaps Yaḥyā would not have been displeased at this. His love of truth was ecumenical in every sense.

This work also reflects the goals and interfaith context of EASTERN CHRISTIAN TEXTS. In 1997, Brigham Young University's Middle Eastern Texts Initiative published the first volume in its Islamic Translation Series. This series met with immediate success and gave rise to a corresponding series to publish works from the Eastern Christian traditions. The proximate goal of these series is to provide high-quality bilingual editions of important ancient religious and philosophical texts. Their ultimate goal is to promote scholarship, understanding, and dialogue, and the values and truths that these texts embody.

Eastern Christian Texts benefits from the expertise of an international advisory board of distinguished scholars whom we wish to thank for their support and advice. Our deepest gratitude is also due those benefactors whose financial support has made this series possible, especially to Brigham Young University and its sponsor, the Church of Jesus Christ of Latter-day Saints. The resources they have dedicated to this endeavor are an expression of their esteem for these texts and for the faith traditions they represent.

—Daniel C. Peterson
Carl W. Griffin
Kristian S. Heal

Preface

Arabic-speaking Christians like Yaḥyā ibn ᶜAdī played a significant role in the translation movement in Baghdad in the ninth and tenth Christian centuries, bringing the Greek classics of science and philosophy into the world of Islam. The movement was a major component of the then burgeoning classical culture of the Islamic world. For translation brings not only texts from one cultural milieu to another, but new ideas and attitudes that stimulate and shape the intellectual life of the world into which they come. Translation also tends to promote tolerance because peoples of diverse ideas and backgrounds are necessarily involved in it. By participating in the translation movement, among other enterprises, Christian scholars and intellectuals in tenth-century Baghdad helped to bring about a measure of tolerance and humane regard in the interreligious affairs of the dominantly Muslim world of the early Islamic commonwealth.

Translation also promotes originality. Because of his love of philosophy and his trust in reason, arguably instilled in him by the very works he translated, Yaḥyā ibn ᶜAdī, like other Christian writers of Arabic in his era, composed works that made the best use possible of the cultural riches the translations provided. He used what they offered to defend the reasonableness of his Christian faith in the Islamic milieu of the world in which he lived, and even to make a modest contribution to philosophical thought in the Aristotelian tradition. Yaḥyā went still further. He wrote a small book that commends humane values in those who would follow the philosophical way of life in an interreligious polity that, within his purview, included those who frequented both mosques and churches. The work now goes under the title it bears here: *The Reformation of Morals*. It is significant that over the centuries the work has been esteemed by both Muslims and Christians.

Yaḥyā's *Reformation of Morals* is not without its limitations. In it the author fails to take into consideration the broader spectrum of the interreligious life of his own time and place. Jewish, Christian, and Muslim populations, along with some others, made up the broad community of the "People of the Book" that the Qur'ān recognizes; Yaḥyā alludes only to Christians and Muslims. He pays no attention at all to non-biblical religious communities. In the world of which he speaks, only men seem to have the potential for full humanity; women are spoken of only in terms of a lesser potential. Philosophically, Yaḥyā's work lacks the intellectual acuity and development to be found in the ethical writings of other scholars in his time, like his teacher al-Fārābī. Yaḥyā writes in a more popular and didactic vein. Nevertheless, *The Reformation of Morals* may be viewed as a philosophically well-informed essay on moral improvement in an "Islamochristian" context that was heir to the religious and philosophical traditions of late antiquity. Its success in its own Arabic-speaking milieu over the centuries can help remind the postmodern reader that shared moral values nurtured by a humane philosophy of human development can foster the growth of a measure of tolerance between the upholders of religious convictions that are inherently critical of one another.

Translation is often a lonely and frustrating task, but the translator is never without a community of supporters. In the present instance, thanks are due to Daniel Peterson, Kristian Heal, Carl Griffin, Morgan Davis, Brian Hauglid, Muhammad Eissa, and the staff of Brigham Young University's Middle Eastern Texts Initiative; their encouragement and timely advice made the English translation of Yaḥyā ibn ʿAdī's *The Reformation of Morals* a possibility. Peter Starr and Bo Holmberg saved the translator from many infelicities of expression and outright errors in translation; they have his profound gratitude. Monica J. Blanchard and Thérèse-Anne Druart, among other colleagues at The Catholic University of America, provided much bibliographical and scholarly support; public thanks are too small a recompense for their help. Finally, thanks be to the doyen of Arab Christian studies in our time, Samir Khalil Samir, S.J., for the superb edition of the Arabic text of *The Reformation of Morals* republished here, from which the English translation has been made.

—Sidney H. Griffith
The Catholic University of America
Washington, D.C.
30 June 2002

Introduction

Yaḥyā ibn ᶜAdī (893–974 C.E.),[1] whose full name is Abū Zakariyyā Yaḥyā ibn ᶜAdī ibn Ḥamīd ibn Zakariyyā al-Takrītī al-Manṭiqī, was a Syrian Orthodox or "Jacobite" Christian who was born in the city of Takrīt in Iraq. As a young man he moved to Baghdad, where he studied with Abū Bishr Mattā ibn Yūnus (ca. 870–ca. 940), the philosopher from the Church of the East,[2] and with the famous Muslim philosopher Abū Naṣr al-Fārābī (ca. 870–950). By the mid-940s Yaḥyā had become a major figure in a new generation of intellectuals in Baghdad. While he earned his living as a professional scribe, he was also for a while one of the leading exponents of the Peripatetic school of thought in the caliph's capital city.[3] He attracted numerous disciples, both Christian and Muslim, not a few of whom went on to become eminent scholars in their own right. Because of this obviously successful scholarly career, Yaḥyā and his circle of intellectual associates have come to be seen by later historians as important participants in the cultural

1. For pre-1970 discussions of Yaḥyā and his works in the standard reference sources for Arab Christian studies, see Georg Graf, *Die Philosophie und Gotteslehre des Jaḥjâ ibn ᶜAdî und späterer Autoren: Skizzen nach meist ungedruckten Quellen* (Münster: Aschendorffschen Buchhandlung, 1910); Augustin Périer, *Yaḥyā ben ᶜAdî: Un philosophe arabe chrétien du Xᵉ siècle* (Paris: Gabalda & Geuthner, 1920); Georg Graf, *Geschichte der christlichen arabischen Literatur* (vol. 2; StT 133; Vatican City: Biblioteca Apostolica Vaticana, 1947), 233–49.

2. Abū Bishr is normally described as a "Nestorian," an adjective of opprobrium used in his own day by the theological adversaries of his community as well as by Muslim writers. It seems best to avoid it in modern scholarly discussion. See Sebastian P. Brock, "The 'Nestorian' Church: A Lamentable Misnomer," *BJRL* 78 (1996): 23–35.

3. See F. E. Peters, *Aristotle and the Arabs: The Aristotelian Tradition in Islam* (New York: New York University Press, 1968), 160–63.

revival during the Buyid age that Joel Kraemer has described as the humanistic renaissance of Islam in its fourth century.[4] And it is for this reason as well that bibliographers both medieval and modern have made every effort to keep track of Yaḥyā's works. In the tenth century his friend, the Muslim bio-bibliographer Muḥammad ibn Isḥāq ibn al-Nadīm (d. 995), recorded his accomplishments in his famous *Fihrist,* and in 1977 Gerhard Endress published an analytical inventory of all the known works of Yaḥyā ibn ᶜAdī.[5]

I
Yaḥyā ibn ᶜAdī *al-Takrītī*[6]

By Yaḥyā ibn ᶜAdī's day, Takrīt in Iraq, located approximately midway along the Tigris River between Baghdad and Mosul, had long been an intellectual and spiritual center of the Jacobite church. Here was the seat of the *maphriān,* since the seventh century the hierarch in charge of Jacobite church affairs in the Persian territories beyond the frontier of the Roman Empire.[7] Nearby was the monastery of Mar Mattai, with its well-known library, an intellectual resource that seems to have served the needs of the entire Syriac-speaking community without regard for denominational identity. In the late eighth century, Catholicos/Patriarch Timothy I (d. 823) of the Church of the East in

4. See Joel L. Kraemer, *Humanism in the Renaissance of Islam: The Cultural Revival during the Buyid Age* (Leiden: Brill, 1986), 104–39. For a brief survey of the Christian participants in this earlier renaissance in the world of Islam, see Khalil Samir, "Rôle des chrétiens dans les renaissances arabes," *Annales de philosophie de l'Université Saint-Joseph* 6 (1985): 1–31.

5. See Bayard Dodge, ed. and trans., *The Fihrist of al-Nadīm: A Tenth-Century Survey of Muslim Culture* (2 vols.; New York: Columbia University Press, 1970), 2:631–32, and *sub nomine;* Gerhard Endress, *The Works of Yaḥyā ibn ᶜAdī: An Analytical Inventory* (Wiesbaden: Dr. Ludwig Reichert Verlag, 1977). See also the important additions and corrections to Endress's *Inventory* in the review by Samir Khalil, "Yaḥyā ibn ᶜAdī (893–974)," *BACh* 3 (1979): 45–63.

6. There is some variation in the sources regarding the *nisbah* of Yaḥyā ibn ᶜAdī. Since Bar Hebraeus, himself from Takrīt and, like Yaḥyā, a Jacobite, assigns him the toponymic *al-Takrītī,* one may be confident that it is likely to be correct. See Gérard Troupeau, "Quelle était la *nisba* de Yaḥyā ibn ᶜAdī?" *Arabica* 41 (1994): 416–18.

7. See J. M. Fiey, "Tagrît: Esquisse d'histoire chrétienne," *OrSyr* 8 (1963): 289–342; repr. in *Communautés syriaques en Iran et Irak dès origines à 1552* (CStS 106; London: Variorum Reprints, 1979).

a letter requests his correspondent Mar Pethion to look for a number of books for him in the library of the monastery of Mar Mattai.[8]

Also natives of Takrīt were Ḥabīb ibn Khidmah Abū Rāʾiṭah (d. before 850)[9] and his nephew, Nonnus of Nisibis (d. after 862),[10] two of the earliest Jacobite intellectuals to engage in the apologetical effort to defend the Christian faith from the religious challenges of Islam. Abū Rāʾiṭah, the first Jacobite we know by name to write Christian theology in Arabic, was in all probability a layman, a *malpōnô* or "teacher," whose role in the community was both to teach Syriac and to function as a catechist, an exegete, and a professional theologian.[11] In his Arabic letters and treatises he wrote to rebut both the theological claims of the Melkites and specifically those of their champion in Arabic, Theodore Abū Qurrah (ca. 755–ca. 830),[12] as well as the Muslim *mutakallimūn* (theologians) of the day who questioned Christian doctrines.[13] Nonnus, who was a deacon, wrote in both Syriac and Arabic. He instructed Syriac-speaking Christians in ways to respond to questions from Muslims about religion, and he commented on important

8. See Timothy's Letter 43, the Syriac text of which is still unpublished, in Vat. Syr. 605, fol. 303v. See also Oskar Braun, "Briefe des Katholikos Timotheos I," *OrChr* 2 (1902): 1–32. On Timothy's role in the translation movement, see Sebastian P. Brock, "Two Letters of the Patriarch Timothy from the Late Eighth Century on Translations from Greek," *Arabic Sciences and Philosophy* 9 (1999): 233–46.

9. See Georg Graf, *Die Schriften des Jacobiten Ḥabīb ibn Ḫidma Abū Rāʾiṭa* (CSCO 130–31; Louvain: Peeters, 1951). See also Sandra Toenies Keating, "Dialogue between Muslims and Christians in the Early 9th Century: The Example of Ḥabīb ibn Khidmah Abū Rāʾiṭah al-Takrītī's Theology of the Trinity," (Ph.D. diss., The Catholic University of America, 2001).

10. See Albert van Roey, *Nonnus de Nisibe, Traité apologétique: Étude, texte et traduction* (BMus 21; Louvain: Peeters, 1948); Sidney H. Griffith, "The Apologetic Treatise of Nonnus of Nisibis," *ARAM* 3 (1991): 115–38.

11. See Keating, "Dialogue," 30–33. Keating rightly points to the parallel between the role of the *malpōnô* in the Syriac-speaking community and that of the *vardapet* in the Armenian community. See Robert W. Thomson, "*Vardapet* in the Early Armenian Church," *Mus* 75 (1962): 367–82.

12. See Sidney H. Griffith, "Reflections on the Biography of Theodore Abū Qurrah," *ParOr* 18 (1993): 143–70.

13. See Seppo Rissanen, *Theological Encounter of Oriental Christians with Islam during Early Abbasid Rule* (Åbo: Åbo Akademi University Press, 1993); Sidney H. Griffith, "'Melkites', 'Jacobites' and the Christological Controversies in Arabic in Third/Ninth-Century Syria," in *Syrian Christians under Islam: The First Thousand Years* (ed. David Thomas; Leiden: Brill, 2001), 9–55.

parts of the scriptures in Arabic, in response to challenges from both Christian and Muslim adversaries.[14]

Members of the large Syriac-speaking Christian families, not only from the environs of Takrīt, but from throughout Iraq, particularly those who were members of the Church of the East, became prominent in the ninth and tenth centuries as physicians, often serving in the caliph's court.[15] Others, often with ties to particular monastic communities, like the families of Dayr Qunnā on the lower Tigris, became professional scribes and administrators who exercised a considerable influence in Islamic society for several generations.[16] Finally, one must mention the numerous Christians in Baghdad and its environs of all three main denominations, the Melkites, Jacobites, and members of the Church of the East, who were actively engaged from the late eighth century in the translation movement that was to play so significant a role in the formation of classical Islamic intellectual culture.[17] Yaḥyā was destined to join their number.

Yaḥyā ibn ʿAdī had his family origins in this milieu of Christian intellectual cultivation in Takrīt, and elsewhere in Iraq, in the late ninth century.[18] We know next to nothing about his personal life except that he must have been a married layman, like Abū Rāʾiṭah in the previous century; he had a son named Zachary, as we learn from his *kunyā* (surname), Abū Zakariyyā. Also like Abū Rāʾiṭah, he may have been a "teacher" *(malpōnô)* in the Syrian Orthodox community. As a young

14. See van Roey, *Nonnus de Nisibe,* and Griffith, "Apologetic Treatise."

15. See Dimitri Gutas, *Greek Thought, Arabic Culture: The Graeco-Arabic Translation Movement in Baghdad and Early ʿAbbasid Society (2nd–4th/8th–10th Centuries)* (London: Routledge, 1998), 118–19, 131–33. See also George Saliba, "Competition and the Transmission of the Foreign Sciences: Ḥunayn at the Abbasid Court," *Bulletin of the Royal Institute for Inter-Faith Studies* 2 (2000): 85–101.

16. See Louis Massignon, "La politique islamo-chrétienne des scribes nestoriens de Deir Qunna à la cour de Bagdad au IXe siècle de notre ère," *VivPen* 2 (1942): 7–14; repr. in *Opera Minora* (ed. Youakim Moubarac; 3 vols.; Beirut: Dar al-Maaref, 1963), 1:250–57. Yaḥyā ibn ʿAdī had at least one student from the Ibn al-Jarrāḥ family from Dayr Qunnā. See Gutas, *Greek Thought,* 72–73, 73 n. 23, 132.

17. See Gutas, *Greek Thought,* esp. 131–33.

18. The best and most complete biographical sketch of Yaḥyā, with a survey of all the sources Christian and Islamic, is in Emilio Platti, *Yaḥyā ibn ʿAdī, théologien chrétien et philosophe arabe: Sa théologie de l'Incarnation* (OLA 14; Leuven: Katholieke Universiteit Leuven, Departement Oriëntalistiek, 1983), 1–53.

man Yaḥyā went to Baghdad to study under the renowned philosopher al-Fārābī (870–950) and under al-Fārābī's teacher, Abū Bishr Mattā ibn Yūnus (d. 940), a member of the Church of the East who is often credited as the founder of the Aristotelian school of Baghdad.[19]

Yaḥyā seems to have spent the rest of his life in Baghdad. He served there as a scribe and bookman, a translator, an Aristotelian philosopher, an apologist for Christian doctrines and practices, and, of course, as a teacher. Like his contemporary Ibn al-Nadīm, professionally he was a copyist and a bookseller. Some sources wrongly claim he was a physician. Anecdotes about him are found in a number of early works, both Islamic and Christian.[20] But by all accounts Yaḥyā was mainly concerned with books; he searched them out relentlessly, bought them, sold them, and copied them. According to Ibn al-Nadīm, Yaḥyā himself said he had copied al-Ṭabarī's complete Qurʾān commentary two times and that it was his practice to copy a hundred leaves every day and night.[21] But Yaḥyā's passion was for books of logic and philosophy; he not only searched for them and copied them, but he translated them from Syriac into Arabic. In this enterprise he followed in the footsteps of a number of Christian predecessors, whose work he often corrected and revised.[22]

As a teacher Yaḥyā ibn ʿAdī spoke and wrote on a number of topics, mostly philosophical and Aristotelian, but also theological and moral. So influential did he become in his time that modern scholars still recognize him as the "head of the Baghdad Aristotelians in the mid-tenth

---

19. See Gutas, *Greek Thought,* 132.

20. See Platti, *Yaḥyā ibn ʿAdī,* 1–53, and Kraemer, *Humanism,* 104–16.

21. See Dodge, *Fihrist of al-Nadīm,* 2:631.

22. For a survey of Yaḥyā's Christian predecessors in the translation movement, see Henri Hugonnard-Roche, "Les traductions du grec au syriaque et du syriaque à l'arabe (à propos de l'*Organon* d'Aristote)," in *Rencontres de cultures dans la philosophie médiévale: Traductions et traducteurs de l'antiquité tardive au XIVe siècle* (ed. Jacqueline Hamesse and Marta Fattori; Louvain-la-Neuve: Université Catholique de Louvain, 1990), 131–47; idem, "L'intermédiaire syriaque dans la transmission de la philosophie grecque à l'arabe: Le cas de l'*Organon* d'Aristote," *Arabic Sciences and Philosophy* 1 (1991): 187–209; Sebastian P. Brock, "The Syriac Commentary Tradition," in *Glosses and Commentaries on Aristotelian Logical Texts: The Syriac, Arabic and Medieval Latin Traditions* (ed. Charles Burnett; London: Warburg Institute, 1993), 3–18; Ephrem-Isa Yousif, *Les philosophes et traducteurs syriaques: D'Athènes à Bagdad* (Paris: Harmattan, 1997). See also the important study of Bénédicte Landron, "Les chrétiens arabes et les disciplines philosophiques," *POC* 36 (1986): 23–45.

century."[23] And in that capacity circles of students and colleagues, both Muslims and Christians, carried on in his tradition after his death.[24] It is especially interesting in this connection to notice what one might call the "ecumenical" character of Yaḥyā's entourage. Not only was it interreligious, in that Muslims and Christians freely intermingled in the pursuit of philosophical knowledge, but from the Christian perspective it was interdenominational as well; Melkites, Jacobites, and members of the Church of the East can all be found among Yaḥyā's associates. Together these Christian and Muslim scholars participated in producing the intellectual culture of the classical period in Islam.

Yaḥyā ibn ᶜAdī died on 13 August 974. He was buried in the church of St. Thomas, in the Daqīq quarter of Baghdad. The inscription on his tomb survives, preserved by the Muslim biographer of famous physicians, Ibn Abī Uṣaybiᶜah. It was inscribed on Yaḥyā's commission by one of his students, his fellow Jacobite Abū ᶜAlī ᶜĪsā ibn Zurᶜa (943–1008), a famous scholar in his own right.[25] The text highlights Yaḥyā's devotion to "knowledge" *(ᶜilm);* it gives the following advice:

> Many a dead man lives on through knowledge,
> while one left behind is dead of ignorance and fecklessness.
> Acquire knowledge to attain immortality;
> do not reckon life in ignorance to be worth anything.[26]

II
Yaḥyā ibn ᶜAdī *al-Manṭiqī*

Yaḥyā's devotion to knowledge and philosophy is what has earned him a reputation among many modern scholars who have been preoccupied with the study of how the Greek sciences passed to the Arabs. As the epithet *al-manṭiqī,* "the logician," implies, Yaḥyā came from within an intellectual tradition that had already cultivated an intense interest

23. Gutas, *Greek Thought,* 101.

24. See Kraemer, *Humanism,* 116–39. See also Ian Richard Netton, *Al-Fārābī and His School* (Richmond, Eng.: Curzon, 1992).

25. See Cyrille Haddad, *ᶜIsa ibn Zurᶜa: Philosophe arabe et apologiste chrétien* (Beirut: Dar al-Kalima, 1971); Kraemer, *Humanism,* 116–23.

26. Aḥmad ibn al-Qāsim ibn Abī Uṣaybiᶜah, *Kitab ᶜuyūn al-anbaʾ fī ṭabaqāt al-aṭibbāʾ* (ed. August Müller; 2 vols.; Cairo & Köningsberg: n.p., 1882–84), 1:235. See Kraemer, *Humanism,* 106.

in Greek logical texts, particularly those based on the logical works of Aristotle and Porphyry's *Isagoge.* This was the so-called "Graeco-Syrian logical curriculum of late antiquity," to borrow a phrase from Dimitri Gutas.[27] Already in pre-Islamic times Syriac-speaking Christians had cultivated this and other aspects of Greek science and philosophy in their schools, both for their own sakes and as aids in the exposition and defense of the several Christian theological allegiances.[28] From his position within this tradition and its extension into the era of the Graeco-Arabic translation movement in the Islamic milieu in which he lived, Yaḥyā ibn ᶜAdī was thus well prepared for a scholarly career. Like his master al-Fārābī, he made logic the substrate of all his other inquiries.[29]

As just a brief review of his bibliography shows, Yaḥyā was much involved with both Aristotle's *Topics* and his *Physics,* the two works that Dimitri Gutas has identified as of crucial interest in what he calls "the exigencies of inter-faith discourse" in the era of the translation movement.[30] As for the *Topics,* which teaches the ways of dispute and dialectic, Yaḥyā was one of several who at sundry times translated it into Arabic; he worked from Isḥāq ibn Ḥunayn's earlier Syriac version.[31] Yaḥyā's interest in the subject matter of the *Physics* is evident in the numerous treatises on various aspects of the study of its contents that can be found in his bibliography. In all his work on these topics he seems to have stayed close to the teaching of Aristotle and his Alexandrian interpreters, a circumstance that earned him some obloquy in later years, when later Muslim philosophers such as Ibn Sīnā (d. 1037) and others voiced their disdain for the work of those they viewed as the staid and unadventuresome Aristotelians of Baghdad.[32]

---

27. Gutas, *Greek Thought,* 62.

28. In this connection one might call attention to the work of the Jacobite Sergius of Resh ᶜAynâ (d. 536) and Paul the Persian (fl. 531–578) of the Church of the East. See Dimitri Gutas, "Paul the Persian on the Classification of the Parts of Aristotle's Philosophy: A Milestone between Alexandria and Bagdad," *Der Islam* 60 (1983): 231–67, and Henri Hugonnard-Roche, "Notes sur Sergius de Rešᶜainā, traducteur du grec en syriaque et commentateur d'Aristote," in *The Ancient Tradition in Christian and Islamic Hellenism* (ed. Gerhard Endress and Remke Kruk; CNWS Publications 50; Leiden: Research School CNWS, 1997), 121–43.

29. See Netton, *Al-Fārābī,* 56.

30. Gutas, *Greek Thought,* 61–74.

31. See ibid., 61.

32. See Shlomo Pines, "La 'philosophie orientale' d'Avicenne et sa polémique contre les Bagdadiens," *AHDL* 27 (1952): 5–37; H.V. B. Brown, "Avicenna and

The enterprise of Yaḥyā ibn ᶜAdī and others to promote the Greek sciences in the Arabic-speaking world of Islam introduced something of an epistemological crisis into the world of the contemporary practitioners of the Islamic religious sciences. Yaḥyā and the philosophers presented the claims of reason in the idiom of the translated, universal (so they claimed) sciences of the Greeks over against the doctrines of the more conventional, Arabic-speaking religious teachers. In Yaḥyā's day, these Muslim teachers were themselves divided into those who championed the exclusive authority of tradition in religious matters and those who allowed a measure of authority to the claims of human reason.[33] The latter were the Muslim *mutakallimūn,* who had built their systems of thought on the rules of theoretical Arabic grammar.[34] A particularly striking instance of the clash between the points of view of the philosophers and the *mutakallimūn* can be seen in the report by one of Yaḥyā's Muslim students, Abū Ḥayyān al-Tawḥīdī (d. 1023),[35] on the debate held in the year 932 between Yaḥyā's teacher, the logician Abū Bishr Mattā ibn Yūnus, and the Muslim theologian and jurist, Abū Saᶜīd al-Sīrāfī.[36] Meanwhile, Yaḥyā himself participated in the larger controversy on the same subject; he wrote a treatise that upholds the views of the logicians and the philosophers against those of the

---

the Christian Philosophers in Baghdad," in *Islamic Philosophy and the Classical Tradition: Essays Presented by His Friends and Pupils to Richard Walzer on His Seventieth Birthday* (ed. S. M. Stern, Albert H. Hourani, and Vivian Brown; Columbia: University of South Carolina Press, 1972), 35–48; Dimitri Gutas, *Avicenna and the Aristotelian Tradition* (Leiden: Brill, 1988), 64–72.

33. See Binyamin Abrahamov, *Islamic Theology: Traditionalism and Rationalism* (Edinburgh: Edinburgh University Press, 1998).

34. See, for example, the Muᶜtazilī system described by Richard M. Frank, *Beings and Their Attributes: The Teaching of the Basrian School of the Muᶜtazila in the Classical Period* (Albany: State University of New York Press, 1978); idem, "The Science of Kalām," *Arabic Sciences and Philosophy* 2 (1992): 9–37.

35. Concerning whom see Kraemer, *Humanism,* 212–22.

36. See D. S. Margoliouth, "The Discussion between Abū Bishr Mattā and Abū Saᶜīd al-Sīrāfī," *JRAS* (1905): 79–129; Muhsin Mahdi, "Language and Logic in Classical Islam," in *Logic in Classical Islamic Culture* (ed. G. E. von Grunebaum; Wiesbaden: Harrassowitz, 1970), 51–83; Gerhard Endress, "The Debate between Arabic Grammar and Greek Logic in Classical Islamic Thought," *Journal for the History of Arabic Science* [Aleppo] 1 (1977): 320–23, 339–51; idem, "Grammatik und Logik: Arabische Philologie und griechische Philosophie im Widerstreit," in *Sprachphilosophie in Antike und Mittelalter* (ed. Burkhard Mojsisch; BSPh 3; Amsterdam: Gruner, 1986), 163–299.

mutakallimūn.[37] He also sometimes wrote on topics of direct interest to the *mutakallimūn,* in which writings he took issue with them. An example is a text in which Yaḥyā refutes the position of an Ashᶜarite theologian on the subject of *al-iktisāb* (acquisition), a theory elaborated by some thinkers of this school in an effort to escape from between the logical horns of the dilemma posed by the partisans of free will versus predestination.[38] Finally, in this connection, there is a report in the *Muntakhab ṣiwān al-ḥikmah* of Abū Sulaymān al-Sijistānī (d. ca. 985),[39] another Muslim student of Yaḥyā ibn ᶜAdī, about an occasion when in a *majlis* (session) Yaḥyā pointedly questioned the significance of the terms *kalām* (speech, theology) and *mutakallim* (speaker, theologian) as they were customarily used to mean only the adepts of religious thought. With some evident sarcasm, he asked, did not the devotees of other disciplines also speak?[40]

In view of the clash between the philosopher-logicians and the *mutakallimūn* in the ninth and tenth centuries in the Arabic-speaking scholarly milieu of Baghdad, many modern commentators have argued that for the philosophers in that milieu, including Yaḥyā ibn ᶜAdī, the use of reason was deemed superior to religion in the search for the answers to life's ultimate questions. In this connection Dimitri Gutas has written, "Just as logic is superior to grammar in that it is universal and supralingual—so Abū Bishr Mattā's and Yaḥyā's argument in defense of logic ran—so also is philosophy, the use of reason, superior to religion in that it is universal and supranational (since each nation has its own religion)."[41] For Joel Kraemer, this view was a basic tenet of the philosophic humanism of the renaissance of Islam in the Buyid period, and he goes on to say that "the chief architects of this philosophic humanism in our period were the Christian philosopher Yaḥyā b. ᶜAdī and his immediate disciples."[42] For Kraemer, Yaḥyā was "first

37. The treatise is published by Gerhard Endress, "Yaḥyā ibn ᶜAdī: Maqāla fī tabyīn al-faṣl bayna ṣināᶜat al-manṭiq al-falsafī wa al-naḥw al-ᶜarabī," *Journal for the History of Arabic Science* [Aleppo] 2 (1978): 181–93.

38. See Shlomo Pines and Michael Schwarz, "Yaḥyā ibn ᶜAdī's Refutation of the Doctrine of Acquisition *(iktisāb),*" in *Studia orientalia memoriae D. H. Baneth dedicata* (Jerusalem: Magnes Press, Hebrew University of Jerusalem, 1979), 49–94, esp. 62–68.

39. See Kraemer, *Humanism,* 139–65.

40. See Platti, *Yaḥyā ibn ᶜAdī,* 12.

41. Gutas, *Greek Thought,* 103.

42. Kraemer, *Humanism,* 6.

and foremost a philosopher,"[43] even in his theological treatises. And he goes so far as to say the following:

> In consistency with Alfarabi's philosophy of religion, according to which religious motifs are symbols of philosophical truths, Ibn ᶜAdī treated theological notions as embodiments of philosophical concepts. . . . He interprets the persons of the Trinity as symbolic representations of Aristotelian ideas: the Father symbolizes the intellect, the Son symbolizes the intellectually cognizing subject, and the Spirit symbolizes the intellectually cognized object.[44]

Clearly, Kraemer holds the view that for Yaḥyā knowledge is better than belief. This idea, expressed by some philosophers in the Aristotelian tradition to which Yaḥyā ibn ᶜAdī belonged, that knowledge is better than belief, can be traced back in the tradition beyond the debate between the philosophers and the Muslim *mutakallimūn* of the tenth century. In the Christian philosophical milieu, it can be found already in the work of the "Nestorian" Paul the Persian in the sixth century.[45] But the question now is, was this truly Yaḥyā's view, even if it can be shown to have been adopted by his master al-Fārābī[46] and seemingly defended even by Abū Bishr Mattā ibn Yūnus? After all, as Dimitri Gutas states, in the Aristotelian logical tradition cultivated in the Syriac schools prior to the time of Islam, "Paul was somewhat of a maverick," who had in fact converted from Christianity to Zoroastrianism at the court of Khusrau Anūshirwân.[47] And in Yaḥyā's day it was the Muslim *mutakallimūn,* the partisans of their own brand of grammatical "rationalism," who were discomfited by the claims of Aristotelian logic. Furthermore, Muslim scholars in general, already since the time of Abū Yūsuf Yaʾqūb ibn Isḥāq al-Kindī (d. 870), were seriously challenged by the seeming conflict between the rival claims

43. Ibid., 106–7.

44. Ibid., 107.

45. See Gutas, "Paul the Persian," 247–49, 254.

46. On this subject al-Fārābī's views are highly nuanced. See now the sensitive study of them by Muhsin S. Mahdi, *Alfarabi and the Foundation of Islamic Political Philosophy* (Chicago: University of Chicago Press, 2001), esp. 208–28. Mahdi writes of al-Fārābī that "what he plans to teach philosophers of his time and his coreligionists is that their religion consists of similitudes of true philosophy" (221). Mahdi makes no mention at all of Yaḥyā ibn ᶜAdī in this book.

47. Gutas, "Paul the Persian," 250.

of reason and revelation precipitated by the translation of Aristotelian logical texts into Arabic.[48]

However, for the Christian theologians of that era, Aristotelian logic had by way of contrast long been an auxiliary discipline. Yaḥyā and the other Christian apologists, like Ḥunayn ibn Isḥāq in the preceding century, were thinking and writing within a tradition that had long since learned to present the claims of their religious convictions in the Greek idiom of Aristotelian logic, even when translated into Syriac or Arabic. What is more, the doctrinal positions that Yaḥyā and the other Christians defended in Syriac or Arabic were themselves initially formulated in Greek philosophical and logical terms. They were constantly being defended by appeal to the logical requirements of the proper definitions of the originally Greek terms, even in their Syriac and Arabic versions. This agenda was still the operative one in the ninth and tenth centuries, in response to the religious claims of Islam, when the challenge for Christians was not so much reason versus revelation, but the development of an appropriately logical and philosophical, not to say theological, vocabulary in Arabic. And it is from this perspective that a thinker like Yaḥyā ibn ᶜAdī would have found the categories of the philosophers far more congenial for his religious, apologetical purposes in Arabic than the methods of the Islamic *mutakallimūn,* although some of his fellow Arab Christian apologists in the previous century did in fact develop what can plausibly be called a Christian *ᶜilm al-kalām* (science of theology) to meet the same challenges.[49] Therefore, it does not seem convincing to claim, along with Joel Kraemer and Dimitri Gutas, that Yaḥyā's interest in logic and philosophy, that is to say, his cultivation of reason, supplanted his devotion to revelation, or that he thought of his "theological notions as embodiments of philosophical concepts."[50] After all, on the religious front Yaḥyā's

48. See Richard M. Frank, "Reason and Revealed Law: A Sample of Parallels and Divergences in Kalâm and Falsafa," in *Recherches d'Islamologie: Recueil d'articles offerts à G. Anawati et L. Gardet par leurs collègues et amis* (BPhL 26; Louvain: Peeters, 1977), 123–38; Gerhard Endress, "The Defense of Reason: The Plea for Philosophy in the Religious Community," *ZGAIW* 6 (1990): 1–49.

49. See Rissanen, *Theological Encounter.* See also the recent volume of collected studies on this phenomenon: Sidney H. Griffith, *The Beginnings of Christian Theology in Arabic: Muslim-Christian Encounters in the Early Islamic Period* (CStS 746; Aldershot, Eng.: Ashgate, 2002).

50. See Kraemer, *Humanism,* 107.

problems were not of the same order as those of Muslim scholars like al-Kindī or al-Fārābī, whose thought he followed so closely in other matters. Rather, Yaḥyā used his logical expertise to defend already established Christian doctrines precisely against the logical attacks of Muslim philosophers. A case in point is his refutation on logical grounds of al-Kindī's attack on the credibility of the doctrine of the Trinity. Al-Kindī refuted the doctrine on the same logical grounds that Yaḥyā used to defend it.[51]

As for the issue of the primacy of reason over revelation, in Yaḥyā's case the mention of it recalls not so much the question as posed within the framework of the concerns of the Muslims al-Kindī or al-Fārābī, but rather the old concern of Georg Graf and Augustin Périer about whether Yaḥyā himself, within the Christian horizon, was primarily a theologian, as Graf thought, or a philosopher, as Périer said.[52] In fact theological concerns seem to have loomed as large for him as did the simply philosophical ones, but there is no evidence that Yaḥyā saw any conflict between the two realms of inquiry. On the contrary, he used his considerable philosophical acumen not only in defense of the doctrines of the Trinity and the Incarnation, as espoused by all the Christians of his day, but also, vigorously, in defense of the veracity of the Christological formulae of his own Syrian Orthodox community against the objections of other Christians, particularly those whom he called "Nestorians," as we shall see below.

Emilio Platti, the modern scholar who has most intensively studied Yaḥyā's theological works, has argued that in them his principal concern was to prove that the traditional doctrines of the Syrian Orthodox church are not contrary to the first principles of reason. Furthermore, Platti has also shown that Yaḥyā was far from being a rationalist pure and simple; he did not argue, for example, like his disciple from the Church of the East, Abū al-Faraj ibn al-Ṭayyib (d. ca. 1055),[53] that a logical demonstration was superior to the evidence of the miracles recorded in the Gospels in affirming the divinity of Christ. Rather, Yaḥyā taught that the Gospel miracles were the primary warrant for the

51. See Augustin Périer, "Un traité de Yahyâ ben ᶜAdî: Défense du dogme de la trinité contre les objections d'al-Kindî," *ROC,* 3d ser., 2 (1920–21): 3–21.

52. See Graf, *Philosophie und Gotteslehre,* 8, and Périer, "Yaḥyâ ben ᶜAdî," 82.

53. See Bénédicte Landron, *Chrétiens et musulmans en Irak: Attitudes nestoriennes vis-à-vis de l'Islam* (Études chrétiennes arabes; Paris: Cariscript, 1994), 108–12.

spread of the Christian faith.[54] Platti has even quoted Yaḥyā to the effect that "ce n'est pas Aristote qui me guide quand il s'agit du christianisme."[55] And in another place Platti has written of Yaḥyā:

> Au moment même où apparaît la question du statut de la révélation par rapport à la sagesse humaine, il se dévoile dans ses options théologiques, refusant d'attacher à la spéculation philosophique une valeur ultime.[56]

So when it comes to the claims of Christian doctrine, it seems best to think of Yaḥyā in the role of a defender of the teachings of the Syrian Orthodox community like Abū Rā'iṭah before him. But in Yaḥyā's hands, Christian theology in Arabic took a new turn. Disdaining the ways of the *mutakallimūn*, both Muslim and Christian, Yaḥyā ibn ʿAdī *al-Manṭiqī* used the rigorous categories of the Aristotelian logician to argue his case. The distinctive feature of Yaḥyā's theological discourse was not to be the rule of theoretical Arabic grammar but the Greek syllogism.

III
Yaḥyā ibn ʿAdī, the Theologian

In addition to his work as a logician, philosopher, and translator, who translated many works of Aristotle and his commentators from Syriac into Arabic, Yaḥyā was also a prolific writer in the area of Christian theology and apologetics.[57] In this connection, his concerns were not limited to the customary topics of the Christian apologetical agenda developed in the previous century; they extended to issues of public morality, as in the *Kitāb tahdhīb al-akhlāq* (Reformation of morals), to

54. See Platti, *Yaḥyā ibn ʿAdī*, 78–79.

55. Ibid., 78.

56. Emilio Platti, "Intellect et révélation chez Ibn ʿAdī: Lecture d'une page d'un petit traité," in *Actes du deuxième congrès international d'études arabes chrétiennes (Oosterhesselen, septembre 1984)* (ed. Khalil Samir; OCA 226; Rome: Pont. Institutum Studiorum Orientalium, 1986), 234.

57. In this connection see the numerous studies of Emilio Platti, in particular: "Deux manuscrits théologiques de Yaḥyā b. ʿAdī," *MIDEO* 12 (1974): 217–29; idem, "Yahyā b. ʿAdī, philosophe et théologien," *MIDEO* 14 (1980): 167–84; idem, "Une cosmologie chrétienne," *MIDEO* 15 (1982): 75–118; idem, *Yaḥyā ibn ʿAdī;* idem, *La grande polémique antinestorienne (et la discussion avec Muhammad al-Misri)* (CSCO 427–28; Louvain: Peeters, 1981); idem, *Abū ʿĪsā al-Warrāq, Yaḥyā ibn ʿAdī: De l'incarnation* (CSCO 490–91; Louvain: Peeters, 1987).

the ethical value of celibacy,[58] and to the larger question of the general human pursuit of happiness and the avoidance of sorrow.[59] But when all is said and done, the defense of the doctrines of the Trinity and the Incarnation loom largest among Yaḥyā ibn ᶜAdī's theological concerns. They are the primary topics in the more than sixty works that Gerhard Endress lists under the heading of "Christian Theology" in his bibliography of Yaḥyā's works.[60]

But Yaḥyā's apologetical task did not begin straightaway with the defense of the central Christian doctrines. Like the Muslim scholars of his day, logically he had first to secure the basic premises of belief in one, creator God. A principal work in this enterprise is Yaḥyā's *Maqālah fī al-tawḥīd* (Essay on monotheism).[61] He wrote it in the spring of the year 940, with a view to providing a definition of the concept of "one" sufficient to justify both the affirmation of one God *(al-tawḥīd),* the central tenet of Islam, and the confession of three *(al-tathlīth)* essential "attributes" *(al-ṣifāt):* "goodness," "wisdom," and "power" *(al-jūd, al-ḥikmah,* and *al-qudrah),*[62] sufficient, in his judgment, to provide a logical presumption in favor of the credibility of the Christian doctrine of the Trinity. An interesting feature of Yaḥyā's argument in this enterprise, as Endress points out, is that the triad of attributes he puts forward has an intellectual pedigree reaching back to the Neoplatonist philosopher Proclus (ca. 410–85) by way of the Syrian mystical theologian, Dionysius the Pseudo-Areopagite (ca. 500).[63] And this circumstance in turn testifies to Yaḥyā's deep-rootedness in the Christian theological tradition of his own religious community.

While Yaḥyā's discussions in a number of treatises of various aspects of the doctrine of the Trinity seem designed to deal principally

---

58. See Vincent Mistrih, "Traité sur la continence de Yaḥyā ibn ᶜAdī, édition critique," *SOC.C* 16 (1981): 1–137.

59. On this topic and its context in the Muslim-Christian interaction, see Sidney H. Griffith, "The Muslim Philosopher al-Kindi and His Christian Readers: Three Arab Christian Texts on 'The Dissipation of Sorrows,'" *BJRL* 78 (1996): 111–27. For purposes of comparison see also Thérèse-Anne Druart, "Philosophical Consolation in Christianity and Islam: Boethius and al-Kindi," *Topoi* 19 (2000): 25–34.

60. See Endress, *Works of Yaḥyā ibn ᶜAdī,* 99–123.

61. Khalil Samir, *Le traité de l'unité de Yaḥyā ibn ᶜAdī (893–974): Étude et édition critique* (PAC; Jounieh, Lebanon: Librairie St. Paul, 1980).

62. See Samir, *Traité de l'unité,* 273–74.

63. See Endress, *Works of Yaḥyā ibn ᶜAdī,* 73.

with objections to the doctrine posed by Muslims,[64] as in the instance of his rebuttal of the arguments put forward by the philosopher al-Kindī, mentioned above,[65] when it comes to the doctrine of the Incarnation, his concern is not only with Islamic objections but also with those of Christian adversaries who were opposed to the teachings of his own Syrian Orthodox church. Chief among them are those of the Church of the East, whom he calls "Nestorians." This circumstance highlights Yaḥyā's role as a teacher in his own community. A notable feature of both of these classes of works is their often personal, dialogical character, whereby he addresses himself to a particular individual who had posed a question to him.[66]

One of the most significant of Yaḥyā ibn ᶜAdī's theological works is his response to Abū ᶜĪsā Muḥammad ibn Hārūn al-Warrāq's *Kitāb fī al-radd ᶜalā al-firaq al-thalāth min al-naṣārā* (Refutation of the three sects of the Christians).[67] In fact, Abū ᶜĪsā al-Warrāq's text survives largely due to generous quotations from it included in Yaḥyā's response. Abū ᶜĪsā al-Warrāq (d. ca. 862) was a prominent Muᶜtazilī *mutakallim* in the first half of the ninth century who is distinguished by his careful reporting of the beliefs of non-Muslim communities in the course of his refutations of their teachings. Due in no small part to his accurate and seemingly sympathetic presentations of the beliefs of others, Abū ᶜĪsā came under a considerable amount of obloquy in the Islamic community, where he was suspected of harboring dualist, even Manichaean, sympathies.[68] From the Christian perspective, he was by far one of the most trenchant

---

64. There are even texts of uncertain authenticity on this theme that are often attributed to Yaḥyā. See, for example, Bo Holmberg, "Notes on a Treatise on the Unity and Trinity of God Attributed to Yaḥyā ibn ᶜAdī," in *Actes du deuxième congrès*, 235–45.

65. See note 51 above.

66. See the sustained study of Yaḥyā's discussions of the Incarnation in Platti, *Yaḥyā ibn ᶜAdī*, esp. 54–133.

67. See Platti, *Abū ᶜĪsā al-Warrāq*. See also Armand Abel, *Abū ᶜĪsā Muḥammad b. Hārūn al-Warrāq, Le livre pour la réfutation des trois sectes chrétiennes* (Bruxelles: Mimeo, 1949); David Thomas, *Anti-Christian Polemic in Early Islam: Abū ᶜĪsā al-Warrāq's "Against the Trinity"* (UCOP 45; Cambridge: Cambridge University Press, 1992).

68. See Josef van Ess, *Theologie und Gesellschaft im 2. und 3. Jahrhundert Hidschra: Eine Geschichte des religiösen Denkens im frühen Islam* (6 vols.; Berlin: de Gruyter, 1991–97), 4:289–94. See also Carsten Colpe, "Anpassung des Manichäismus an den Islam (Abū ᶜĪsā al-Warrāq)," *ZDMG* 109 (1959): 82–91; Wilferd Madelung,

and incisive of Muslim polemicists against Christian doctrines. So it is not surprising that even a century after his time, a scholar of the stature of Yaḥyā ibn ʿAdī felt obliged to refute his charges point by point, often, as mentioned above, quoting long excerpts from his work in the process. Indeed it is in response to Abū ʿĪsā's challenges that Yaḥyā presented some of his own most carefully reasoned, logical defenses of the credibility of the Christian doctrines of the Trinity and the Incarnation.[69]

So effective were Yaḥyā ibn ʿAdī's apologetical works in the eyes of other Christian writers in Arabic that large portions of them were excerpted for inclusion in compilations of texts on doctrinal topics made by apologists in later times. Particularly notable among them were the Coptic scholars of the thirteenth century, especially such well-known ones as al-Ṣafī ibn al-ʿAssāl (d. before 1260) and Muʾtaman ibn al-ʿAssāl (d. after 1275), as well as the noted compiler of the following century, Abū al-Barakāt ibn Kabar (d. 1324).[70]

IV
Yaḥyā ibn ʿAdī and the *Kitāb tahdhīb al-akhlāq*

One of the more interesting essays to come from the pen of Yaḥyā ibn ʿAdī is the remarkable text *Tahdhīb al-akhlāq,* a treatise on the improvement of morals in which he teaches that virtue itself suffices to attain the happiness of which human nature is capable. For centuries

---

"Abū ʿĪsā al-Warrāq über die Bardesaniten, Marcioniten und Kantäer," in *Studien zur Geschichte und Kultur des Vorderen Orients: Festschrift für Berthold Spuler* (ed. Hans R. Roemer and Albrecht Noth; Leiden: Brill, 1981), 210–24; repr. in *Religious Schools and Sects in Medieval Islam* (CStS 213; London: Variorum Reprints, 1985); David Thomas, "Abū ʿĪsā al-Warrāq and the History of Religions," *JSS* 41 (1996): 275–90; Dominique Urvoy, *Les penseurs libres dans l'Islam classique* (Paris: Albin Michel, 1996), 102–17.

69. See Emilio Platti, "Les objections de Abū ʿĪsā al-Warrāq concernant l'incarnation et les réponses de Yaḥyā ibn ʿAdī," *QSA* 5–6 (1987–88): 661–66; idem, "La doctrine des chrétiens d'après Abū ʿĪsā al-Warrāq dans son traité sur la Trinité," *MIDEO* 20 (1991): 7–30; idem, "Yaḥyā b. ʿAdī and His Refutation of al-Warrāq's Treatise on the Trinity in Relation to His Other Works," in *Christian Arabic Apologetics during the Abbasid Period (750–1258)* (ed. Samir Khalil Samir and Jørgen S. Nielsen; SHR 63; Leiden: Brill, 1994), 172–91.

70. See Emilio Platti, "Une compilation théologique de Yaḥyā ibn ʿAdī par al-Ṣafī ibn al-ʿAssāl," *MIDEO* 13 (1977): 291–303. See also Platti, *Yaḥyā ibn ʿAdī,* 33–53.

this work has circulated in the Arabic-speaking world of Islam. It represents such a high degree of cultural integration on the part of a Christian writer in the Islamic milieu that a Muslim scholar of modern times, Naji al-Takriti, has written about the treatise, properly attributed, and without any apparent sense of irony, that "perhaps the most important feature of *Tahdhīb al-akhlāq* is that it was one of the earliest books on Islamic [*sic*] ethical philosophy."[71] At the very least one may be able to regard it as a concrete instance on the part of an Arab Christian writer of that "extremely fertile exchange of ideas with Muslim philosophers" of which Franz Rosenthal spoke in his study of the classical heritage in Islam.[72] As such it may also be seen as a Christian contribution to the burgeoning Arabic/Islamic intellectual culture of the early Abbasid period.

By now about twenty manuscript copies of all or part of Yaḥyā ibn ᶜAdī's *Kitāb tahdhīb al-akhlāq* are known, and Samir Khalil Kussaim has not so long ago published a critical edition of the Arabic text, which he says in the introduction is, by his count, the twentieth printed edition of the work.[73] Over the long course of its textual history, the work has sometimes been attributed by Muslim scribes and editors to such lofty figures as al-Jāḥiẓ (d. 868), Ibn al-Haytham (d. 1041), and Muḥyī al-Dīn ibn al-ᶜArabī (d. 1240), to name only the most famous of them. In modern scholarship Samir Khalil Samir has forcefully argued in behalf of the work's authenticity as Yaḥyā's composition, noting that over the centuries Christian scribes have consistently attributed the text to Yaḥyā.[74] Gerhard Endress simply concludes, "There is no intrinsic evidence against the authorship of Yaḥyā ibn ᶜAdī."[75]

---

71. Naji al-Takriti, *Yaḥyā ibn ᶜAdī: A Critical Edition and Study of His* Tahdhīb al-akhlāq (Beirut: Oueidat, 1978), 222. In this same connection one might note that al-Shahrastānī, in his *Kitāb al-milal wa al-niḥal,* was happy to list Abū Zakariyyā Yaḥyā ibn ᶜAdī among the philosophers of Islam. See Troupeau, "Quelle était la *nisba?*"

72. Franz Rosenthal, *The Classical Heritage in Islam* (London: Routledge & Kegan Paul, 1975), 9.

73. Samir Khalil Kussaim, *Yaḥyā ibn ᶜAdī (893–974): Tahdhīb al-aḫlāq* (Beirut: CEDRAC, 1994), 5.

74. Khalil Samir, "Le *Tahḏīb al-aḫlāq* de Yaḥyā b. ᶜAdī (m. 974) attribué à Ǧāḥiẓ et à Ibn al-ᶜArabī," *Arabica* 21 (1974): 111–38; Samir Khalil, "Nouveaux renseignements sur le *Tahḏīb al-aḫlāq* de Yaḥyā ibn ᶜAdī et sur le 'Taymūr aḫlāq 290,'" *Arabica* 26 (1979): 158–78.

75. Endress, *Works of Yaḥyā ibn ᶜAdī,* 84.

The problem has been not so much that there are actual reasons to attribute the work to anyone else, but that the title as we now have it does not appear on the earliest list of Yaḥyā's works. Instead, a work entitled *Siyāsat al-nafs* (Governance of the soul) appears there,[76] repeating a phrase that in fact often appears in the text itself. But another phrase also appears in the text: *tahdhīb al-akhlāq*. In the course of the transmission of the text over the centuries, it seems that the latter phrase eventually came to be used as the work's title, perhaps under the influence of the titles of similar works of other authors in the wider culture. An example of another such work would be the somewhat more philosophical *Tahdhīb al-akhlāq* of the Muslim author and younger contemporary of Yaḥyā ibn ᶜAdī, Aḥmad ibn Muḥammad Miskawayh (932–1030), who, like Yaḥyā, spent much of his scholarly life in Baghdad.[77] The currency of works of similar titles, in fact, might well have been the reason for the attribution by some Muslim scribes and editors of Yaḥyā's always popular work to Arabic writers with more immediate name recognition and higher credentials in Islamic circles, and who were known to have written works with comparable titles. In any case, subsequent to Samir Khalil's exhaustive studies of more than twenty years ago, no recent scholar, Muslim or otherwise,[78] now questions Yaḥyā's authorship of the *Tahdhīb al-akhlāq* that is attributed to him.

While a number of scholarly studies of particular issues raised in Yaḥyā's *Tahdhīb al-akhlāq* have been published in recent decades,[79] only two monographs have been devoted to the work. One is the Cambridge Ph.D. dissertation of Dr. Naji al-Takriti, which includes a critical edition of the text together with a study of the sources of Yaḥyā's

76. See ibid., 85.

77. See Constantine K. Zurayk, *Tahdhīb al-akhlāq li Abi ᶜAlī Aḥmad ibn Muḥammad Miskawayh* (Beirut: American University of Beirut, 1966); idem, trans., *Miskawayh, The Refinement of Character* (Beirut: American University of Beirut, 1968). See also Mohammed Arkoun, trans., *Miskawayh (320/21–420), Traité d'éthique* (2d ed.; Damas: Institut Français de Damas, 1988).

78. Dr. Naji al-Takriti independently came to the same conclusion in *Critical Edition and Study,* 11–20.

79. In two places Majid Fakhry has furnished a general sketch of the contents of the work: Majid Fakhry, *A History of Islamic Philosophy* (2d ed.; StOC 5; New York: Columbia University Press, 1983), 192–96; idem, "Aspects de la pensée morale de Yaḥyā ibn ᶜAdī," *Annales de philosophie de l'Université Saint-Joseph* 6 (1985): 121–30.

ideas and modes of expression, as well as a comparison of his thought with that of his contemporaries and with the Islamic intellectual tradition more generally.[80] The other monograph, by Marie-Thérèse Urvoy, includes, in addition to a critical edition of the text, a thoroughgoing introductory study and a French translation of the whole work, heretofore the only translation of it into a Western language.[81]

Both al-Takriti and Urvoy concentrate their analyses of the *Tahdhīb al-akhlāq* on an examination of the sources of Yaḥyā ibn ʿAdī's ethical ideas, highlighting in particular what they consider to be the three predominant frames of reference behind the work: pre-Islamic Arabic tradition as refracted in early Islamic discourse, the Persian tradition of "mirrors for princes," and, principally, the Greek philosophical tradition, so major a part of Yaḥyā's own scholarly concerns. Given the undoubtedly Hellenistic flavor of the *Tahdhīb al-akhlāq* as a whole and its debts to the early Arabic expressions of views usually attributed to Plato, Aristotle, Galen, and Yaḥyā's own master, al-Fārābī, it is nevertheless clear that in the ensemble the work is not simply a conventional re-presentation of already familiar doctrines. On the one hand, the recognition of the work's distinctiveness prompted Richard Walzer, ever the reductive source critic, to say of the structure of Yaḥyā's composition that "this scheme probably depends ultimately on some lost pre-neoplatonic Greek original."[82] Urvoy, on the other hand, speaks of the "syncretism of Ibn ʿAdī" that goes much farther than just the sum of the ideas of his sources.[83] And the same author goes on to say that Yaḥyā's work has a markedly different character from the ethical compositions of later Muslim writers, who never mention Yaḥyā's work, not even Miskawayh, who wrote his own *Kitāb tahdhīb al-akhlāq* in the same city not fifty years later.[84] In other words, one might just as well say that Yaḥyā ibn ʿAdī, writing in the idiom of his own day and

80. Al-Takriti, *Critical Edition and Study*. See note 71 above.

81. Marie-Thérèse Urvoy, *Traité d'éthique d'Abû Zakariyyâʾ Yahyâ Ibn ʿAdi: Introduction, texte et traduction* (Études chrétiennes arabes; Paris: Cariscript, 1991).

82. Richard Walzer, "Akhlāk," *EI*[2] 1:328.

83. See Urvoy, *Traité d'éthique*, 43.

84. Mohammed Arkoun, the modern scholar who has most intensively studied Miskawayh's work, says that he was trained by students of Yaḥyā ibn ʿAdī and must have known his works. See Mohammed Arkoun, *L'humanisme arabe au IVe/Xe siècle: Miskawayh, philosophe et historien* (2d ed.; EtMu 12; Paris: Vrin, 1982), 97–98.

using the scholarly resources available to him, composed an original work with its own purposes, in view of the social dimensions of his own time and place.

A brief outline of the work is in order. The *Tahdhīb al-akhlāq* is short; it is really no more than a pamphlet of some fifty pages in most editions. The topical outline features five principal sections:[85]

A. The Definition of Human Moral Qualities

Yaḥyā begins from the premise that human fulfillment and perfection, which he believes one can use the discerning mind to achieve, requires one to become well trained in good moral qualities and to extirpate evil ones. So first of all he must define what he means by a "moral quality" *(khulq, khuluq,* pl. *akhlāq).*[86] Following Galen, he says,

> A moral quality [*al-khuluq*] is a state [*ḥāl*] proper to the soul, in which a man performs his actions without deliberation or study. (1.5)[87]

The problem, according to Yaḥyā, is that while moral qualities may be good or bad, inborn or acquired, in fact evil overcomes most people

85. See Endress, *Works of Yaḥyā ibn ʿAdī,* 85.

86. It is difficult to find *le mot juste* in English for this Arabic term, which has been used by the early Arab translators of philosophical texts to translate the Greek term ἦθος (pl. ἤθη). Customarily, in English, the word "character" is used to render the Greek word. See, for example, F. E. Peters, *Greek Philosophical Terms: A Historical Lexicon* (New York: New York University Press, 1967), 66. But it hardly seems to be an appropriate equivalent in the present context. Urvoy uses "caractère" in French; al-Takriti uses "character" in English, but the usage is awkward. The phrase "moral quality" seems more apt; one might also speak of a "moral disposition," or a "trait of character," or, in the plural, simply of "morals" or "ethics."

87. All in-text references are to part and paragraph number in the present edition. Both Urvoy, *Traité d'éthique,* 25, and al-Takriti, *Critical Edition and Study,* 203, point out that Yaḥyā has borrowed this definition of the "moral quality" from the Arabic translation of Galen's treatise Περὶ ἠθῶν, now lost in the original Greek. See Paul Kraus, ed., *Kitāb al-akhlāq li-Gālīnūs* (Majallat kulliyat al-adāb 5; Dirāsāt fī tāʾrīkh al-tarjama fī al-islām 1; Cairo: Fuad I University, 1937), 25. For an English translation of the relevant passage see J. N. Mattock, "A Translation of the Arabic Epitome of Galen's Book Περὶ Ἠθῶν," in *Islamic Philosophy and the Classical Tradition,* 236: "A trait of character is a state of the soul that induces a man to perform the actions of the soul without consideration or precise knowledge."

in the world, and so there is a need in society for kings, laws, and systems of ethics to encourage the acquisition and practice of the good moral qualities and the extirpation of the bad ones. Consequently, Yaḥyā gives the reader to understand that the person who can aptly be described as "someone of reformed morals" *(al-muhadhdhab al-akhlāq)* would be the most appreciative reader of his book, because when such a person "finds his own moral qualities listed in books and described as good, this summons him to persevere in his good behavior and to make progress in his conduct" (1.4).[88] But by definition, moral qualities are states proper to the soul, so one must first consider how they relate to the soul.

B. The Tripartite Soul

Following the Platonic tradition he inherited, Yaḥyā distinguishes three "faculties" *(quwā)* in the soul, and he maintains that the soul, with these faculties, is "the necessary cause for the differentiation of the moral qualities." He goes on to say,

> The soul has three faculties, and they are also named souls: the appetitive soul, the irascible soul, and the rational soul. All of the moral qualities emanate from these faculties. (2.1)

From this point, Yaḥyā proceeds to give a brief characterization of the inclinations and instincts of each of the three "souls" or "faculties." Along the way one learns that the moral qualities *(al-akhlāq)* inhere in the souls as "habits" *(al-ᶜādāt)*, and that "the necessary cause for the differentiation of people's habits . . . [is] the differentiation of the states [*aḥwāl*] of the soul" (2.5), that is to say, the differentiation of the moral qualities as characterized by each of the three faculties of the soul, since moral qualities are themselves states of the soul. Just as the faculties of the soul are "appetitive," "irascible," and "rational," so are the moral qualities and their corresponding habits, as states of the soul, characterized as appetitive, irascible, and rational. Some of these moral qualities and habits are good and commendable, and some of them are evil and to be avoided; the good ones are "virtues" *(faḍāʾil*, sing. *faḍīlah)* and the evil ones are "vices" *(radhāʾil*, sing. *radhīlah)*.

---

88. Yaḥyā also puts the phrases "complete man" *(al-insān al-tāmm)* and "someone of reformed morals" *(al-muhadhdhab al-akhlāq)* in apposition with one another (see 1.3).

According to Yaḥyā, the rational soul, which distinguishes man from the animals, is also the faculty "by which he deems good deeds to be good and bad deeds to be bad." Furthermore, "by means of it a man has the ability to reform [*yuhadhdhib*] the remaining two faculties (that is, the appetitive and the irascible), to control them and to restrain them" (2.11). So the "reformation of morals" *(tahdhīb al-akhlāq)* is the work of the rational soul. This "reformation" *(tahdhīb)* itself, according to Yaḥyā, is a process of "refinement" *(taʾdīb);* he uses the two terms in apposition with one another[89] and in parallel phrases. He says, for example, that "it is necessary for a man to refine [*yuʾaddib*] his appetitive soul and to reform it [*yuhadhdhibahā*]" (2.5). This process of reformation and refinement under the guidance of the rational soul, according to Yaḥyā, is what allows the one who practices it to become "someone of reformed morals" *(al-muhadhdhab al-akhlāq).*[90] Such a person can then aptly be described as "someone confirmed in humanity [*insāniyyah*], someone who is deservedly a natural leader" (2.15). Later in the treatise, as we shall see, Yaḥyā will speak of such a person as the "perfect man" *(al-insān al-kāmil),* a "complete man" *(al-insān al-tāmm).* But first he reviews the particular virtues and vices that are the principal moral qualities he thinks call for attention in the context of his discussion of the reformation of morals.

C. Virtues and Vices

Yaḥyā provides a list of twenty virtues and twenty vices, each of which he defines and describes in some detail. The virtues are abstinence, contentment, self-control, forbearance, modesty, friendship, compassion, fidelity, honesty, keeping secrets, humility, joy, truthfulness, benevolence, generosity, courage, emulation, perseverance in difficulties, high ambition, and justice. The vices are debauchery, greed, profligacy, folly, levity (including impudence), passion, harshness, perfidy, dishonesty, divulging secrets (including character defamation), arrogance, sullenness, lying, malevolence (including resentment), niggardliness, cowardice, envy, anxiety in the face of adversity, lack of ambition, and injustice (3.1–41).

From the perspective of the historian, perhaps the first thing that strikes the reader of this list is its idiosyncratic character. On the one

89. See, for example, 2.5 and 2.10.
90. See 1.3, 1.4, and 4.7.

hand, it does not correspond exactly to any earlier scholar's list of virtues and vices; it does not follow the Greek philosophical practice of listing the virtues under the headings of the four cardinal virtues, followed, for example, by Miskawayh, whose treatise *Tahdhīb al-akhlāq* is otherwise in a number of respects comparable to the one bearing the same name by his older contemporary, Yaḥyā ibn ᶜAdī.[91] On the other hand, the virtues and vices on Yaḥyā's list can also be found discussed in much the same terms by other writers to whom he clearly owes a debt, such as Galen, al-Fārābī, and perhaps al-Rāzī, not to mention Aristotle and the Platonic tradition. There are also parallels to be found with Persian ethical traditions and even the lore of the ancient Arabs.[92] But when all is said and done, the fact remains that Yaḥyā's list is singular, reflecting the requirements of his own purposes and the distinctive profile of his own thought, whatever may have been his intellectual debt to his predecessors.

One notable feature of Yaḥyā's discussion of the virtues and vices is his practice, after having defined each one of them as a moral quality, of making distinctions in terms of their commendability or abhorrence and repugnance by reference to the social status of the persons who might possess them. In this connection he distinguishes in particular between kings and "leaders" *(al-ruʾasāʾ)* or "prominent people" *(al-ᶜuẓamāʾ)* on the one hand, and ordinary people, or even lower-class people, on the other hand. In some instances he makes similar distinctions between men and women, young and old. According to Yaḥyā, a moral quality may be more or less commendable according to the social rank of the person who acquires it and more or less reprehensible on the basis of the same consideration. A good example of this relativistic point of view may be seen in his discussion of the vice of "niggardliness" *(al-bukhl)*. He says,

> Niggardliness is refusing to come to the aid of someone who asks for it when one has the capacity to aid him. This moral quality is abhorrent for everyone, but it is less abhorrent for women. . . . As for the rest of the people, niggardliness disgraces them, especially kings and leaders. Niggardliness is loathsome for them much more than it is for their subjects; it is degrading in the exercise of their

91. See Zurayk, *Tahdhīb al-akhlāq,* 16–30; idem, *Refinement of Character,* 15–26.

92. These parallels and their sources have been discussed by Urvoy, *Traité d'éthique,* 27–38, and al-Takriti, *Critical Edition and Study,* 234–39.

> kingship because for them it cuts off ambition and makes them loathsome to their subjects. (3.36)

Yaḥyā's preoccupying concern for the ruling classes is evident in this quotation, along with other social considerations in the assessment of the degree of abhorrence to be assigned to the moral quality. The same considerations are taken into account in assessing the commendability of virtues, as may be seen in the discussion of the virtue of "forbearance" *(al-ḥilm)*. Yaḥyā says,

> Forbearance is abstention from taking vengeance in the heat of anger in spite of having the capacity for it. This situation is commendable as long as it does not lead to a breach of honor or to bad policy. It is especially good for leaders and kings because they are the ones most capable of taking revenge on those who anger them. The forbearance of a lower-class person toward someone of a higher class is not to be reckoned as a virtue, assuming that he is in a position actually to encounter him. For, even if he holds back, it will only be reckoned as fear and not as forbearance. (3.5)

Social considerations also prompted Yaḥyā to distinguish four moral qualities that cannot be included on either the list of virtues or the list of vices because in some cases they are virtues, but in others they are vices. These moral qualities are love of honor, love of pomp and splendor, overcompensation for praise, and renunciation (see 3.42–45). It will be instructive to quote his discussion of "renunciation" *(al-zuhd)* because it includes references to two classes of people for whom Yaḥyā has a high regard. He says,

> Renunciation is having little desire for money and goods, for accumulation and acquisition. It is choosing to be satisfied with what supports bare life, making light of this world and its goods and pleasures. It is paying little attention to the higher social orders, deeming kings and their kingdoms of small importance, along with the owners of money and their money. This moral quality is to be considered very good, but it is for scholars, monks, religious leaders, orators, preachers, and whoever gives people an interest in eternal life. It is not to be deemed good for kings and leaders, nor is it appropriate for them. For, when a king makes his practice of renunciation public, he becomes deficient. The reason is that his reign achieves its full purpose only with the collection of money and goods, and the accumulation of them, so that he might defend his realm with them,

> conserve its assets, and come to the aid of his subjects. This is contrary to the practice of renunciation. So, if he abandons the accumulation [of goods], his reign becomes futile, and he will summarily be numbered among the most inadequate of the kings who deviate from the way of right government. (3.45)

In this passage not only can social considerations be seen to play a determining role in Yaḥyā's thinking about a particular moral quality, but his concern for the right conduct of the ruling class is evident, as well as his concern for a meaningful place in society for scholars and religious leaders. We shall return to this theme below. First we must consider the program Yaḥyā puts forward for instilling virtues and extirpating vices.

D. *The Way of Reformation*

Yaḥyā has a definite program to commend for the reformation of morals. Having discussed the virtues and vices, he then advises the reader that "whoever does not take the trouble to control himself, and to examine his faults, is not free of many faults, even if he does not perceive them and does not advert to them" (4.1). So the obvious requirement is to find a way to acquire the virtues and to extirpate the vices. But first Yaḥyā calls attention to the fact that the ordinary person is wont to think that people vary only in terms of money and possessions rather than in terms of virtue. He points out that, to the contrary, money only provides social status and economic power, and he claims that so far is it from enhancing virtue, it may even play a role in exposing and promoting one's vices by providing the means for indulging them (see 4.2–7). So what is really wanted, according to Yaḥyā, is a program of training in good morals and of making their practice habitual. Consistent with the earlier teaching in the treatise, Yaḥyā then reminds the reader that such a program consists in subjecting the appetitive and the irascible souls and their faculties to the control of the rational soul.

The program Yaḥyā commends for the rational control of each of the three souls and their faculties has some common elements (see 4.9–29). For the subjection of the appetitive and the irascible souls, he recommends keeping the objective of the virtue to be acquired constantly in mind as well as the repulsive quality of the vices that would otherwise characterize a person's habitual conduct. He suggests that one frequent the *majālis* (sessions) of the best and brightest people so as to emulate their practice. He counsels against intoxication, listening to music, and gluttony at some length. He commends constant vigilance and mindfulness of the virtuous goal to be achieved. In the end, for Yaḥyā, "the basis of the enterprise to reform morals and to control the appetitive and the irascible souls is the rational soul. All the ways of behaving [*al-siyāsāt*] are in this soul" (4.22).

Several times in the course of his discussion Yaḥyā recommends reading books as a significant part of the process of acquiring virtue. After speaking of the importance of keeping good company he says, "One must also be continually studying books on morality and deportment as well as accounts of ascetics, monks, hermits, and pious people" (4.11). To do so, for Yaḥyā, is an indispensable part of advancing in the "rational sciences" *(al-ʿulūm al-aqliyyah),* which he thinks are necessary for the strengthening of the rational soul. He says,

> When one studies the rational sciences, refines his study of them, examines the books on morality and deportment, and lingers over them, his soul will awaken, take cognizance of its appetites, recover from its indolence, perceive its virtues, and reject its vices. (4.23)

Finally, in connection with reading books, Yaḥyā says, "Anyone who has a love for his own morals must start with the study of the books on morals and deportment, then with schooling himself in the exact sciences" (4.23). For Yaḥyā, in the end, the program for acquiring virtues and extirpating vices, for making the virtues habitual, and for suppressing the troubling powers of the appetitive and the irascible souls is "to improve the rational soul, to empower it, to embellish it with virtues, refinement, and good deeds" (4.25). He calls this program "a tool for self-management" *(ʾālat al-siyāsah)* and a workable "vehicle of practice" *(markab al-riyāḍah)* (4.25). Its purpose is to provide that "discernment" *(tamyīz)* of good and bad habits that is based on the acquisition of the "rational sciences" and the "refinement of one's critical thinking" *(tadqīq al-fikr)* (see 4.26). The end product is the perfect man.

E. The Perfect Man

Yaḥyā says, "The complete man [*al-insān al-tāmm*] is one whom virtue does not bypass, whom vice does not disfigure" (5.2). He thinks that only rarely does a man actually fulfill this definition, but he believes it is possible for him to do so. And when it happens he says of such a man, "It is the angels he resembles more than he resembles men" (5.2). He can be characterized, says Yaḥyā, as one who is "passionate for the image of perfection [*li-ṣūrat al-kamāl*]" (5.3). For Yaḥyā, the terms "completeness" or "fulfillment" *(al-tamām)* and "perfection" *(al-kamāl)* together express the hoped-for moral condition of the complete/fulfilled man. And he says that the way to achieve it is to cultivate a solicitude for what the modern reader can only call the "philosophical life" as it was practiced in late antiquity.[93] Yaḥyā himself does not use this expression. Rather, he says that the way for the "complete man" to arrive at perfection is for him to adopt the following program of action:

> To direct his attention to the study of the "exact sciences" [*al-ᶜulūm al-ḥaqīqiyyah*]; to make it his goal to grasp the quiddities of existing things, to disclose their causes and occasions, and to search out their final ends and purposes. He shall not pause in his labor at any particular end without giving some consideration to what is beyond that end. He shall make it his badge of honor, night and day, to read books on morals, to scrutinize books of biographies and of policies. He shall devote himself to implementing what virtuous people have bidden to be implemented and what the sages who have gone before have advised to be made habitual. He shall also acquire a modicum of the discipline of grammar and rhetoric and be endowed with a measure of eloquence and oratorical felicity. He shall always frequent the sessions [*majālis*] of scholars and sages and continually associate with modest and abstinent people. (5.4)

Yaḥyā goes on immediately to say that this profile of the perfect man fits only subjects and commoners. Kings and leaders, who for Yaḥyā are not always or even often perfect men,[94] have additional responsibilities. They are charged with seeking the company and the counsel of scholars and sages and also with supporting them and encouraging them. For the rest, whoever would be perfect must "make for himself a rule [*qānūn*] according to which he will restrict himself" (5.7) in response to the pressures of the appetitive and irascible powers of his soul. Yaḥyā gives

---

93. See the provocative discussion in Pierre Hadot, *Philosophy as a Way of Life* (Oxford: Blackwell, 1995). More on this below.

94. See Jad Hatem, "Que le roi ne peut être un homme parfait selon Yāḥyā ibn ᶜAdī," *Annales de philosophie de l'Université Saint-Joseph* 6 (1985): 89–104; idem, "Fī ᵓanna al-malika lā yastaṭīᶜu anna yakūna insānan tāmman," *Al-Machriq* 66 (1992): 161–77.

special attention to the need to control the appetite for food and drink. And he speaks at considerable length about money and its dangers. He says, "Money is only to be wanted for the sake of something else; it is not to be sought for its own sake" (5.8). And the something else he has in mind, at least for the money of kings and leaders, is the support of scholars, ascetics, and the poor. But he teaches that even the poor should be generous with what little they have.

Positively, Yaḥyā ibn ᶜAdī teaches that the lover of perfection must habitually love all people. And he bases this obligation on his teaching about the rational soul. He says,

> Men are a single tribe [*qabīl*], related to one another; humanity unites them. The adornment of the divine power is in all of them and in each one of them, and it is the rational soul. By means of this soul man becomes man. It is the nobler of the two parts of man, which are the soul and the body. So man in his true being is the rational soul, and it is a single substance [*jawhar*] in all men. All men in their true being are a single thing [*shayʾun wāḥidun*], but they are many in persons [*al-ashkhāṣ*]. Since their souls are one, and love is only in the soul, all of them must then show affection for one another and love one another. This is a natural disposition [*ṭabīʿah*] in men as long as the irascible soul does not lead them on. (5.14–15)

From this point Yaḥyā goes on to mention the dangers inherent in the exercise of political or military power, and he promotes a commendable openness about faults and failings, especially among kings and leaders. He warns that such things can never really be kept secret. Finally, he counsels the reader never to be content with any degree of perfection he thinks he may possess; there is always one beyond it. Yaḥyā says, "The man farthest from fulfillment is the one who is content with the deficiency his soul possesses" (5.22).

Throughout this portion of the text, as earlier, a considerable amount of attention is paid to kings and leaders, detailing how they of all people stand to profit from the reformation of their morals. While they have all the inducements to pleasure and vice in this world, Yaḥyā says,

> The most successful of them, when his soul aspires to human fulfillment and yearns for authentic sovereignty, knows that a king is the most worthy to become the most complete person of his time, more virtuous than his officers and subjects. So it should be easy for him to disengage from evil appetites and to forgo vile pleasures. (5.6)

In another place Yaḥyā says,

> The complete man is a leader by nature. If a king is fulfilled, embodying good moral qualities, including all the virtuous traits, he is a king by nature. If he is deficient, he is a king by force. (5.21)

In Yaḥyā's day, the Buyid period of Islamic history,[95] rulers were not noticeably "perfect" or "complete" in any moral sense of the words. Nevertheless, Yaḥyā envisioned a moral as well as a practical role in society for kings and leaders. More specifically, he saw it as an important part of their responsibility to dole out money fairly and to support the poor, the scholarly, and the devout. Yaḥyā said of kings that, after consolidating their power,

> They should give to scholars according to their classes, they should assign them salaries from their own private monies, and they should reward anyone who perseveres in knowledge and refinement. They should deal kindly with the weak and the poor, and they should search out the strangers and the alienated. They should be solicitous for ascetics and devout people, and they should allot them proportionately a share of their goods and their flocks. (5.11)

V
The "Philosophical Life" in Yaḥyā ibn ᶜAdī's View

Having reviewed the contents of Yaḥyā ibn ᶜAdī's *Kitāb tahdhīb al-akhlāq* in its five clearly distinguishable sections, one is finally in a position to consider its broader dimensions. What is it about Yaḥyā's own circumstances, and those of his time, that prompted him to write this somewhat uncharacteristic work, which goes much further, to paraphrase Marie-Thérèse Urvoy again, than just the sum of the ideas of his sources?[96] Yaḥyā himself did not clearly spell out his purposes, but perhaps we can discern them in part by trying, as it were, to read between the lines.

In spite of the constant mention of kings and leaders, it seems clear that Yaḥyā did not think of himself as writing in the "mirror for princes" tradition, after the manner of the Persian convert to Islam, Ibn al-Muqaffaᶜ (d. 757), to whose works he may nevertheless have

95. See Roy Mottahedeh, *Loyalty and Leadership in an Early Islamic Society* (rev. ed.; London: Tauris, 2001).

96. See note 83 above.

been somewhat indebted.[97] Rather, given his manifest preference for scholars, monks, and ascetics in society and his own devotion to philosophy, it makes better sense to think that Yaḥyā wrote the *Tahdhīb al-akhlāq* for the instruction of prospective students and future leaders in society more generally, be they Christians or Muslims, in order to inculcate in them the requisite moral attitude for the practice of the philosophical way of life. In this connection one might recall the likely influence on Yaḥyā of his master al-Fārābī, who saw character training, based on a consideration of the powers of the soul, as a requisite preparation for the study of logic and philosophy. Indeed, from this perspective, it is tempting to think of Yaḥyā's *Tahdhīb al-akhlāq* as practically a textbook for the program called for in the *Epistle on What Ought to Precede the Study of Philosophy,* often attributed to al-Fārābī. There one finds the following paragraph, virtually a brief description of the work Yaḥyā actually wrote:

> Before studying philosophy one must reform the character traits of the appetitive soul in order that there will only be truly virtuous appetite, rather than a desire which is falsely believed to be virtuous, such as pleasure or the love of domination. This is obtained by means of character reformation not only in words but also in deeds. Then, one will reform one's rational soul in order that it understand the way of truth by means of which one is safe from error and from being deceived. This is obtained by schooling in the science of demonstration.[98]

From an entirely different perspective, one modern commentator, Jad Hatem, thinks that what Yaḥyā has to say about kings and leaders in the *Tahdhīb al-akhlāq* can fairly well be described as "foncièrement polémique."[99] That is to say, he proposes that what Yaḥyā has written can be considered a protest against the actual behavior of the ruling classes in the Islamic society of his day. Therefore, says Hatem, one should not think, as some have surmised, that in this work Yaḥyā is inculcating the ideas of his master al-Fārābī about the moral training of the philosopher-king.[100] Rather, according to Hatem, one should

97. In this connection see the remarks of Urvoy, *Traité d'éthique,* 16–19.

98. Quoted from Thérèse-Anne Druart, "Al-Fārābī, Ethics, and First Intelligibles," *Documenti e studi sulla tradizione filosofica medievale* 8 (1997): 410. See also ibid., 411 n. 29.

99. Hatem, "Que le roi ne peut être un homme parfait," 94.

100. Ibid., 90.

conclude that Yaḥyā's real purpose was both the practical one of encouraging moral education in the multireligious society of the Islamic world in the tenth century and the polemical one of convicting the rulers of that same society of actual injustice. This purpose would then explain the very down-to-earth quality of the work, with its unusual sensitivity to the different ethical requirements of people in different roles in society. According to Hatem, it is not a highly theoretical work, not even as much so as Miskawayh's *Tahdhīb al-akhlāq*. On this reading, one might suppose that it was at least part of Yaḥyā's purpose to present a *dhimmī*'s plea for justice in an Islamic society—a feature of the work that may help explain the publication of its many new editions in modern times, largely under Christian auspices,[101] while Muslim scholars, often laboring under similarly oppressive conditions, have themselves been quick to credit the work's significance.

Yaḥyā's real heroes are not in fact kings and leaders, but "scholars" *(ahl al-ᶜilm)*, "monks" *(al-ruhbān)*, and "ascetics" *(al-zuhhād)*. He says that "what is to be considered good for them is clothing of hair and coarse material, traveling on foot, obscurity, attendance at churches and mosques and so forth, and an abhorrence for luxurious living" (3.43). One notes the interreligious character of this last remark, invoking, as it does, both churches and mosques. In another place Yaḥyā says of the scholars, monks, and ascetics that it is their task to "give people an interest in eternal life" (3.45). This is just about as close as he comes to an overtly religious theme in this whole treatise. It is true that he does speak of the rational soul as "the adornment of the divine power" (5.14) in a man and that he ends the work with the prayer, "Praised be the One who endows the intellect always and forever. Amen" (5.27). But when all is said and done, Yaḥyā, who in other works was a formidable apologist for Christian doctrines and practices, is in the *Kitāb tahdhīb al-akhlāq* overtly content to commend virtue and human perfection for its own sake, with reason as its arbiter. In this work, Yaḥyā promoted what he calls "humanity" *(al-insāniyyah)*,[102] that is to say, humane behavior in the social sphere that he must have thought to be a prerequisite for the well-being of both philosophy and religion in society.

---

101. One modern edition was published by the late Syrian Orthodox Patriarch Ignatius Aphram I Barsoum (1887–1957) when he was still Metropolitan Archbishop of his church in Syria and Lebanon: Mar Severius Afram Barṣaum, "Jaḥjā ibn ᶜAdī's Treatise on Character Training," *AJSL* 45 (1928): 1–129.

102. See the term used in two places, 2.15 and 5.14.

To translate Yaḥyā ibn ᶜAdī's Arabic term *al-insāniyyah* by the English word "humanism," with all its modern political and philosophical connotations, would be to go too far. Doubtless he used the term in much the same meaning as did his master al-Fārābī. The latter spoke of *al-insāniyyah* "in the sense of the quality that human beings have in common, or human nature; [for him] it also signifies being truly human, in the sense of realizing the end or perfection of man qua man, often synonymous with the exercise of reason."[103] Hence the preoccupation of the philosophers in the Arabic-speaking world of Yaḥyā ibn ᶜAdī's day to promote the claims of reason and philosophy; to this extent Yaḥyā seems to have shared their concern for the sake of promoting truly humane behavior in society.

As for the place of Yaḥyā ibn ᶜAdī's *Tahdhīb al-akhlāq* in the larger context of the development of ethical thought in the Arabic-speaking world of Islam in the tenth century, it is notable that Aristotle's *Nichomachean Ethics* does not seem to have exerted any considerable influence on the work, as one might have expected. Nor is there much concern for the development of a systematic ethics at all, on the order of the concerns of earlier Arab philosophers such as al-Kindī, al-Rāzī, or even al-Fārābī.[104] In this connection, Thérèse-Anne Druart, pointing to the rhetorical flourishes in the work and to the effort to persuade the reader that is so obvious a feature of the style of the *Tahdhīb al-akhlāq,* thinks that Yaḥyā's treatise is not a work of ethics at all. Rather, she thinks that Yaḥyā's *Tahdhīb al-akhlāq,* like the work of the same name by Miskawayh, fits better in the category of *adab* literature.[105]

The *adab,* or "humane," behavior that Yaḥyā commends in the *Tahdhīb al-akhlāq,* and especially his preference for the role of monks and ascetics in society, brings to mind Yaḥyā's other prominent work with a moral concern, the so-called *Treatise on Continence.*[106] In this work, written more in Yaḥyā's customary, syllogistic style than is the case in the *Tahdhīb al-akhlāq,* he argues as "the protagonist of the Christians"

---

103. Kraemer, *Humanism,* 10 n. 14.

104. See Thérèse-Anne Druart, "Al-Kindi's Ethics," *RMet* 47 (1993): 329–57; eadem, "The Ethics of al-Razi (865–925?)," *Medieval Philosophy and Theology* 6 (1997): 47–71; eadem, "Al-Fārābī," 403–23; eadem, "Philosophical Consolation."

105. See Thérèse-Anne Druart, "La philosophie morale arabe et l'antiquité tardive," *BEO* 48 (1996): 185.

106. See Mistrih, "Traité sur la continence." The Arabic term behind "la continence" is *al-ᶜiffah,* which in this translation of the *Tahdhīb al-akhlāq* is always rendered as "abstinence."

(dāᶜī al-naṣārā) that the practice of "avoiding a preoccupation with the aspiration to procreate"[107] on the part of some special people in society is not only not immoral, as his adversaries claim, but in fact is a commendable practice conducive to acquiring "the virtue that brings one close to God."[108] For Yaḥyā such a virtue is the perfection of the rational faculty in man and it is "the acquisition of the exact sciences and divine wisdom."[109] Or, as he put it in another place in the treatise, "The most virtuous thing in a man is the acquisition of the exact sciences and divine knowledge."[110] One notices immediately the openly religious dimension of this treatise, in notable contrast to the *Tahdhīb al-akhlāq*. Not only is there the concern for the attainment of "divine" knowledge or wisdom, but brief prayers for Yaḥyā's interlocutors are scattered throughout the text. And while on the one hand he does say, "I think that Aristotle, Plato, and Socrates were the most excellent in terms of making choices, the most perfect in conduct, and more successful than any of the other practitioners of philosophy and religion,"[111] on the other hand, in another place in the same treatise, he speaks of Christ and his apostles as paragons of virtue, who practiced abstinence from procreation as a means of pursuing a higher good.[112]

In the *Treatise on Continence* the philosophical way of life that Yaḥyā commends is virtually monastic. In the *Kitāb tahdhīb al-akhlāq* the closest he comes to adumbrating the monastic ideal is his remark that when someone achieves the status of the perfect, complete man, "it is the angels he resembles more than he resembles men" (5.2). Nevertheless, given the ancient Christian penchant for equating monasticism with the practice of the philosophy of Christ, and Yaḥyā's own agenda for promoting Christian thought and doctrine, it is worth wondering if the philosophical life in Yaḥyā ibn ᶜAdī's view did not owe as much to the influence of the monastic ideal as it did to the more secular philosophical tradition to which he was also an heir. If so, one could think of the *Tahdhīb al-akhlāq* as a distinctly Christian contribution to the moral education of those in the interreligious society of tenth-century Baghdad who were destined to become kings and leaders in

---

107. Mistrih, "Traité sur la continence," 14.
108. Ibid., 14 and passim.
109. Ibid., 25.
110. Ibid., 37.
111. Ibid., 46.
112. Ibid., 61–62.

their polity. They are charged with the imperative to acquire virtues for the sake of promoting the philosophical way of life, especially among the scholars, monks, and ascetics in the churches and mosques of the caliphate. It is not so much the program of al-Fārābī as it is an ancient Christian ideal translated into the Islamic milieu.

Note on the Text and Translation

The Arabic text of Yaḥyā ibn ʿAdī's *Tahdhīb al-akhlāq* published here is based on the critical edition by Samir Khalil Kussaim, *Yaḥyā ibn ʿAdī (893–974): Tahdhīb al-aḫlāq* (Beirut: CEDRAC, 1994). Marginal pagination in the Arabic references this edition, and I have retained its divisions and headings while introducing new paragraphing and paragraph numbers. The translation aims accurately to express the thought of Yaḥyā ibn ʿAdī in a literal rendering of the Arabic, consistent with the requirements of intelligible English expression.

THE REFORMATION OF MORALS

هَذا كِتَابُ

«تَهْذِيبِ الأَخْلاقِ»

تَأْلِيفُ الحَكِيمِ الأَجَلِّ الفَاضِلِ

أَبِي زَكَرِيّا يَحْيَى بْنِ عَدِيٍّ

قَدَّسَ اللّهُ رُوحَهُ. قَالَ:

This is the text of

The Reformation of Morals,

a work of the illustrious, eminent, wise man,

Abū Zakariyyā Yaḥyā ibn ʿAdī.

May God hallow his spirit.

He spoke as follows.

◆

[القِسْمُ الأَوَّل] p. 16

[مُقَدِّمَاتُ الكِتَاب]

1. اِعلَمْ أَنَّ الإِنْسَانَ، مِنْ بَيْنِ سَائِرِ الحَيَوانِ، ذُو فِكْرٍ وتَمْيِيزٍ. وهُوَ أَبداً يُحِبُّ مِنَ الأُمُورِ أَفْضَلَهَا، ومِنَ المَرَاتِبِ أَشْرَفَهَا، ومِنَ المُقْتَنَيَاتِ أَنْفَسَهَا، إِذَا لَمْ يَعْدِلْ عَنِ التَّمْيِيزِ في اخْتِيَارِهِ، ولَمْ يَغْلِبْهُ هَوَاهُ في اتِّبَاعِ أَغْرَاضِهِ.

2. وأَوْلَى مَا اخْتَارَهُ الإِنْسَانُ لِنَفْسِهِ، ولَمْ يَقِفْ دُونَ بُلُوغِ الغَايَةِ مِنْهُ، ولَمْ
يَرْضَ بالتَّقْصِيرِ عَنْ نِهَايَتِهِ، تَمَامُه وكَمَالُه. ومِنْ تَمَامِ الإِنْسَانِ وكَمَالِهِ أَنْ يَكُونَ مُرْتَاضاً p. 17
بِمَكَارِمِ الأَخْلاقِ ومَحَاسِنِهَا، ومُتَنَزِّهاً عَنْ مَسَاوِئِهَا ومَقَابِحِهَا، آخِذاً في جَمِيعِ أَحْوالِهِ بِقَوَانِينِ الفَضَائِلِ، عَادِلاً في كُلِّ أَفْعَالِهِ عَنْ طُرُقِ الرَّذَائِلِ. وإِذَا كَانَ ذَلِكَ كَذَلِكَ، كَانَ وَاجِباً عَلَى الإِنْسَانِ أَنْ يَجْعَلَ قَصْدَهُ اكْتِسَابَ كُلِّ شِيمَةٍ سَلِيمَةٍ مِنَ المَعَايِبِ، ويَصْرِفَ هِمَّتَهُ إِلَى اقْتِنَاءِ كُلِّ خِيمٍ كَرِيمٍ خَالِصٍ مِنَ الشَّوَائِبِ، وأَنْ يَبْذُلَ جَهْدَهُ في اجْتِنَابِ كُلِّ خَصْلَةٍ مَكْرُوهَةٍ رَدِيئَةٍ، ويَسْتَفْرِغَ وُسْعَهُ في اطِّرَاحِ كُلِّ خَلَّةٍ مَذْمُومَةٍ دَنِيئَةٍ؛ حَتَّى
يَحُوزَ الكَمَالَ بتَهْذِيبِ خَلائِقِهِ، ويَكْتَسِيَ حُلَلَ الجَمَالِ بِدَمَاثَةِ شَمَائِلِهِ، ويُبَاهِيَ بحَقٍّ أَهْلَ p. 18
السُّؤْدُدِ والفَخْرِ، ويَلْحَقَ بِالذُّرَى مِنْ دَرَجَاتِ النَّبَاهَةِ والمَجْدِ. إِلاَّ أَنَّ المُبْتَدِئَ بِطَلَبِ

Part One

People have dispensations, most often toward evil but can be trained to strive & do good & virtuous deeds

Prolegomena to the text

1. Understand that man, of all the animals, is possessed of critical thinking and the power of discrimination. When he does not digress from discrimination in making his choices, and when his craving to follow his own inclinations does not overcome him, he always wants the best things, the noblest stations in life, and the most precious acquisitions.

2. The worthiest thing a man chooses for himself is his own fulfillment and perfection; he will not stop short of attaining the highest degree of it, nor will he be content with any failure to achieve its final reach. Part of a man's fulfillment and perfection is to be well trained in honorable and good moral qualities, to refrain from evil and wrong ones, in all his circumstances to uphold the canons of virtue, and in all his actions to turn aside from the ways of vice. Therefore, it is necessary for a man to make it his intention to acquire every manner of disposition that is free of faults and to turn his resolution to procuring every noble quality that is clear of blemishes. He should make an effort to avoid every vile, detestable trait and exhaust his capacity to discard every base, objectionable characteristic, so that he might attain perfection by the reformation of his morals. So also that he might be beautifully attired in the gentleness of his good qualities and be able actually to compete with the people of power and glory, to reach the top grades of fame and grandeur. However, sometimes the beginner in the quest

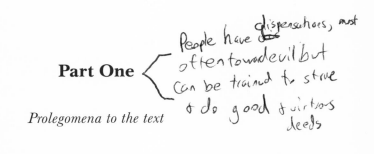

هَذِهِ المَرْتَبَةِ ، والرَّاغِبَ في بُلُوغِ هَذِهِ المَنْزِلَةِ ، رُبَّمَا خَفِيَتْ عَلَيْهِ الخِلَالُ المُسْتَحْسَنَةُ الَّتِي
بُغْيَتُهُ تَحَرِّيهَا ، ولَمْ تَتَمَيَّزْ لَهُ مِنَ المُسْتَقْبَحَةِ الَّتِي غَرَضُهُ تَوَقِّيهَا .

3. فَمِنْ أَجْلِ ذَلِكَ ، وَجَبَ أَنْ نَقُولَ في الأَخْلَاقِ قَوْلاً ، نُبَيِّنُ فِيهِ : مَا الخُلُقُ ،
وَمَا عِلَّتُهُ ، وكَمْ أَنْوَاعُهُ وأَقْسَامُهُ ؛ وَمَا المَرْضِي مِنْهَا ، المَغْبُوطُ صَاحِبُهُ ، والمُتَخَلِّقُ بِهِ ،
p. 19 وَمَا المُسْتَثْنَى مِنْهَا ، المَمْقُوتُ فَاعِلُهُ ، والمُتَوَسِّمُ بِهِ ؛ لِيَسْتَرْشِدَ بذَلِكَ مَنْ كَانَتْ لَهُ هِمَّةٌ
سَنِيَّةٌ تَسْمُو إِلَى مُبَارَاةِ أَهْلِ الفَضْلِ ، ونَفْسٌ أَبِيَّةٌ تَنْبُو عَنْ مُسَاوَاةِ أَهْلِ الدَّنَاءَةِ والنَّقْصِ .
ونَدُلُّ أَيْضاً عَلَى طَرِيقِ الارْتِيَاضِ بالمَحْمُودِ مِنْ أَنْوَاعِهِ ، والتَّدَرُّبِ بِهِ ، وتَنَكُّبِ المَذْمُومِ
مِنْهَا ، وتَجَنُّبِهِ ؛ حَتَّى يَصِيرَ لِلْمُرْتَاضِ بِهِ دَيْدَناً وعَادَةً ، وسَجِيَّةً وطَبْعاً ؛ لِيَهْتَدِيَ بِهِ مَنْ
نَشَأَ عَلَى الأَخْلَاقِ السَّيِّئَةِ ، وأَلِفَهَا ، وجَرَى عَلَى العَادَاتِ الرَّدِيئَةِ ، وأَنِسَ بِهَا . ونَصِفُ
p. 20 أَيْضاً الإِنْسَانَ التَّامَّ ، المُهَذَّبَ الأَخْلَاقِ ، المُحِيطَ بِجَمِيعِ المَنَاقِبِ الخُلُقِيَّةِ ، وطَرِيقَتَهُ الَّتِي
يَصِلُ بِهَا إِلَى التَّمَامِ ، وتَحْفَظُ عَلَيْهِ الكَمَالَ ؛ لِيَشْتَاقَ إِلَى صُورَتِهِ مَنْ تَشَوَّفَ إِلَى الرُّتْبَةِ
العُلْيَا ، ويَحِنَّ إِلَى احْتِذَاءِ سِيرَتِهِ مَنِ اسْتَشْرَفَ الغَايَةَ القُصْوَى .

4. وقَدْ يَتَنَبَّهُ أَيْضاً بِمَا نَذْكُرُهُ مَنْ كَانَتْ لَهُ عُيُوبٌ قَدِ اشْتَبَهَتْ عَلَيْهِ ، وهُوَ
مَعَ ذَلِكَ يَظُنُّ أَنَّهُ في غَايَةِ الكَمَالِ . فَإِنَّ مَنْ هَذِهِ حَالُهُ ، إِذَا تَكَرَّرَ عَلَيْهِ ذِكْرُ الأَخْلَاقِ
المَكْرُوهَةِ ، تَيَقَّظَ لِمَا فِيهِ مِنْ ذَلِكَ ، وأَنِفَ مِنْهُ ، واجْتَهَدَ في تَرْكِهِ والتَّنَزُّهِ عَنْهُ . وكَذَلِكَ ،
p. 21 إِذَا تَصَفَّحَ الأَخْلَاقَ المَحْمُودَةَ مَنْ كَانَ جَامِعاً لأَكْثَرِهَا ، عَادِماً لِبَعْضِهَا ، قَرِمَ إِلَى التَّخَلُّقِ
بِذَلِكَ البَعْضِ الَّذِي هُوَ عَادِمٌ لَهُ ، وتَاقَتْ نَفْسُهُ إِلَى الإِحَاطَةِ بِجَمِيعِهَا . وقَدْ يَنتَفِعُ مِمَّا
نَذْكُرُهُ أَيْضاً مَنْ كَانَ في غَايَةِ التَّمَامِ والكَمَالِ . فَإِنَّ المُهَذَّبَ الأَخْلَاقِ ، الكَامِلَ الآلَاتِ ،
الجَامِعَ المَحَاسِنِ ، إِذَا مَرَّ بِسَمْعِهِ ذِكْرُ الخَلَائِقِ الجَمِيلَةِ والمَنَاقِبِ النَّفِيسَةِ ، ورَأَى أَنَّ تِلْكَ

for this rank (someone wanting to arrive at this status) is unaware of the commendable character traits which he desires, for they are not clearly distinct from the repugnant traits against which he guards himself.

3. Therefore, it is necessary that we say something about moral qualities, in the course of which we will clarify what a moral quality is and what the cause of it is and how many are its kinds and divisions. We shall mention those that are the most gratifying—the possessor of which is fortunate to be morally shaped by them—as well as those that are to be renounced, since people who put them into action are detestable for being characterized by them. It is so that by this means one might be well guided who has a high resolve and aspires to compete with the people of virtue and a lofty soul who dislikes equality with vile and deficient people. We shall also point out the way to train oneself in the most laudable manner, to practice it in its different kinds, as well as how to avoid the most objectionable way and to steer clear of it, so that one becomes well schooled as a matter of habit, custom, character, and natural disposition. Then, too, by the same token, one who has grown up with bad morals, who has become fond of them, and who has continued in bad habits and has become accustomed to them, will be rightly guided. We shall also give a description of the perfect man, someone of reformed moral qualities, comprising all the moral virtues. We shall describe the way by which he achieves fulfillment and which sustains perfection for him, so that those who gaze at the high rank will yearn to be like him, and so that those who keep their eyes on the farthest goal will long to imitate him.

4. Those, too, who have faults that are obscure to them, who nevertheless suppose that they are at the acme of perfection, may be alerted to what we shall have to say. When the recitation of the abhorrent moral qualities is reiterated for someone in this situation, he awakens to those of them that are within him, he rejects them, and makes every effort to abandon them and to get beyond them. So it is also when someone studies the praiseworthy moral qualities; if he is one who has assembled most of them but lacks some of them, he longs to be morally formed in that which he lacks, and his soul yearns to comprise them all. Even those who are at the acme of fulfillment and perfection may gain profit from what we shall have to say. For someone of reformed morals who is accomplished in the means and possesses good character, when the talk of seemly moral traits and valuable virtues comes to his ears and he sees

هِيَ عَادَتُهُ وسَجَايَاهُ، كَانَتْ لَهُ بِذَلِكَ لَذَّةٌ عَجِيبَةٌ، وفَرْحَةٌ مُبْهِجَةٌ؛ كما أَنَّ المَمْدُوحَ يُسَرُّ إذَا ذَكَرَ المَادِحُ مَحَاسِنَهُ، ونَشَرَ فَضَائِلَهُ. وأَيْضاً فَإِنَّهُ، إذَا وَجَدَ أَخْلاقَهُ مُدَوَّنَةً في الكُتُبِ، مَوْصُوفَةً بِالحُسْنِ، كَانَ ذَلِكَ دَاعِياً إلَى الاسْتِمْرَارِ عَلَى سِيرَتِهِ، والإصْرَارِ عَلَى طَرِيقَتِهِ.

[في أَخْلاَقِ الإِنْسَانِ] p. 22

5. وهَذَا حِينَ ابْتِدَائِنَا بِذِكْرِ الأَخْلاَقِ، فَنَقُولُ: إنَّ الخُلُقَ هُوَ حَالٌ لِلنَّفْسِ، بِهِ يَفْعَلُ الإنْسَانُ أَفْعَالَهُ بِلاَ رَوِيَّةٍ، ولاَ اخْتِيَارٍ. والخُلُقُ قَدْ يَكُونُ في بَعْضِ النَّاسِ غَرِيزَةً وطَبْعاً، وفي بَعْضِ النَّاسِ لاَ يَكُونُ إلاَّ بِالرِّيَاضَةِ والاجْتِهَادِ. كَالسَّخَاءِ قَدْ يُوجَدُ في كَثِيرٍ مِنَ النَّاسِ، مِنْ غَيْرِ رِيَاضَةٍ ولاَ تَعَمُّدٍ؛ وكَالشَّجَاعَةِ والحِلْمِ والعِفَّةِ والعَدْلِ، وغَيْرِ
ذَلِكَ مِنَ الأَخْلاَقِ المَحْمُودَةِ. وكَثِيرٌ مِنَ النَّاسِ يُوجَدُ فِيهِمْ ذَلِكَ: فَمِنْهُمْ مَنْ يَصِيرُ إِلَيْهِ p. 23
بِالرِّيَاضَةِ، ومِنْهُمْ مَنْ يَبْقَى عَلَى عَادَتِهِ، ويَجْرِي عَلَى سِيرَتِهِ.

6. فَأَمَّا الأَخْلاَقُ المَذْمُومَةُ، فَإِنَّهَا مَوْجُودَةٌ في كَثِيرٍ مِنَ النَّاسِ، كَالبُخْلِ والجُبْنِ والظُّلْمِ والتَّشَرُّرِ. فَإِنَّ هَذِهِ العَادَاتِ غَالِبَةٌ عَلَى أَكْثَرِ النَّاسِ، مَالِكَةٌ لَهُمْ. بَلْ قَلَّمَا يُوجَدُ في النَّاسِ مَنْ يَخْلُو مِنْ خُلُقٍ مَكْرُوهٍ، ويَسْلَمُ مِنْ جَمِيعِ العُيُوبِ، ولَكِنَّهُمْ يَتَفَاضَلُونَ
في ذَلِكَ. وكَذلِكَ في الأَخْلاَقِ المَحْمُودَةِ، قَدْ يَخْتَلِفُ النَّاسُ ويَتَفَاضَلُونَ. إلاَّ أَنَّ p. 24
المَجْبُولِينَ عَلَى الأَخْلاَقِ الجَمِيلَةِ قَلِيلُونَ جِدّاً، والمُبْغِضِينَ لَهَا كَثِيرُونَ. فَأَمَّا المَجْبُولُونَ عَلَى الأَخْلاَقِ السَّيِّئَةِ، فَأَكْثَرُ النَّاسِ. لأَنَّ الغَالِبَ عَلَى طَبِيعَةِ الإِنْسَانِ الشَّرُّ.

that they are his own habitual practice and disposition, he experiences a marvelous pleasure and a pleasant joy, just as someone who is praised is delighted when the one praising him mentions his good character and announces his virtues. Then, when he finds his own moral qualities listed in books and described as good, this summons him to persevere in his good behavior and to make progress in his conduct.

On man's moral qualities

5. Now it is time for us to begin specifying the moral qualities, so we say the following: A moral quality is a state proper to the soul, in which a man performs his actions without deliberation or study. A moral quality may come to be in some people as a natural impulse or disposition and in others only by way of practice and effort. So, generosity may be found in a great many people, without practice or the making of a resolution; and so also courage, forbearance, abstinence, justice, and others of the praiseworthy moral qualities. This may be found to be the case in a great many people, some of them coming to it by practice, others maintaining it by habit and carrying on according to their customary way of acting.

6. As for the blameworthy moral qualities, they too are to be found in a great many people, such as niggardliness, cowardice, injustice, and malevolence. These habits overwhelm most people, dominating them. In fact, seldom is there to be found among people someone who is free of any abhorrent moral quality and unimpaired by any fault. Rather, they rival one another in the matter. Likewise, in regard to the praiseworthy moral qualities, people differ and they rival one another. However, those naturally disposed to the good moral qualities are very few, and the ones who detest them are many. Most people are naturally disposed to the bad moral qualities, given the fact that evil predominates over human nature.

٧. وذَلِكَ أَنَّ الإنْسَانَ ، إذَا اسْتَرْسَلَ مَعَ طَبْعِهِ ، ولَمْ يَسْتَعْمِلِ الفِكْرَ ولاَ
التَّمييزَ ، ولاَ الحَيَاءَ ولاَ التَّحَفُّظَ ، كَانَ الغَالِبُ عَلَيْهِ أَخْلاقَ البَهَائِمِ. وذَلِكَ أَنَّ الإنْسَانَ ،
p. 25 إِنَّمَا يَتَمَيَّزُ عَنِ البَهَائِمِ بِالفِكْرِ والتَّمييزِ. فَإِذَا لَمْ يَسْتَعْمِلْهَا ، كَانَ مُشَارِكاً لِلبَهَائِمِ في
عَادَاتِهَا ، والشَّهَوَاتُ مُسْتَوْلِيَةٌ عَلَيْهِ ، والحَيَاءُ غَائِبٌ عَنْهُ ، والغَضَبُ يَسْتَفِزُّهُ ، والسَّكِينَةُ
غَيْرُ حَاضِرَةٍ لَهُ ، والحِرْصُ والإحْتِشَادُ دَيْدَنُهُ ، والشَّرَهُ لا يُفَارِقُهُ. فَالنَّاسُ مَطْبُوعُونَ
عَلَى الأَخْلاقِ الرَّدِيئَةِ ، مُنْقَادُونَ لِلشَّهَوَاتِ الدَّنِيئَةِ.

٨. ولِذَلِكَ وَقَعَ الافْتِقَارُ إلى الشَّرَائِعِ والسُّنَنِ والسِّيَاسَاتِ المَحْمُودَةِ ، وعَظُمَ
الانْتِفَاعُ بالمُلُوكِ الحَسَنِي السِّيرَةِ ، لِيَرْدَعُوا الظَّالِمَ عَنْ ظُلْمِهِ ، ويَمْنَعُوا الغَاضِبَ عَنْ
p. 26 غَضَبِهِ ، ويُعَاقِبُوا الفَاجِرَ عَلى فُجُورِهِ ، ويَقْمَعُوا الجَائِرَ حَتَّى يَعُودَ إِلَى الاعْتِدَالِ في
جَمِيعِ أُمُورِهِ.

٩. فَالأَخْلاقُ المَكْرُوهَةُ في طِبَاعِ النَّاسِ. إلاَّ أَنَّ مِنْهُمْ مَنْ يَتَظَاهَرُ بِهَا ، ويَنْقَادُ
لَهَا ، وهُمْ أَشْرَارُ النَّاسِ. ومِنْهُم مَنْ يَتَنَبَّهُ (بِجُودَةِ الفِكْرِ وقُوَّةِ التَّمييزِ) عَلَى قُبْحِهَا ،
فَيَأْنَفُ مِنْهَا ويَتَصَنَّعُ لاِجْتِنَابِهَا ؛ وذَلِكَ يَكُونُ عَنْ طَبْعٍ كَرِيمٍ ، ونَفْسٍ شَرِيفَةٍ. ومِنْهُمْ مَنْ لا
p. 27 يَتَنَبَّهُ لِذَلِكَ ؛ إلاَّ أَنَّهُ ، إذَا نُبِّهَ عَلَيْهِ ، أَحَسَّ بِقُبْحِهِ ، فَرُبَّمَا حَمَلَ نَفْسَهُ عَلَى تَرْكِهِ. ومِنْهُمْ
مَنْ ، إذَا تَنَبَّهَ لِمَا فِيهِ مِنَ النَّقَائِصِ أو نُبِّهَ عَلَيْهَا ، ورَامَ العُدُولَ عَنْهَا ، تَعَذَّرَ عَلَيْهِ ذَلِكَ ،
ولَمْ يُطَاوِعْهُ طَبْعُهُ ، وإِنْ كَانَ مُؤْثِراً لِلعُدُولِ عَنْهَا ، مُجْتَهِداً في ذَلِكَ. وهَذِهِ الطَّائِفَةُ
تَحْتَاجُ إِلَى أَنْ تُرْشَدَ إِلَى طَرِيقِ التَّدَرُّبِ والتَّعَمُّلِ لِلعَادَاتِ المَحْمُودَةِ ، حَتَّى تَصِيرَ إِلَيهَا
عَلَى التَّدْرِيجِ. ومِنَ النَّاسِ مَنْ ، إذا تَنَبَّهَ عَلَى الأَخْلاقِ الرَّدِيئَةِ أَوْ نُبِّهَ عَلَيْهَا ، فَلا يَحِنُّ
إِلَى تَجَنُّبِهَا ، ولاَ تَسْمَحُ نَفْسُهُ لِمُفَارَقَتِهَا ، بَلْ يُؤْثِرُ الإصْرَارَ عَلَيْهَا ، مَعَ عِلْمِهِ بِرَدَاءَتِهَا

7. That is because, when a man gives himself up to his nature and exercises neither critical thought nor discrimination, neither a sense of shame nor wariness, what predominates over him is the morality of the animals. That is because a man is only distinguished from the animals by thought and discrimination. When he does not put them to use, he begins to share with the animals in their habits. Desires gain mastery over him, shame vanishes from him, anger incites him, tranquility has left him, greed and avarice are his habitual practice, and ravenousness never withdraws from him. People are disposed to bad morals, inclined to yield to base desires.

8. Therefore, the need arises for laws, norms, and laudable policies. And the advantage of kings of good conduct is immense. They will dissuade the wrongdoer from his wrong, they will hold back the angry man from his anger, they will punish the immoral man for his immorality, and they will restrain the tyrant to the point that he reverts to moderation in all his affairs.

9. Abhorrent moral qualities are in the natures of people. The fact is that there are some people who put them on display and are led by them; they are the worst of people. There are some people who (by reason of the good quality of their thought and the power of discrimination) take notice of the foulness of these things, and so they disdain them and devise means to avoid them. That comes from an honorable nature and a noble soul. There are some people who take no notice of the matter; but when they are put on notice, they perceive the foulness, and so sometimes their soul brings them to renunciation. There are also some people who, when they notice some failings or are put on notice about them and they want to refrain from them, find it is too difficult for them. Their nature does not comply with their wishes, even though they prefer to refrain from these things and they make an effort to do so. This group needs to be guided to the way to be trained and to work hard for praiseworthy habits, so that they might come into them step by step. There are also some people who, when they become aware of bad morals or are put on notice about them, do not yearn to avoid them. Their soul does not allow them to disengage themselves from them. Rather, they prefer to persist in them, concomitant with their knowledge of their viciousness and foulness. There

p. 28 وقُبْحِها . وهَذِهِ الطَّائِفَةُ لَيْسَ إلَى تَهْذِيبِهَا طَرِيقٌ ، إلاَّ بالْقَهْرِ والتَّخْوِيفِ والعُقُوبَةِ ، إنْ لَمْ
يَرْدَعْهَا التَّرْهِيبُ .

10. فَأمَّا الأَخْلاَقُ المَحْمُودَةُ ، فَإنَّهَا ، وإنْ كَانَتْ في بَعْضِ النَّاسِ غَرِيزَةً ، فَلَيْسَتْ في جَمِيعِهِمْ . وإنَّ البَاقِينَ قَدْ يُمْكِنُ أَنْ يَصِيرُوا إلَيْهَا بِالتَّدَرُّبِ والرِّيَاضَةِ ، ويَتَرَقَّوْا إلَيْهَا بالاِعْتِيَادِ والأُلْفِ . ومَعَ هَذِهِ الحَالِ ، فقَدْ يَكُونُ في النّاسِ مَنْ لا يَقْبَلُ طَبْعُهُ
p. 29 العَادَاتِ الحَسَنَةَ ، ولاَ الخُلُقَ الجَمِيلَ ؛ وذَلِكَ يَكُونُ لِرَداءَةِ جَوْهَرِهِ وخُبْثِ عُنْصُرِهِ . وهَذِهِ الطَّائِفَةُ مِنْ جُمْلَةِ الأَشْرَارِ ، الَّذِينَ لاَ يُرْجَى صَلاَحُهُمْ . وكَثِيرٌ مِنَ النَّاسِ مَنْ يَقْبَلُ كَثِيراً مِنَ الأَخْلاَقِ المَحْمُودَةِ ، ويَنْبُو طَبْعُهُ عَنْ بَعْضِهَا . ولَيْسَ يُعَدُّ هَذَا شِرِّيراً ، بَلْ تَكُونُ رُتْبَتُهُ في الخَيْرِ بِحَسَبِ مَحَاسِنِهِ .

is no way for the reformation of this group, except by force, fright, and punishment, if intimidation does not impede them.

10. As for the praiseworthy moral qualities, although they are innate in some people, they are not innate in all of them. It may be possible for the remainder to attain them by drill and by practice and to advance in them by forming habits and by accustoming themselves to them. But, concomitantly, there may also be people whose nature is not receptive to good habits or to any good moral quality. That will be due to their bad substance and the wickedness of their stock. This group, of all the bad ones, are those whose improvement is not even to be hoped for. But many people are receptive to many of the praiseworthy moral qualities, even though their nature shies away from some of them. These are not to be reckoned bad. Rather, their rank is to be among the good, commensurate with their merits.

[القِسْمُ الثَّانِي]

[العِلَّةُ المُوجِبَةُ لِاخْتِلَافِ الأَخْلَاقِ هِيَ قُوَى النَّفْس]

1. فَأَمَّا العِلَّةُ المُوجِبَةُ لِاخْتِلَافِ الأَخْلَاقِ، فَهِيَ النَّفْسُ. وَلِلنَّفْسِ ثَلَاثُ

قُوًى، وَهِيَ تُسَمَّى أَيْضاً نُفُوساً؛ وَهِيَ النَّفْسُ الشَّهْوَانِيَّةُ، وَالنَّفْسُ الغَضَبِيَّةُ، وَالنَّفْسُ

5 النَّاطِقَةُ. وَجَمِيعُ الأَخْلَاقِ تَصْدُرُ عَنْ هَذِهِ القُوَى. فَمِنْهَا مَا يَخْتَصُّ بِإِحْدَاهِنَّ، وَمِنْهَا

مَا يَشْتَرِكُ فِيهَا قُوَّتَانِ، وَمِنْهَا مَا يَشْتَرِكُ فِيهَا القُوَى الثَّلَاثُ. وَمِنْ هَذِهِ القُوَى مَا يَكُونُ

لِلْإِنْسَانِ وَغَيْرِهِ مِنَ الحَيَوَانِ، وَمِنْهَا مَا يَخْتَصُّ بِهِ الإِنْسَانُ فَقَطْ.

[النَّفْسُ الشَّهْوَانِيَّةُ]

2. أَمَّا النَّفْسُ الشَّهْوَانِيَّةُ، فَهِيَ لِلْإِنْسَانِ وَلِسَائِرِ الحَيَوَانِ. وَهِيَ الَّتِي تَكُونُ

10 بِهَا جَمِيعُ اللَّذَّاتِ وَالشَّهَوَاتِ الجِسْمَانِيَّةِ، كَالقَرَمِ إِلَى المَآكِلِ وَالمَشَارِبِ وَالمُبَاضَعَةِ. وَهَذِهِ

النَّفْسُ قَوِيَّةٌ جِدّاً: مَتَى لَمْ يَقْهَرْهَا الإِنْسَانُ وَيُؤَدِّبْهَا، مَلَكَتْهُ وَاسْتَوْلَتْ عَلَيْهِ. فَإِذَا

اسْتَوْلَتْ عَلَيْهِ، عَسُرَ تَهْذِيبُهَا، وَصَعُبَ قَمْعُهَا وَتَذْلِيلُهَا. فَإِذَا تَمَكَّنَتْ هَذِهِ النَّفْسُ مِنَ

Part Two

The faculties of the soul are the necessary cause for the differentiation of the moral qualities

1. The necessary cause for the differentiation of the moral qualities is the soul. The soul has three faculties, and they are also named souls: the appetitive soul, the irascible soul, and the rational soul. All of the moral qualities emanate from these faculties. Some moral qualities are specific to a particular faculty; in some, two faculties participate; and, in some of them, the three faculties participate. Some faculties belong to man and to the other animals, and some are specific to man alone.

The appetitive soul

2. The appetitive soul belongs to man and to the rest of the animals. It is the one in which all the pleasures and bodily appetites come to be, such as the desire for food and drink and for having sexual intercourse. This soul is extremely powerful. Whenever a man does not subjugate it and discipline it, it dominates him and gains the mastery over him. And, when it gains the mastery over him, to reform it is difficult; to curb it and to subdue it is hard. When this soul gains possession

الإِنْسَانِ، وَمَلَكَهُ، وَانْقَادَ لَهَا، كَانَ بِالبَهَائِمِ أَشْبَهَ مِنْهُ بِالنَّاسِ. لِأَنَّ أَغْرَاضَهُ وَمَطْلُوبَاتِهِ وَهِمَّتَهُ تَصِيرُ أَبَداً مَصْرُوفَةً إِلَى الشَّهَوَاتِ وَاللَّذَّاتِ فَقَطْ. وَهَذِهِ هِيَ عَادَاتُ البَهَائِمِ.

3. وَمَنْ يَكُونُ بِهَذِهِ الصِّفَةِ، يَقِلُّ حَيَاؤُهُ، وَيَكْثُرُ خُرْقُهُ، وَيَسْتَوْحِشُ مِنْ أَهْلِ الفَضْلِ، وَيَمِيلُ إِلَى الخَلَوَاتِ، وَيَنْقَبِضُ عَنِ المَجَالِسِ الحَفْلَةِ، وَيُبْغِضُ أَهْلَ العِلْمِ،

p. 33

5 وَيَشْنَأُ أَهْلَ الوَرَعِ وَالنُّسُكِ، وَيَوَدُّ أَصْحَابَ الفُجُورِ، وَيَسْتَحِبُّ الفَوَاحِشَ، وَيُكْثِرُ مِنْ ذِكْرِهَا، وَيَلَذُّ بِاسْتِمَاعِهَا، وَيُسَرُّ بِمُعَاشَرَةِ السُّفَهَاءِ، وَيَغْلِبُ عَلَيْهِ الهَزَلُ وَكَثْرَةُ اللَّهْوِ. وَقَدْ يَصِيرُ مَنْ هَذِهِ حَالُهُ إِلَى الفُجُورِ، وَارْتِكَابِ الفَوَاحِشِ، وَالتَّعَرُّضِ لِلْمَحْظُورَاتِ. وَرُبَّمَا دَعَتْهُ مَحَبَّةُ اللَّذَّاتِ إِلَى اكْتِسَابِ الأَمْوَالِ مِنْ أَقْبَحِ وُجُوهِهَا. وَرُبَّمَا حَمَلَتْهُ نَفْسُهُ عَلَى الغَضَبِ، وَالتَّلَصُّصِ، وَالخِيَانَةِ، وَأَخْذِ مَا لَيْسَ لَهُ بِحَقٍّ. فَإِنَّ اللَّذَّاتِ لَا تَتِمُّ إِلَّا

10 بِالأَمْوَالِ وَالأَغْرَاضِ. فَمُحِبُّ اللَّذَّاتِ، إِذَا تَعَذَّرَتْ عَلَيْهِ الأَمْوَالُ مِنْ وُجُوهِهَا، جَسَّرَتْهُ شَهْوَتُهُ عَلَى اكْتِسَابِهَا مِنْ غَيْرِ وُجُوهِهَا.

p. 34

4. وَمَنْ تَنْتَهِي بِهِ شَهَوَاتُهُ إِلَى هَذَا الحَدِّ، فَهُوَ أَسْوَأُ النَّاسِ حَالاً، وَهُوَ مِنَ الأَشْرَارِ الَّذِينَ يُخَافُ خُبْثُهُمْ، وَيُسْتَوْحَشُ مِنْهُمْ، وَيُسْتَرْوَحُ إِلَى البُعْدِ عَنْهُمْ. وَيَصِيرُ وَاجِباً، عَلَى مُتَوَلِّي السِّيَاسَاتِ، تَقْوِيمُهُمْ وَتَأْدِيبُهُمْ وَإِبْعَادُهُمْ وَنَفْيُهُمْ، حَتَّى لَا يَخْتَلِطُوا

15 بِالنَّاسِ. فَإِنَّ، فِي اخْتِلَاطِ مَنْ هَذِهِ صِفَتُهُ بِالنَّاسِ، مَضَرَّةً لَهُمْ، وَخَاصَّةً لِأَحْدَاثِهِمْ. فَإِنَّ الحَدَثَ سَرِيعُ الِانْطِبَاعِ، وَنَفْسُهُ مَجْبُولَةٌ عَلَى المَيْلِ إِلَى الشَّهَوَاتِ. فَإِذَا شَاهَدَ غَيْرَهُ مُرْتَكِباً لَهَا، مُسْتَحْسِناً لِلِانْهِمَاكِ فِيهَا، مَالَ هُوَ أَيْضاً إِلَى الِاقْتِدَاءِ بِهِ وَإِلَى

p. 35

مُسَاعَدَةِ لَذَّتِهِ. وَأَمَّا مَنْ مَلَكَ نَفْسَهُ الشَّهْوَانِيَّةَ وَقَهَرَهَا، كَانَ ضَابِطاً لِنَفْسِهِ، عَفِيفاً

of a man and dominates him, and he yields to it, he becomes more like the animals than like men, because his aims, his demands, and his ambition come always to be devoted to appetites and pleasures alone. These are the habits of the animals.

3. A person of this description is one whose shame is sparse and whose folly abounds. He feels distaste for people of virtue, and he has a liking for seclusion. He shuts himself off from social gatherings, and he loathes people of knowledge. He hates people of godliness and piety, while he is fond of the companions of debauchery and deems lewdness lovable. He frequently mentions it and is delighted to hear about it. He is happy in the company of the foolish; joking and amusement take control of him. Someone in this situation may end up debauched, pursuing lewdness, and venturing into the forbidden. Sometimes the love of pleasure induces him to acquire wealth in the foulest of ways. Sometimes his soul moves him to anger, to engage in thievery and treachery, to take that to which he has no right. For pleasure is never complete except in wealth and fame. So, when wealth in the proper way is too difficult for the lover of pleasure, his appetite emboldens him to acquire it improperly.

4. Someone whose appetites bring him ultimately to this extremity is the worst of people, in terms of his condition. He is one of those evil ones whose malevolence is to be feared, for whom one has a distaste; and one is glad to be far from them. It becomes necessary for those in authority to correct them, to discipline them, to banish them, and to ostracize them so that they will not associate with people. The association of someone of this description with people is something harmful to them, and particularly to the youths among them. For a youth is quick to be impressed, and his soul is disposed to be inclined to the appetites. When he sees someone else in pursuit of them, condoning indulgence in them, he likewise is inclined to imitate him and to assist in his pleasure. Whoever dominates his appetitive soul and subjugates it is in control

فِي شَهَوَاتِهِ، مُحْتَشِماً مِنَ الفَواحِشِ، مُتَوَقِّياً مِنَ المَحْظُورَاتِ، مَحْمُودَ الطَّرِيقَةِ، في جَمِيعِ مَا يَتَعَلَّقُ بِاللَّذَّاتِ.

5. فَالعِلَّةُ المُوجِبَةُ لِاخْتِلَافِ عَادَاتِ النَّاسِ، في شَهَوَاتِهِمْ ولَذَّاتِهِمْ، وعِفَّةِ بَعْضِهِمْ وفُجُورِ بَعْضِهِمْ، هِيَ اخْتِلَافُ أَحْوَالِ النَّفْسِ الشَّهْوَانِيَّةِ. فَإِنَّهَا، إذا كَانَتْ مُهَذَّبَةً مُؤَدَّبَةً، كَانَ صَاحِبُهَا عَفِيفاً ضَابِطاً لِنَفْسِهِ. وإذا كَانَتْ مُهْمَلَةً مُرْسَلَةً، مَالِكَةً لِصَاحِبِهَا، كَانَ صَاحِبُهَا فَاجِراً شِرِّيراً. وإِذَا كَانَتْ مُتَوَسِّطَةَ الحَالِ، كَانَتْ رُتْبَةُ p. 36 صَاحِبِهَا في العِفَّةِ كَرُتْبَتِهَا في التَّأَدُّبِ. فَمِنْ أَجْلِ ذَلِكَ، وَجَبَ أَنْ يُؤَدِّبَ الإِنْسَانُ نَفْسَهُ الشَّهْوَانِيَّةَ ويُهَذِّبَهَا. حَتَّى تَصِيرَ مُنْقَادَةً لَهُ، فَيَكُونَ هُوَ مَالِكُهَا؛ فَيَسْتَعْمِلَهَا في حَاجَاتِهِ الَّتي لاَ غِنَى عَنْهَا، ويَكُفَّهَا عَمَّا لاَ حَاجَةَ بِهِ إِلَيْهِ مِنَ الشَّهَوَاتِ الرَّدِيئَةِ واللَّذَّاتِ الفَاحِشَةِ.

[النَّفْسُ الغَضَبِيَّة]

6. فَأَمَّا النَّفْسُ الغَضَبِيَّةُ، فَيَشْتَرِكُ فِيهَا أَيْضاً الإِنْسَانُ وسَائِرُ الحَيَوَانِ. وهِيَ p. 37 الَّتي يَكُونُ بِهَا الغَضَبُ، والجُرْأَةُ، ومَحَبَّةُ الغَلَبَةِ. وهَذِهِ النَّفْسُ أَقْوَى مِنَ النَّفْسِ الشَّهْوَانِيَّةِ وأَضَرُّ بِصَاحِبِهَا، إذَا مَلَكَتْهُ وَانْقَادَ لَهَا. فَإِنَّ الإِنْسَانَ، إِذَا انْقَادَ لِلنَّفْسِ الغَضَبِيَّةِ، كَثُرَ غَضَبُهُ، وظَهَرَ خُرْقُهُ، واشْتَدَّ حِقْدُهُ، وعَدِمَ حِلْمُهُ ووَقَارُهُ، وقَوِيَتْ جُرْأَتُهُ، وتَسَرَّعَ عِنْدَ الغَضَبِ إِلَى الاِنْتِقَامِ والإِيقَاعِ بِمُغْضِبِهِ، والوُثُوبِ بِخُصُومِهِ، فَأَسْرَفَ في العُقُوبَةِ، وزَادَ في التَّشَفِّي، فَأَكْثَرَ السَّبَّ وأَفْحَشَ فِيهِ. فَإذَا اسْتَمَرَّتْ هَذِهِ العَادَاتُ بِالإِنْسَانِ، كَانَ بِالسِّبَاعِ أَشْبَهَ مِنْهُ بِالنَّاسِ.

of himself, modest in his appetites, bashful about lewdness, on his guard about what is forbidden, praiseworthy in the way he deals with everything connected with pleasure.

5. The necessary cause for the differentiation of people's habits in connection with their appetites and their pleasures—the modesty of some of them and the debauchery of others—is the differentiation of the states of the appetitive soul. When it is reformed and disciplined, its possessor is an abstinent man, in control of himself. When it is neglected and let go, dominating its possessor, its possessor is an evil debauchee. When it is in an intermediate state, the rank of its possessor in abstinence is according to the soul's rank in discipline. For this reason, it is necessary for a man to refine his appetitive soul and to reform it so that it becomes obedient to him and he comes to be its master. Then he will employ it for those needs of his which he cannot do without, and he will restrain it from those bad appetites and lewd pleasures for which he has no need.

The irascible soul

6. Both man and the rest of the animals also participate in the irascible soul. In it are anger, recklessness, and the love of victory. This soul is more powerful than the appetitive soul and more injurious to its possessor when it gains the mastery over him and he yields to it. When a man yields to the irascible soul, his anger is excessive, his folly becomes evident, his rancor is strengthened, his gentleness and dignity are nonexistent, and his recklessness becomes powerful. He rushes in anger to avenge himself, to attack anyone who angers him, and to pounce on his opponents. He exceeds all bounds in punishment and grows intense in satisfying his thirst for revenge. He constantly curses and uses obscene language. When these habits persist in a man, he comes more to resemble the beasts of prey than he does men.

p. 38 7. ورُبَّمَا حَمَلَ قَوْماً عَلَى حَمْلِ السِّلَاحِ، ورُبَّمَا أَقْدَمُوا عَلَى القَتْلِ والجَرْحِ، ورُبَّمَا وَثَبُوا بِالسِّلاحِ عَلَى إِخْوَانِهِمْ وأَوْلِيَائِهِمْ، وعَبِيدِهِمْ وخَدَمِهِمْ، عِنْدَ الغَضَبِ مِنَ اليَسِيرِ مِنَ الأُمُورِ. ورُبَّمَا غَضِبَ مَنْ هذِهِ حَالَتُهُ، ولَمْ يَقْدِرْ عَلَى الاِنْتِقَامِ مِنْ خَصْمِهِ، فَيَعُودُ بِالضَّرْبِ والسَّبِّ والأَلَمِ عَلَى نَفْسِهِ: فَمِنْهُمْ مَنْ يَلْطِمُ وَجْهَهُ، ويَنْتِفُ لِحْيَتَهُ، ويَعَضُّ يَدَهُ، ويَسُبُّ نَفْسَهُ، ويَذْكُرُ عِرْضَهُ.

8. وأَيْضاً، فَإِنَّ مَنْ تَمْلِكُهُ النَّفْسُ الغَضَبِيَّةُ، يَكُونُ مُحِبّاً لِلغَلَبَةِ، مُتَوَثِّباً عَلَى مَنْ آذَاهُ، مُقْدِماً عَلَى كُلِّ مَنْ نَاوَأَهُ، طَالِباً لِلتَّرَؤُّسِ مِنْ غَيْرِ وَجْهِهِ. فَإِذَا لَمْ يَتَمَكَّنْ
p. 39 مِنَ الرِّئَاسَةِ، تَوَصَّلَ إِلَيْهَا بِالحِيَلِ الخَبِيثَةِ، فَاسْتَعْمَلَ كُلَّ مَا يُمْكِنُهُ مِنَ الشَّرِّ. وهَذِهِ الأَفْعَالُ تُوَرِّطُ صَاحِبَهَا، وتُوقِعُهُ في المَهَاوِي والمَهَالِكِ. فَإِنَّ مَنْ وَثَبَ عَلَى النَّاسِ، وَثَبُوا عَلَيْهِ؛ ومَنْ خَاصَمَهُمْ، خَاصَمُوهُ؛ ومَنْ أَقْدَمَ عَلَيهِمْ، أَقْدَمُوا عَلَيْهِ؛ ومَنْ تَشَرَّرَ عَلَيْهِمْ، قَصَدُوهُ بِالشَّرِّ. ورُبَّمَا سَفِهَ الإِنْسَانُ عَلَى خَصْمِهِ، وكَانَ الخَصْمُ أَسْفَهَ مِنْهُ. فَإِنْ نَالَهُ بِسُوءٍ، قَابَلَهُ ذَاكَ بِأَكْثَرِ مِنْهُ. وقَدْ يَغْلِبُ عَلَى مَنْ هَذِهِ حَالُهُ الحَسَدُ، والحِقْدُ، والقِحَةُ، واللَّجَاجُ، والجَوْرُ. وقَدْ تَحْمِلُ هَؤُلَاءِ مَحَبَّةُ الغَلَبَةِ، وطَلَبُ الرِّئَاسَةِ، عَلَى
p. 40 اكْتِسَابِ الأَمْوَالِ مِنْ غَيْرِ وُجُوهِهَا، وأَخْذِهَا بِالغَضَبِ والغَلَبَةِ والظُّلْمِ. ورُبَّمَا قَتَلُوا، عَلَى مَحَبَّةِ الغَلَبَةِ، مَنْ يُنَاوِئُهُمْ؛ وقَدْ يَفْعَلُونَ ذَلِكَ مِنْ غَيْرِ رَوِيَّةٍ، فَيَؤُولُ الأَمْرُ بِهِمْ إِلَى البَوَارِ والاِسْتِئْصَالِ.

9. فَأَمَّا مَنْ سَاسَ نَفْسَهُ الغَضَبِيَّةَ، وأَدَّبَهَا، وقَمَعَهَا، كَانَ رَجُلاً حَلِيماً، وَقُوراً، عَادِلاً، مَحْمُودَ الطَّرِيقَةِ. فَالعِلَّةُ المُوجِبَةُ لِاخْتِلَافِ عَادَاتِ النَّاسِ، في غَضَبِهِمْ وخُرْقِهِمْ، وحِلْمِ بَعْضِهِمْ، وسَفَاهَةِ بَعْضٍ، هِيَ اخْتِلَافُ أَحْوَالِ النَّفْسِ الغَضَبِيَّةِ. فَإِذَا

7. Sometimes he incites people to carry weapons; sometimes they have the audacity to kill and to wound; and sometimes, for the most insignificant of reasons, they rush in anger with weapons against their own brothers, patrons, slaves, and servants. Sometimes, someone in this state gets angry and is unable to take vengeance against his opponent. So he turns the blows, the cursing, and the affliction back on himself. There are those of them who strike their own faces, pluck out their own beards, and bite their own hands; they also revile themselves and impugn their own honor.

8. Then, too, one whom the irascible soul rules has the wish to dominate, pouncing on anyone who harms him, attacking everyone who stands up to him, seeking to acquire authority improperly. When he does not possess any authority, he gains access to it by means of evil strategies, and so he makes use of any wrong thing that he can. These kinds of actions get the one who performs them into trouble and plunge him into pitfalls and perils. For, if someone pounces on people, they pounce on him; if he quarrels with them, they quarrel with him; if he attacks them, they attack him; if he is malevolent toward them, they want him to be harmed. Sometimes, when a man is insolent toward his opponent, the opponent becomes even more insolent than he is. If he then harms him, that one counters with a worse harm. And sometimes envy, malice, impudence, obstinacy, and outrage overwhelm someone in this condition. Sometimes the wish to dominate and the search for authority bring these people to acquire wealth unethically, to take it with anger, subjugation, and ill treatment. Sometimes, on account of the wish to dominate, they kill whoever opposes them. Sometimes they will do this without any deliberation, and the matter brings them eventually to perdition and annihilation.

9. Someone who governs his irascible soul, disciplines it, and bridles it becomes a gentle, dignified, and just man, praiseworthy for his way of life. So the necessary cause for the differentiation of people's habits in regard to their anger and their folly, as well as the gentleness of some of them and the silliness of some, is the difference of the states of the

كَانَتْ مُذَلَّلَةً مَقْهُورَةً ، كَانَ صَاحِبُهَا حَلِيماً وَقُوراً . وإذَا كَانَتْ مُهْمَلَةً مُسْتَوْلِيَةً عَلى
صَاحِبِهَا ، كَانَ صَاحِبُهَا غَضُوباً ، سَفِيهاً ، ظَلُوماً ، غَشُوماً . وإذَا كَانَتْ مُتَوَسِّطَةَ p. 41
الحَالِ ، كَانَ صَاحِبُهَا مُتَوَسِّطَ الحَالِ ، رُتْبَتُهُ في الحِلْمِ كَرُتْبَةِ نَفْسِهِ الغَضَبِيَّةِ في التَّأَدُّبِ .
فَمِنْ أَجْلِ ذَلِكَ ، وَجَبَ أَنْ يُرَوِّضَ الإنْسَانُ نَفْسَهُ الغَضَبِيَّةَ ، حَتَّى تَنْقَادَ لَهُ ، فَيَمْلِكُهَا
وَيَسْتَعْمِلُهَا في المَوَاضِعِ الَّتي يَجِبُ اسْتِعْمَالُهَا فِيهَا .

10. ولِهَذِهِ النَّفْسِ أَيْضاً فَضَائِلُ مَحْمُودَةٌ ، كَالأَنَفَةِ مِنَ الأُمُورِ الدَّنِيئَةِ ، ومَحَبَّةِ
الرِّئَاسَةِ الحَقِيقِيَّةِ ، وطَلَبِ المَرَاتِبِ العَالِيَةِ . وهَذِهِ الأَخْلَاقُ المَحْمُودَةُ هِيَ مِنْ أَفْعَالِ
النَّفْسِ الغَضَبِيَّةِ . فَإِذَا مَلَكَ الإنْسَانُ هَذِهِ النَّفْسَ ، بِالتَّأْدِيبِ والتَّهْذِيبِ ، واسْتَعْمَلَهَا في p. 42
الأُمُورِ الجَمِيلَةِ ، وكَفَّهَا عَنِ الأَفْعَالِ المَكْرُوهَةِ ، كَانَ حَسَنَ الحَالِ مَحْمُودَ الطَّرِيقَةِ .

[النَّفْسُ النَّاطِقَة]

11. فَأَمَّا النَّفْسُ النَّاطِقَةُ ، فَهِيَ الَّتي بِهَا يَتَمَيَّزُ الإنْسَانُ مِنْ جَمِيعِ الحَيَوانِ .
وهِيَ الَّتي بِهَا يَكُونُ الفِكْرُ والذِّكْرُ ، والتَّمْيِيزُ والفَهْمُ . وهِيَ الَّتي عَظُمَ بِهَا
شَرَفُ الإنْسَانِ ، وعَظُمَتْ هِمَّتُهُ ، فَأُعْجِبَ بِنَفْسِهِ . وهِيَ الَّتي بِهَا يَسْتَحْسِنُ
المَحَاسِنَ ويَسْتَقْبِحُ المَقَابِحَ . وبِهَا يُمْكِنُ الإنْسَانُ أَنْ يُهَذِّبَ قُوَّتَيْهِ البَاقِيَتَيْنِ (وهُمَا p. 43
الشَّهْوَانِيَّةُ والغَضَبِيَّةُ) ، ويَضْبِطَهُمَا ، ويَكُفَّهُمَا . وبِهَا يُفَكِّرُ في عَوَاقِبِ الأُمُورِ ، فَيُبَادِرُ
بِاسْتِدْرَاكِهَا مِنْ أَوَائِلِهَا .

12. ولِهَذِهِ النَّفْسِ أَيْضاً فَضَائِلُ ورَذَائِلُ . أَمَّا فَضَائِلُهَا ، فَاكْتِسَابُ العُلُومِ
والآدَابِ ؛ وكَفُّ صَاحِبِهَا عَنِ الرَّذَائِلِ والفَوَاحِشِ ؛ وقَهْرُ النَّفْسَيْنِ الأُخْرَيَيْنِ وتَأْدِيبُهُمَا ؛

irascible soul. When it is subdued and subjugated, its possessor is gentle and dignified. When it is neglected, overpowering its possessor, its possessor is irascible, impudent, tyrannical, and unjust. When it occupies an intermediate state, its possessor occupies an intermediate state; his rank in gentleness is comparable with the rank of his irascible soul in being disciplined. Therefore, it is necessary that a man train his irascible soul to the point that it yields to him, so that he rules it and makes use of it in those situations in which its use is necessary.

10. This soul also has some praiseworthy virtues, such as scorn for the baser things, love of genuine authority, and the pursuit of the higher ranks. These praiseworthy moral qualities are among the actions of the irascible soul. So, when a man dominates this soul by means of discipline and reforming action, makes use of it for good things, and holds it back from abhorrent deeds, he is in good condition and commendable for his way of life.

The rational soul

11. The rational soul is the one by means of which man is distinguished from all the animals. It is the one by which thought, memory, discrimination, and understanding happen. It is the one by which man's nobility grows great and his determination grows strong, so that he can be proud of himself. It is the one by which he deems good deeds to be good and bad deeds to be bad. By means of it, a man has the ability to reform the remaining two faculties (that is, the appetitive and the irascible), to control them, and to restrain them. With it, he also ponders the results of his undertakings, so he is prompt to put them aright from their beginnings.

12. This soul also has virtues and vices. Its virtues are the acquisition of knowledge and refinement, the restraint of its owner from vices and lewdness, the subjugation of the other two souls, and the disciplining

وسِيَاسَةُ صَاحِبِهَا في مَعَاشِهِ ومَكْسَبِهِ، ومُرُوءَتِهِ وتَجَمُّلِهِ؛ وحَثُّ صَاحِبِهَا عَلَى فِعْلِ الخَيْرِ، والتَّوَدُّدِ، والرِّقَّةِ، وسَلامَةِ النِّيَّةِ، والحِلْمِ، والحَيَاءِ، والنُّسْكِ، والعِفَّةِ؛ وطَلَبُ p. 44 الرِّئاسَةِ مِنَ الوُجُوهِ الجَمِيلَةِ. وأَمَّا رَذائِلُهَا، فَالخُبْثُ والحِيلَةُ والخَدِيعَةُ والمَلَقُ والمكْرُ والحَسَدُ والتَّشَرُّرُ والرِّيَاءُ. وهَذِهِ النَّفْسُ هِيَ لِجَمِيعِ النَّاسِ. إلاَّ أَنَّ مِنْهُمْ مَنْ تَغلِبُ عَلَيْهِ فَضَائِلُهَا، فيَسْتَحْسِنُهَا ويَسْتَعْمِلُهَا. ومِنْهُمْ مَنْ تَغلِبُ عَلَيْهِ رَذَائِلُهَا، فيأْلَفُهَا ويَسْتَمِرُّ عَلَيْهَا. ومِنْهُمْ مَنْ تَجْتَمِعُ فِيهِ بَعْضُ الفَضَائِلِ، وبَعْضُ الرَّذَائِلِ.

13. وهَذِهِ العَادَاتُ قَدْ تكُونُ فى كَثِيرٍ مِنَ النَّاسِ سَجِيَّةً وطَبْعاً، لا بتَكَلُّفٍ. فَأَمَّا المَطْبُوعُ عَلَى العَادَاتِ الجَمِيلَةِ مِنْهَا، فَيَكُونُ لِقُوَّةِ نَفْسِهِ النَّاطِقَةِ وشَرَفِ عُنْصُرِهِ. p. 45 وأَمَّا المَطْبُوعُ عَلَى العَادَاتِ المكْرُوهَةِ، فَلِضُعْفِ نَفْسِهِ النَّاطِقَةِ وسُوءِ جَوْهَرِهِ. وأَمَّا الَّذي تَجْتَمِعُ فِيهِ فَضَائِلُ ورَذَائِلُ، فَهُوَ الَّذِي تَكُونُ نَفْسُهُ النَّاطِقَهُ مُتَوَسِّطَةَ الحَالِ.

14. وقَدْ يَكْتَسِبُ أَكْثَرُ النَّاسِ هَذِهِ العَادَاتِ، وجَمِيعَ الأَخْلاقِ، جَمِيلَهَا وقَبِيحَهَا، اكْتِسَاباً. وذَلِكَ يَكُونُ بِحَسَبِ مَنْشَأِ الإِنْسَانِ، وأَخْلاقِ مَنْ يُحِيطُ بِهِ ويُشَاهِدُهُ، وبِحَسَبِ رُؤَسَاءِ وَقْتِهِ، ومَنْ يُشَارُ إلَيْهِ بِالنَّبَاهَةِ، ويُغْبَطُ عَلَى رُتْبَتِهِ. فَإِنَّ الحَدَثَ والنَّاشِئَ يَكْتَسِبُ الأَخْلاقَ، مِمَّنْ يُكْثِرُ مُلابَسَتَهُ ومُخَالَطَتَهُ، ومِنْ أَبَوَيْهِ وأَهْلِهِ p. 46 وعَشِيرَتِهِ. فإِذَا كَانَ هَؤلاءِ سَيِّئِي الأَخْلاقِ، مَذْمُومِي الطَّرِيقَةِ، كَانَ الحَدَثُ والنَّاشِئُ بَيْنَهُمْ أَيْضاً سَيِّئَ الأَخْلاقِ، مَكْرُوهَ العَادَاتِ. وإِذَا لَحَظَ الحَدَثُ أَيْضاً أَهْلَ الرِّئاسَةِ ومَنْ فَوْقَهُ، وغَبَطَهُمْ عَلَى مَرَاتِبِهِمْ، آثَرَ التَّشَبُّهَ بِهِمْ، والتَّخَلُّقَ بأَخْلاقِهِمْ. فإِنْ كَانُوا مُهَذَّبِي الأَخْلاقِ، حَسَنِي السِّيرَةِ، كَانَ المُتَشَبِّهُ بِهِمْ حَسَنَ الأَخْلاقِ، مَرْضِيَّ الطَّرِيقَةِ. فإِنْ كَانُوا أَشْرَاراً جُهّالاً، خَرَجَ الغَابِطُ لَهُمْ، السَّالِكُ طَرِيقَهُمْ، شِرِّيراً جَاهِلاً. وهَذِهِ الحَالُ هِيَ

of them. Also included are the management of the possessor's livelihood and his profit, manliness, and good behavior, prompting the possessor to do good; to show affection, friendliness, soundness of intention, gentleness, shyness, devout behavior, and modesty, and to seek authority in fair ways. Its vices are malevolence, subterfuge, deception, flattery, cunning, envy, defamation, and hypocrisy. All people have this soul. However, in some its virtues dominate, so they approve of them and put them into action. In some its vices dominate, so they become accustomed to them and persist in them. In some people, certain virtues and certain vices combine.

13. These habits may come about in many people spontaneously, as a result of a natural disposition, and not through effort. In the case of someone naturally disposed to good habits, it is due to the strength of his rational soul and the nobility of his lineage. As for someone naturally disposed to abhorrent habits, it is due to the weakness of his rational soul and the bad condition of his substance. In the case of someone in whom virtues and vices combine, his rational soul is in the intermediate state.

14. Most people can acquire these habits and all the moral qualities, good and bad. It will depend on the upbringing of the man, on the moral qualities of anyone with whom he is familiar and whom he observes. It will also depend on the leaders of his time, on those noted for celebrity and envied for their rank. The young person will acquire morality from anyone who is frequently on intimate terms with him and who associates with him, as well as from his parents, his family, and his relatives. So, when they are people of bad morals and of a blameworthy way of life, the young person among them will also be someone of bad morals and of abhorrent habits. When the youth also observes people of authority, and whoever is above him, and envies them on account of their ranks, he chooses to imitate them and to model himself morally on their morals. If they are people of reformed morals and good lifestyle, he, modeled on them, becomes someone of good morals, with a pleasing way of life. If they are ignorant evildoers, the one who is envious of them and who acts like them emerges as an ignorant evildoer. This is the moral state of

أَخْلاقَ أَكْثَرِ النَّاسِ ؛ فَإِنَّ الجَهْلَ ، والشَّرَّ ، والخُبْثَ ، والشَّرَهَ ، والحَسَدَ ، غَالِبٌ عَلَيْهِمْ . p. 47 والنَّاسُ بِالطَّبْعِ يَقْتَدِي بَعْضُهُمْ بِبَعْضٍ ، ويَحْتَذِي التَّابِعُ أَبَداً سِيرَةَ المَتْبُوعِ . وإِذَا كَانَ الغَالِبُ عَلَيْهِمِ الشَّرَّ والجَهْلَ ، كَانَ وَاجِباً أَنْ يَقْتَدِيَ أَحْدَاثُهُمْ وأَوْلادُهُمْ وأَتْبَاعُهُمْ بِهِمْ .

15. فَالعِلَّةُ المُوجِبَةُ لاخْتِلافِ أَخْلاقِ النَّاسِ ، في سِيَاسَاتِهِمْ وفَضَائِلِهِمْ ، وغَلَبَةِ الخَيْرِ والشَّرِّ عَلَيْهِمْ ، هِيَ اخْتِلافُ قُوَّةِ النَّفْسِ النَّاطِقَةِ فِيهِمْ . إِذَا كَانَتْ خَيِّرَةً فَاضِلَةً ، قَاهِرَةً لِلنَّفْسَيْنِ البَاقِيَتَيْنِ ، كَانَ صَاحِبُهَا خَيِّراً عَادِلاً ، حَسَنَ السِّيرَةِ . وإِذا p. 48 كَانَتْ شِرِّيرَةً خَبِيثَةً ، مُهْمِلَةً لِلنَّفْسَيْنِ الأُخْرَيَيْنِ ، كَانَ صَاحِبُهَا شِرِّيراً خَبِيثاً جَاهِلاً . فَمِنْ أَجْلِ ذَلِكَ ، وَجَبَ أَنْ يُعْمِلَ الإِنْسَانُ فِكْرَهُ ، ويُمَيِّزَ أَخْلاقَهُ ، ويَخْتَارَ مِنْهَا مَا كَانَ مُسْتَحْسَاناً جَمِيلاً ، ويَنْفِيَ مِنْهَا مَا كَانَ مُسْتَنْكَراً قَبِيحاً ، ويَحْمِلَ نَفْسَهُ عَلَى التَّشَبُّهِ بِالأَخْيَارِ ، ويَتَجَنَّبَ كُلَّ التَّجَنُّبِ عَادَاتِ الأَشْرَارِ . فَإِنَّهُ ، إِذَا فَعَلَ ذَلِكَ ، صَارَ بِالإِنْسَانِيَّةِ مُتَحَقِّقاً ، ولِلرِّئَاسَةِ الذَّاتِيَّةِ مُسْتَحِقّاً .

most people: ignorance, evildoing, malevolence, greed, and envy; it predominates in them. By nature, people emulate one another. The follower always copies the behavior of the leader. When what overwhelms the leaders is evildoing and ignorance, it is inevitable that their youths, their children, and their subordinates will emulate them.

15. So the necessary cause for the differentiation of people's moral qualities in their conduct and their virtues, in the dominance of good and evil over them, is the differentiation of the strength of the rational soul in them. When it is good and virtuous, subduing the other two souls, its possessor is good, just, and fair in his behavior. When it is evil and malevolent, negligent of the other two souls, its possessor is evil, malevolent, and ignorant. Therefore, a man must put his thinking capacity to work, distinguish his moral qualities, and choose what is deemed to be good and fair. He must reject what is deemed to be objectionable and repugnant, bring himself to become similar to the best people, and utterly avoid the habits of the worst people. When he does this, he becomes someone confirmed in humanity, someone who is deservedly a natural leader.

[القِسْمُ الثَّالِث]

p. 49

[في الأَخْلاَقِ الحَسَنَةِ والرَّدِيئَة]

[فِي الأَخْلاَقِ الحَسَنَةِ]

1. فَأَمَّا أَنْوَاعُ الأَخْلاقِ وأَقْسَامُهَا ، ومَا المُسْتَحْسَنُ مِنْهَا ، ومَا المُسْتَحَبُّ اعْتِيَادُهُ ، ويُعَدُّ فَضَائِلَ ، ومَا المُسْتَقبَحُ مِنْهَا ، المكْرُوهُ ، ويُعَدُّ نَقَائِصَ ومَعَايِب ، فَهِيَ الأَنْوَاعُ الَّتِي نَحْنُ وَاصِفُوهَا .

أَمَّا الَّتِي تُعَدُّ فَضَائِلَ ،

فَإِنَّ مِنْهَا العِفَّةُ

p. 50 **2.** وهِيَ ضَبْطُ النَّفْسِ عَنِ الشَّهَوَاتِ ؛ وقَسْرُهَا عَلَى الاكْتِفَاءِ بِمَا يُقِيمُ أَوَدَ الجَسَدِ ، ويَحْفَظُ صِحَّتَهُ فَقَطْ ؛ واجْتِنَابُ السَّرَفِ والتَّقْصِيرِ في جَمِيعِ اللَّذَّاتِ ، وقَصْدُ الاِعْتِدَالِ. وأَنْ يَكُونَ مَا يُقْتَصَرُ عَلَيْهِ مِنَ الشَّهَوَاتِ عَلَى الوَجْهِ المُسْتَحَبِّ ، المُتَّفَقِ عَلَى

Part Three

On the good and the bad moral qualities

On the good moral qualities

1. We shall describe the kinds of moral qualities and their classes. There are those that are to be considered good, that it is desirable to acquire, and that are to be reckoned virtues; and there are those that are to be considered repugnant, that are abhorrent, and that are to be reckoned defects and faults.

As for those reckoned to be virtues:

ABSTINENCE

2. It is the soul's control of the appetites, and the constraint of them to be satisfied with what furnishes the body with the means of subsistence and preserves its health, and no more. It is also the avoidance of intemperance, the curtailment of all pleasures, and the endeavor to be moderate. Furthermore, the appetites to which one is restricted should be indulged in a commendable manner, agreeable with their

ارْتِضَائِهِ، وفي أَوْقَاتِ الْحَاجَةِ الَّتِي لا غِنَى عَنْهَا، وعَلَى القَدْرِ الَّذِي لا يُحْتَاجُ إِلَى أَكْثَرَ

مِنْهُ، ولا يَحْرُسُ النَّفْسَ والقُوَّةَ أَقَلَّ مِنْهُ. وهذِهِ الحَالُ هِيَ غَايَةُ العِفَّةِ.

p. 51
ومِنْهَا القَنَاعَةُ

3. وهِيَ الاقْتِصَارُ عَلَى مَا سَنَحَ مِنَ العَيْشِ؛ والرِّضَى بِمَا تَسَهَّلَ مِنَ المَعَاشِ؛

5   وتَرْكُ الحِرْصِ عَلَى اكْتِسَابِ الأَمْوَالِ، وطَلَبِ المَرَاتِبِ العَالِيَةِ؛ مَعَ الرَّغْبَةِ في جَمِيعِ

ذَلِكَ، وإِيثَارِهِ والمَيْلِ إِلَيْهِ؛ وقَهْرُ النَّفْسِ عَلَى ذَلِكَ، والتَّقَنُّعُ بِاليَسِيرِ مِنْهُ. وهَذَا

الخُلُقُ مُسْتَحْسَنٌ مِنْ أَوْسَاطِ النَّاسِ وأَصَاغِرِهِمْ. فَأَمَّا المُلُوكُ والعُظَمَاءُ، فَلَيْسَ ذَلِكَ

مُسْتَحْسَناً مِنْهُمْ، ولا تُعَدُّ القَنَاعَةُ مِنْ فَضَائِلِهِمْ.

p. 52
ومِنْهَا التَّصَوُّنُ

10   4. وهُوَ التَّحَفُّظُ مِنَ التَّبَذُّلِ. فمِنَ التَّصَوُّنِ التَّحَفُّظُ مِنَ الهَزْلِ القَبِيحِ،

ومُخَالَطَةِ أَهْلِهِ، وحُضُورِ مَجَالِسِهِ؛ وضَبْطُ اللِّسَانِ مِنَ الفُحْشِ، وذِكْرِ الخَنَى والمَزْحِ

والسُّخْفِ، وخَاصَّةً في المَحَافِلِ ومَجَالِسِ المُحْتَشِمِينَ. ولا أُبَّهَةَ لِمَنْ يُسْرِفُ في المَزْحِ،

ويَفْحُشُ فِيهِ. ومِنَ التَّصَوُّنِ أَيْضاً، الاِنْقِبَاضُ مِنْ أَدْنِيَاءِ النَّاسِ وأَصَاغِرِهِمْ، ومُصَادَقَتِهِمْ

ومُجَالَسَتِهِمْ؛ والتَّحَرُّزُ مِنَ المَعَايِشِ الزَّرِيَّةِ، واكْتِسَابِ الأَمْوَالِ مِنَ الوُجُوهِ الخَسِيسَةِ؛

p. 53
15   والتَّرَفُّعُ عَنْ مَسْأَلَةِ الحَاجَاتِ لِلَّئَامِ النَّاسِ وسَفَلَتِهِمْ، والتَّوَاضُعِ لِمَنْ لا قَدْرَ لَهُ؛ والإِقْلالُ

مِنَ البُرُوزِ مِنْ غَيْرِ حَاجَةٍ؛ والتَّبَذُّلِ بِالجُلُوسِ في الأَسْوَاقِ وقَوَارِعِ الطُّرُقِ، مِنْ غَيْرِ

satisfaction, in moments of indispensable need. They should be indulged according to a measure: no more than what is needed, no less than what safeguards soul and strength. This situation is the goal of abstinence.

CONTENTMENT

3. It is restricting oneself to what life affords, being satisfied with what comes easily from one's means, and abandoning the endeavor to acquire wealth and to seek high rank, concomitant with the desire for all this, the predilection for it, and the inclination toward it. It is the constraint of the soul on this account and being content with a little of it. This moral quality is commendable for the middle and lower classes of people. It is not commendable for kings and leaders. Contentment is not to be reckoned among their virtues.

SELF-CONTROL

4. It is guarding against carelessness. So it is part of self-control to guard against repugnant joking, against keeping company with those who engage in it, and against frequenting their company. It is restraining the tongue from lewdness and from obscene, hilarious, and foolish speech, especially in the assemblies and gatherings of decent people. One who goes to excess in joking and acts in a lewd manner has nothing to be proud of. It is part of self-control to keep away from inferior and lower-class people, from their friendship and their gatherings. It is to be on one's guard against despicable ways of life and the acquisition of wealth by contemptible means. It is to be too high-minded to inquire about what is of concern to ignoble, lowly people or to debase oneself before those who have no standing. It is to reduce the frequency of needless public show or of frittering away one's time by sitting in the streets and main roads without necessity.

اضْطِرَارٍ. فَإِنَّ الإِكْثَارَ مِنْ ذَلِكَ لا يَخْلُو مِنَ العُيُوبِ؛ وأَعْظَمُ النَّاسِ قَدْراً مَنْ ظَهَرَ اسْمُهُ، وخَفِيَ شَخْصُهُ.

ومِنْهَا الحِلْمُ

5. وهُوَ تَرْكُ الانْتِقامِ عِنْدَ شِدَّةِ الغَضَبِ، مَعَ القُدْرَةِ عَلَى ذَلِكَ. وهَذِهِ الحَالُ مَحْمُودَةٌ، مَا لَمْ تُؤَدِّ إِلَى ثَلْمِ جَاهٍ، أَوْ فَسَادِ سِيَاسَةٍ. وهِيَ بِالرُّؤَسَاءِ والمُلُوكِ p. 54 أَحْسَنُ، لأَنَّهُم أَقْدَرُ عَلَى الانْتِقامِ مِنْ مُغْضِبِيهِمْ. ولا يُعَدُّ فَضِيلَةً حِلْمُ الصَّغِيرِ عَنِ الكَبِيرِ، وإِنْ كَانَ قَادِراً عَلَى مُقابَلَتِهِ في الحَالِ؛ فَإِنَّهُ، وإِنْ أَمْسَكَ عَنْهُ، فإِنَّمَا يُعَدُّ ذَلِكَ خَوْفاً لاَ حِلْماً.

ومِنْهَا الوَقَارُ

6. وهُوَ الإِمْسَاكُ عَنْ فُضُولِ الكَلامِ، والعَبَثِ، وكَثْرَةِ الإِشَارَةِ والحَرَكَةِ فِيمَا يُسْتَغْنَى عَنِ التَّحَرُّكِ فِيهِ؛ وقِلَّةُ الغَضَبِ؛ والإِصْغَاءُ عِنْدَ الاِسْتِفْهَامِ؛ والتَّوَقُّفُ عِنْدَ الجَوَابِ؛ والتَّحَفُّظُ مِنَ التَّسَرُّعِ والمُبَادَرَةِ في جَمِيعِ الأُمُورِ. ومِنْ قَبِيلِ الوَقَارِ أَيْضاً p. 55 الحَيَاءُ. وهُوَ غَضُّ الطَّرْفِ، والانْقِبَاضُ عَنِ الكَلاَمِ، حِشْمَةً لِلْمُسْتَحْيَا مِنْهُ. وهَذِهِ العَادَةُ مَحْمُودَةٌ، مَا لَمْ تَكُنْ عَنْ عِيٍّ ولاَ عَجْزٍ.

To do this too much is not an act free of blame. The greatest people in terms of importance are ones whose names are widely published but whose persons are concealed.

FORBEARANCE

5. It is abstention from taking vengeance in the heat of anger, in spite of having the capacity for it. This situation is commendable as long as it does not lead to a breach of honor or to bad policy. It is especially good for leaders and kings because they are the ones most capable of taking revenge on those who anger them. The forbearance of a lower-class person toward someone of a higher class is not to be reckoned as a virtue, assuming that he is in a position actually to encounter him. For, even if he holds back, it will only be reckoned as fear and not as forbearance.

MODESTY

6. It is refraining from an excess of speech and mockery, from too much gesticulation and bodily motion in situations in which there is no need to be moving around. It is being sparing of anger, paying attention when a question is posed, pausing for the answer, and guarding against haste and hurry in all affairs. A species of modesty is bashfulness. It is the lowering of the eyes and the withholding of speech out of shame for something deemed to be embarrassing. This habit is commendable, as long as it does not result from incapacity and weakness.

وَمِنْهَا الوُدُّ

7. وهُوَ المَحَبَّةُ المُعْتَدِلَةُ، مِنْ غَيْرِ اتِّبَاعِ الشَّهْوَةِ. والوُدُّ مُسْتَحْسَنٌ مِنَ الإِنْسَانِ، إذَا كَانَ وُدُّهُ لأَهْلِ الفَضْلِ والنُبْلِ، وذَوِي الوَقَارِ والأُبَّهَةِ، والمُتَمَيِّزِينَ مِنَ النَّاسِ. فَأَمَّا التَّوَدُّدُ إلى أَرْذَالِ النَّاسِ وأَصَاغِرِهِمْ، والأَحْدَاثِ والنِّسْوَانِ، ومَا شَابَهَهُمْ، وأَهْلِ الخَلاعَةِ، فَمَكْرُوهٌ جِدّاً. وأَحْسَنُ الوُدِّ مَا نَسَجْتَهُ بَيْنَ مِنْوَالَيْنِ مُتَنَاسِبَي الفَضْلِ، وهُوَ أَوْثَقُ الوُدِّ وأَثْبَتُهُ. فَأَمَّا مَا كَانَ ابْتِدَاؤُهُ اجْتِمَاعاً عَلَى هَزْلٍ، أَوْ لِطَلَبِ لَذَّةٍ، فَلَيْسَ p. 56 مَحْمُوداً، ولَيْسَ بِبَاقٍ، ولاَ ثَابِتٍ.

وَمِنْهَا الرَّحْمَةُ

8. وهُوَ خُلُقٌ مُرَكَّبٌ مِنَ الْوُدِّ والجَزَعِ. والرَّحْمَةُ لاَ تَكُونُ إلاَّ لِمَنْ تَظْهَرُ مِنْهُ، لِرَاحِمِهِ، خَلَّةٌ مَكْرُوهَةٌ، إمَّا نَقِيصَةٌ في نَفْسِهِ، وإمَّا مِحْنَةٌ عَارِضَةٌ. فَالرَّحْمَةُ هِيَ مَحَبَّةٌ لِلْمَرْحُومِ، مَعَ جَزَعٍ مِنَ الحَالِ الَّتِي مِنْ أَجْلِهَا رُحِمَ. وهَذِهِ الحَالُ مُسْتَحْسَنَةٌ، مَا لَمْ تَخْرُجْ بِصَاحِبِهَا عَنِ العَدْلِ، ولَمْ تَنْتَهِ بِهِ إلى الجَوْرِ، وإلَى فَسَادِ السِّيَاسَةِ. فَلَيْسَ p. 57 بِمَحْمُودٍ رَحْمَةُ القَاتِلِ عِنْدَ القَوَدِ، والجَانِي عِنْدَ القِصَاصِ.

وَمِنْهَا الوَفَاءُ

9. وهُو الصَّبْرُ عَلَى مَا يَبْذُلُهُ الإِنْسَانُ مِنْ نَفْسِهِ، ويَرْهَنُ بِهِ لِسَانَهُ؛ والخُرُوجُ مِمَّا يَضْمَنُهُ، وإنْ كَانَ مُجْحِفاً بِهِ. فَلَيْسَ يُعَدُّ وَفِيّاً مَنْ لَمْ تَلْحَقْهُ بِوَفَائِهِ أَذِيَّةٌ، وإنْ قَلَّتْ. وكُلَّمَا أَضَرَّ بِهِ الدُّخُولُ تَحْتَ مَا يَحْكُمُ بِهِ عَلَى نَفْسِهِ، كَانَ أَبْلَغَ في الوَفَاءِ. وهَذَا الخُلُقُ

FRIENDSHIP

7. It is temperate love, without the pursuit of passion. Friendship is something right for man, when his friendship is with people of worth and nobility, of modesty and self-respect, who are the most discriminating of people. As for cultivating friendship with depraved, lower-class people; with youths, women, and such like; and with profligate people, it is extremely abhorrent. The best friendship is one you weave between two looms of corresponding worth. It is the most reliable friendship and the most firm. One begun by a shared liking for fun or for pleasure seeking is not commendable, nor is it lasting, nor firm.

COMPASSION

8. It is a composite moral quality, made up of friendship and concern. Compassion is roused only for someone in whom an abhorrent lack becomes apparent to the one who would show him compassion. It may be a defect in his soul or an accidental affliction. Compassion is love for the one to whom compassion is shown, along with a concern for the situation for which he is to be shown compassion. This disposition is to be deemed good as long as it does not estrange its possessor from justice and does not lead him to injustice and to the impairment of good policy. So compassion for a killer on the occasion of his execution is not commendable, nor for a felon on the occasion of retribution.

FIDELITY

9. It is steadfastness in what a man expends of himself and for which he gives his word as a pledge. It is leaving behind what gives him security, even if it is to his own detriment. One is not reckoned faithful who incurs no harm by reason of his fidelity, even if it is only small. Whenever stepping forward into something he judges to be for the good of his own soul brings him harm, one is the more developed

p. 58

مَحْمُودٌ ، يَنْتَفِعُ بِهِ جَمِيعُ النَّاسِ . فَإِنَّ مَنْ عُرِفَ بِالوَفَاءِ ، كَانَ مَقْبُولَ القَوْلِ فِي جَمِيعِ مَا يَعِدُ بِهِ . وَمَنْ كَانَ مَقْبُولَ القَوْلِ ، كَانَ عَظِيمَ الجَاهِ . إِلَّا أَنَّ انْتِفَاعَ المُلُوكِ بِهَذَا الخُلُقِ أَكْثَرُ ، وَحَاجَتَهُمْ إِلَيْهِ أَشَدُّ . فَإِنَّهُ ، مَتَى عُرِفَ مِنْهُمْ قِلَّةُ الوَفَاءِ ، لَمْ يُوثَقْ بِمَوَاعِيدِهِمْ ، وَلَمْ تَتِمَّ أَغْرَاضُهُمْ ، وَلَمْ يَسْكُنْ إِلَيْهِمْ جُنْدُهُمْ وَأَعْوَانُهُمْ .

5 وَمِنْهَا أَدَاءُ الأَمَانَةِ

10. وَهُوَ التَّعَفُّفُ عَمَّا يَتَصَرَّفُ الإِنْسَانُ فِيهِ ، مِنْ مَالٍ وَغَيرِهِ ، وَمَا يُوثَقُ بِهِ عَلَيْهِ ، مِنَ الأَغْرَاضِ والحُرَمِ ، مَعَ القُدْرَةِ عَلَيْهِ ؛ وَرَدُّ مَا يُسْتَوْدَعُ إِلَى مُودِعِهِ .

p. 59

وَمِنْهَا كِتْمَانُ السِّرِّ

11. وَهَذَا الخُلُقُ مُرَكَّبٌ مِنَ الوَقَارِ وأَدَاءِ الأَمَانَةِ . فَإِنَّ إِخْرَاجَ السِّرِّ [هُوَ]

10 مِنْ فُضُولِ الكَلَامِ ؛ وَلَيْسَ بِوَقُورٍ مَنْ تَكَلَّمَ بِالفُضُولِ . وَأَيْضاً ، فَكَمَا أَنَّهُ مَنِ اسْتُودِعَ مَالاً فَأَخْرَجَهُ إِلَى غَيْرِ مُودِعِهِ ، فَقَدْ خَفَرَ الأَمَانَةَ ، كَذَلِكَ مَنِ اسْتُودِعَ سِرّاً فَأَخْرَجَهُ إِلَى غَيْرِ صَاحِبِهِ ، فَقَدْ خَفَرَ الأَمَانَةَ . وَكِتْمَانُ السِّرِّ مَحْمُودٌ مِنْ جَمِيعِ النَّاسِ ، وَخَاصَّةً مِمَّن يَصْحَبُ السُّلْطَانَ . فَإِنَّ إِخْرَاجَهُ أَسْرَارَهُ ، مَعَ أَنَّهُ قَبِيحٌ فِي نَفْسِهِ ، يُؤَدِّي إِلَى ضَرَرٍ

p. 60

عَظِيمٍ يَدْخُلُ عَلَيْهِ مِنْ سُلْطَانِهِ .

in fidelity. This moral quality is laudable; everyone will profit from it. Whoever is known for fidelity will be taken at his word in everything he promises. Whoever is taken at his word has great dignity. However, the advantage for kings in this moral quality is greater, and their need for it is stronger. For, when some of them are known to have little fidelity, they are not trusted when they make promises, their objectives are not achieved, and their army and their officials do not have faith in them.

HONESTY

10. It is abstaining from the free use of money or whatever one is entrusted with—be they goods or women to be safeguarded—over which one has power. It is also the return of what is deposited to its depositor.

KEEPING SECRETS

11. It is a composite moral quality made up of modesty and honesty. Divulging secrets is due to excessive talking, and whoever talks to excess is not modest. Moreover, someone who is entrusted with a secret that he imparts to someone other than the one who first mentioned it betrays a trust in the same way that someone does who is entrusted with money that he pays out to someone other than the one who deposited it. Keeping a secret is commendable for everyone, but especially for anyone who is a ruler's companion. For him to divulge his secrets is not only bad in itself, but it will also result in great harm accruing to him from his ruler.

وَمِنْهَا التَّوَاضُعُ

12. وَهُوَ تَرْكُ التَّرَؤُّسِ، وَإِظْهَارُ الخُمُولِ، وَكَرَاهِيَةُ التَّعْظِيمِ وَالزِّيَادَةِ فِي الإكْرَامِ. وَأَنْ يَتَجَنَّبَ الإنْسَانُ المُبَاهَاةَ بِمَا فِيهِ الفَضَائِلُ، وَالمُفَاخَرَةَ بِالجَاهِ وَالمَالِ؛ وَأَنْ يَتَحَرَّزَ مِنَ الإعْجَابِ وَالكِبْرِ. وَلَيْسَ يَكُونُ التَّوَاضُعُ إلَّا فِي أَكَابِرِ النَّاسِ وَرُؤَسَائِهِمْ،

5   وَأَهْلِ الفَضْلِ وَالعِلْمِ. وَأَمَّا سِوَى هَؤُلَاءِ، فَلَيْسَ يَكُونُونَ مُتَوَاضِعِينَ؛ لِأَنَّ الضَّعَةَ هِيَ مَحَلُّهُمْ وَمَرْتَبَتُهُمْ، فَهُمْ غَيْرُ مُتَصَنِّعِينَ لَهَا.

وَمِنْهَا البِشْرُ

13. وَهُوَ إظْهَارُ السُّرُورِ بِمَنْ يَلْقَاهُ الإنْسَانُ مِنْ إخْوَانِهِ، وَأَوِدَّائِهِ، وَأَصْحَابِهِ، وَأَوْلِيَائِهِ، وَمَعَارِفِهِ، وَالتَّبَسُّمُ عِنْدَ اللِّقَاءِ. وَهَذَا الخُلُقُ مُسْتَحْسَنٌ مِنْ جَمِيعِ النَّاسِ،

10   وَهُوَ مِنَ المُلُوكِ وَالعُظَمَاءِ أَحْسَنُ. فَإِنَّ البِشْرَ مِنَ المُلُوكِ تَتَآلَفُ بِهِ قُلُوبُ الرَّعِيَّةِ وَالأَعْوَانِ وَالحَاشِيَةِ، وَيَزْدَادُ بِهِ تَحَبُّبًا إِلَيْهِمْ. وَلَيْسَ سَعِيدًا مِنَ المُلُوكِ مَنْ كَانَ مُبْغَضًا إِلَى رَعِيَّتِهِ. وَرُبَّمَا أَدَّى ذَلِكَ إِلَى فَسَادِ أَمْرِهِ وَزَوَالِ مُلْكِهِ.

وَمِنْهَا صِدْقُ اللَّهْجَةِ

14. وَهُوَ الإخْبَارُ عَنِ الشَّيْءِ عَلَى مَا هُوَ بِهِ. وَهَذَا الخُلُقُ مُسْتَحْسَنٌ، مَا لَمْ

15   يُؤَدِّ إِلَى ضَرَرٍ مُجْحِفٍ. فَإِنَّهُ لَيْسَ بِمُسْتَحْسَنٍ صِدْقُ الإنْسَانِ، إِنْ سُئِلَ عَنْ فَاحِشَةٍ كَانَ ارْتَكَبَهَا؛ فَإِنَّهُ لَا يَفِي حُسْنُ صِدْقِهِ بِمَا يَلْحَقُهُ فِي ذَلِكَ مِنَ العَارِ وَالمَنْقَصَةِ البَاقِيَةِ اللَّازِمَةِ. وَكَذَلِكَ لَيْسَ يَحْسُنُ صِدْقُهُ، إِذَا سُئِلَ عَنْ مُسْتَجِيرٍ اسْتَجَارَهُ فَأَخْفَاهُ؛ وَلَا

HUMILITY

12. It is renouncing the assumption of superiority and displaying a low social profile, as well as an antipathy toward aggrandizement and toward the multiplication of honors. It is also that a man avoids boasting about anything in which there is some merit, or vaunting his social standing or wealth, and that he is on his guard against conceit and arrogance. Humility can only come to be in the most important people and their leaders, in people of virtue and knowledge. Others are not exercising humility because lowliness is their station and rank, and so they are not feigning it.

JOY

13. It is showing happiness to whomever one meets, be they brothers, friends, companions, associates, or acquaintances, and smiling when one meets them. This moral quality is to be deemed good for all people; for kings and important people it is especially good. When kings have joy, the hearts of the subjects, the assistants, and the retinue are attuned to one another because of it, and because of it he grows in affection for them. No king is happy who is angry with his subjects. It sometimes leads to the perversion of his condition and the end of his rule.

TRUTHFULNESS

14. It is giving information about something as it actually is. This moral quality is to be considered good as long as it does not lead to some ruinous damage. For a man's truthfulness is not to be considered good if, when he is asked about some lewd act which he has committed, his good truthfulness does not compensate for any shame or inherently lasting loss that attaches to him because of it. Likewise, his telling the truth will not be good when he is asked about someone who has taken refuge with him and whom he has concealed, nor when he is asked about

إِنْ سُئِلَ عَنْ جِنَايَةٍ، مَتَى صَدَقَ فِيهَا عُوقِبَ عَلَيْهَا عُقُوبَةً مُؤْلِمَةً. وَالصِّدْقُ مُسْتَحْسَنٌ

مِنْ جَمِيعِ النَّاسِ، وَهُوَ مِنَ المُلُوكِ وَالعُظَمَاءِ أَحْسَنُ؛ بَلْ لَا يَسَعُهُمُ الكَذِبُ، مَا لَمْ يَعُدِ

الصِّدْقُ عَلَيْهِم بِضَرَرٍ.

وَمِنْهَا سَلَامَةُ النِّيَّةِ

p. 63

15. وَهُوَ اعْتِقَادُ الخَيْرِ بِجَمِيعِ النَّاسِ، وَتَنَكُّبُ الخُبْثِ وَالغِيلَةِ وَالمَكْرِ

وَالخَدِيعَةِ. وَهَذَا الخُلُقُ مَحْمُودٌ مِنْ جَمِيعِ النَّاسِ، إِلَّا أَنَّهُ لَيْسَ يَصْلُحُ لِلْمُلُوكِ التَّخَلُّقُ بِهِ

دَائِمًا؛ وَلَا يَتِمُّ المُلْكُ، إِلَّا بِاسْتِعْمَالِ المَكْرِ وَالحِيَلِ وَالاغْتِيَالِ مَعَ الأَعْدَاءِ. وَلَكِنَّهُ يَحْسُنُ

بِهِم اسْتِعْمَالُهُ مَعَ أَوْلِيَائِهِمْ وَأَصْفِيَائِهِمْ وَأَهْلِ طَاعَتِهِمْ.

وَمِنْهَا السَّخَاءُ

p. 64

16. وَهُوَ بَذْلُ المَالِ، مِنْ غَيْرِ مَسْأَلَةٍ وَلَا اسْتِحْقَاقٍ. وَهَذَا الخُلُقُ مُسْتَحْسَنٌ،

مَا لَمْ يَنْتَهِ إِلَى السَّرَفِ وَالتَّبْذِيرِ. فَإِنَّ مَنْ بَذَلَ جَمِيعَ مَا يَمْلِكُهُ لِمَنْ لَا يَسْتَحِقُّهُ، لَا يُسَمَّى

سَخِيًّا، بَلْ يُسَمَّى مُبَذِّرًا مُضَيِّعًا. وَالسَّخَاءُ فِي سَائِرِ النَّاسِ فَضِيلَةٌ مُسْتَحْسَنَةٌ؛ وَأَمَّا

فِي المُلُوكِ، فَأَمْرٌ وَاجِبٌ. لِأَنَّ البُخْلَ يُؤَدِّي إِلَى الضَّرَرِ العَظِيمِ فِي مُلْكِهِمْ، وَالسَّخَاءُ

وَالبَذْلُ يَرْتَهِنُ بِهِ قُلُوبَ الرَّعِيَّةِ وَالجُنْدِ وَالأَعْوَانِ، فَيَعْظُمُ الانْتِفَاعُ بِهِ.

a felony for which, if he tells the truth about it, he will be punished grievously. Truthfulness is to be considered good for all people, but it is best for kings and important people. As a matter of fact, lying will never suit them, as long as telling the truth does not do them damage.

BENEVOLENCE

15. It is belief in the good in all men, and the shunning of wickedness, treachery, trickery, and betrayal. This moral quality is commendable for everyone, except that it is not right for kings always to be informed by it. The function of kingship is not complete without the exercise of trickery, artifice, and the abduction of enemies. However, it is good for them to exercise [benevolence] toward those close to them, their best friends, and the people subject to them.

GENEROSITY

16. It is spending money without asking questions or considering worthiness. This moral quality is to be deemed good as long as it does not end up in extravagance and squandering. For whoever spends everything he owns on someone who does not deserve it is not to be called a generous man, but a squanderer and a wastrel. Generosity is a virtue to be deemed good in the generality of people. In kings it is a necessity, because avarice will lead to great harm in their exercise of kingship, while generosity and expenditure will secure the hearts of the subjects, the army, and the officials; and then the profit from it will grow large.

ومِنْهَا الشَّجَاعَةُ

17. وهِيَ الإِقْدَامُ عَلَى المكَارِهِ والمَهَالِكِ، عِنْدَ الحَاجَةِ إلَى ذَلِكَ؛ وثَبَاتُ الجَأْشِ عِنْدَ المَخَاوِفِ، والاِسْتِهَانَةُ بِالمَوْتِ. وهَذَا الخُلُقُ مُسْتَحْسَنٌ مِنْ جَمِيعِ النَّاسِ، p. 65 وهُوَ بِالمُلُوكِ وأَعْوَانِهِم أَلْيَقُ وأَحْسَنُ؛ بَلْ لَيْسَ بِمُسْتَحِقٍّ لِلْمُلْكِ مَنْ عَدِمَ هَذِهِ الخَلَّةَ. وأَكْثَرُ النَّاسِ أَخْطَاراً، وأَحْوَجُهُمْ إلَى اقْتِحَامِ الغَمَرَاتِ، هُمُ المُلُوكُ. فَالشَّجَاعَةُ مِنْ أَخْلاقِهِم الْخَاصَّةِ بِهِمْ.

ومِنْهَا المُنَافَسَةُ

18. وهِيَ مُنَازَعَةُ النَّفْسِ إلى التَّشَبُّهِ بِالغَيْرِ، فِيمَا يراهُ لَهُ، ويَرْغَبُ فِيهِ لِنَفْسِهِ؛ والاِجْتِهَادُ في التَّرَقِّي إلَى دَرَجَةٍ أَعْلَى مِنْ دَرَجَتِهِ. وهَذَا الخُلُقُ مَحْمُودٌ، إذَا كَانَتِ المُنَافَسَةُ في الفَضَائِلِ، والمَرَاتِبِ العَالِيَةِ، ومَا يُكْسِبُ مَجْداً وسُؤْدُداً. p. 66 فَأَمَّا في غَيْرِ ذَلِكَ (مِنِ اتِّبَاعِ الشَّهَوَاتِ، والمُبَاهَاةِ بِاللَّذَّاتِ، والزِّينَةِ، والبِزَّةِ)، فَمَكْرُوهٌ جِدّاً.

ومِنْهَا الصَّبْرُ عِنْدَ الشَّدَائِدِ

19. وهَذَا الخُلُقُ مُرَكَّبٌ مِنَ الوَقَارِ والشَّجَاعَةِ. ومُسْتَحْسَنٌ جِدّاً، مَا لَمْ يَكُنِ الجَزَعُ نَافِعاً، ولاَ الحُزْنُ والقَلَقُ مُجْدِياً، ولاَ الحِيلَةُ والاِجْتِهَادُ دَافِعَةً ضَرَرَ تِلْكَ الشَّدَائِدِ. فَمَا أَحْسَنَ الصَّبْرَ، إذَا عَدِمَتِ الحِيلَةُ! ومَا أَقْبَحَ الجَزَعَ، إذَا لَمْ يَكُنْ مُفِيداً!

COURAGE

17. It is boldness in the face of adversities and perils when there is a need for it, steadiness of heart in fearful situations, and scorn for death. This moral quality is to be deemed good for everyone. It is best and most fitting in kings and their officials. Indeed, anyone who lacks this quality is not entitled to kingship. While the most important people are in perilous situations, kings are the ones in greatest need to plunge into hardships. Courage is one of the moral qualities particular to them.

EMULATION

18. It is the soul's struggle to become like someone else in regard to something which one sees in him and which one wants for oneself. It is the effort to advance to a rank higher than one's own rank. This moral quality is commendable when the emulation is for virtues and high ranks, and what one might obtain of power and glory. As for emulation of other things (to do with following the appetites, and boasting of pleasures, finery, and clothes), it is exceedingly abhorrent.

PERSEVERANCE IN DIFFICULTIES

19. This is a composite moral quality, made up of modesty and courage. It is to be deemed exceedingly good as long as apprehension does not become a means of profit, or grief and disquiet something lucrative, and subterfuge and strain do not become the way to deter the injury of these difficulties. How good is perseverance when subterfuge is absent! How bad is apprehension when it is not beneficial!

p. 67 ومِنْهَا عِظَمُ الهِمَّةِ

20. وهُوَ اسْتِصْغارُ مَا دُونَ النِّهَايَةِ مِنْ مَعَالِي الأُمُورِ؛ وطَلَبُ المَرَاتِبِ السَّامِيَةِ؛ واسْتِحْقَارُ مَا يَجُودُ بِهِ الإنْسَانُ عِنْدَ العَطِيَّةِ؛ والاِسْتِخْفَافُ بأَوْسَاطِ الأُمُورِ، وطَلَبُ الغَايَاتِ؛ والتَّهَاوُنُ بِمَا يَمْلِكُهُ؛ وبَذْلُ مَا يُمْكِنُهُ لِمَنْ يَسْأَلُهُ، مِنْ غَيْرِ امْتِنَانٍ ولا اعْتِدَادٍ بِهِ. وهذَا الخُلُقُ مِنْ أَخْلاقِ المُلُوكِ خَاصَّةً؛ وقَدْ يَحْسُنُ بِالرُّؤَسَاءِ والعُظَمَاءِ، ومَنْ تَسْمُو نَفْسُهُ إلى مَرَاتِبِهِمْ. ومِنْ عِظَمِ الهِمَّةِ الأَنَفَةُ، والحَمِيَّةُ، والغَيْرَةُ. p. 68 فَالأَنَفَةُ هِيَ نُبُوُّ النَّفْسِ عَنِ الأُمُورِ الدَّنِيئَةِ. والحَمِيَّةُ والغَيْرَةُ جمِيعاً هُمَا الغَضَبُ عِنْدَ الإحْسَاسِ بِالنَّقْصِ. وإنَّمَا تَلْحَقُ الإنْسَانَ الغَيْرَةُ عَلَى الحُرَمِ، لأَنَّ في التَعَرُّضِ لَهُنَّ عَاراً ومَنْقَصَةً؛ فَإنَّ المُتَعَرِّضَ لِلْحُرَمِ مُهْتَضِمٌ لِصَاحِبِهِنَّ، ومُتَصَرِّفٌ في غَيْرِ حَقٍّ لَهُ؛ والاِهْتِضَامُ نَقِيصَةٌ. ومِنْ عِظَمِ الهِمَّةِ الأَنَفَةُ مِنَ الاِهْتِضَامِ ودُخُولِ النَّقْصِ. وهَذَا الخُلُقُ مُسْتَحْسَنٌ مِنْ جَمِيعِ النَّاسِ.

ومِنْهَا العَدْلُ

21. وهُوَ التَّقَسُّطُ اللاَّزِمُ لِلاِسْتِوَاءِ، واسْتِعْمَالُ الأُمُورِ في مَوَاضِعِهَا، وأَوْقَاتِهَا، ووُجُوهِهَا، ومَقَادِيرِهَا، مِنْ غَيْرِ سَرَفٍ ولا تَقْصِيرٍ، ولا تَقْدِيمٍ ولا تَأْخِيرٍ.

p. 69 [في الأَخْلاقِ الرَّدِيئَةِ]

فَأَمَّا الأَخْلاقُ الرَّدِيئَةُ، الَّتِي تُعَدُّ نَقَائِصَ ومَعَايِبَ،

HIGH AMBITION

20. It is disdain for anything short of the ultimate in exalted matters. It seeks high rank, thinks nothing of what a man liberally gives as a gift. It disdains mediocre things, seeks the apogee, attaches little importance to what one owns, and spends what one owns on anyone who asks for it without obligation or reckoning. This moral quality is one of the moral qualities of kings in particular, but it may also be good for leaders, for important people, and for anyone whose soul strives to be in their ranks. Part of high ambition is pride, vehemence, and jealousy. Pride is the soul's repugnance for demeaning things. Vehemence and jealousy taken together are anger at the perception of deficiency. Jealousy taken alone affects a man in connection with women to be safeguarded. Because being involved with them is a disgrace and a wrong, the one involved with women to be safeguarded does an injustice to their master and conducts himself unfairly toward him. Perpetrating this wrong is a fault. Being too proud for wrongdoing or for incurring fault is part of high ambition. This moral quality is to be deemed good for everyone.

JUSTICE

21. It is the requisite distribution [of goods] to achieve parity and the use of things in their proper places, times, ways, and measures, without excess or diminution, preferment or deferment.

On the bad moral qualities

As for the bad moral qualities, which are to be reckoned as defects and faults, they are the following:

فَإِنَّ مِنْهَا الْفُجُورُ

22. وهُوَ الانْهِمَاكُ في الشَّهَوَاتِ ، والاِسْتِكْثَارُ مِنْهَا ؛ والتَّوَفُّرُ عَلى اللَّذَّاتِ ، والإِدْمَانُ عَلَيْهَا ؛ وَارْتِكَابُ الفَوَاحِشِ ، والمُجَاهَرَةُ بِهَا وبِالجُمْلَةِ ، السَّرَفُ في جَمِيعِ الشَّهَوَاتِ. وهَذَا الخُلُقُ مَكْرُوهٌ جِدّاً ، يَهْدِمُ الحَيَاءَ ، ويَذْهَبُ بِمَاءِ الْوَجْهِ ، ويَخْرِقُ حِجَابَ الحِشْمَةِ.

p. 70 ومِنْهَا الشَّرَهُ

23. وهُوَ الحِرْصُ عَلَى اكْتِسَابِ الأَمْوَالِ وجَمْعِهَا ، وطَلَبِهَا مِنْ كُلِّ وَجْهٍ ، وإِنْ قَبُحَ التَّعَسُّفُ في اكْتِسَابِهَا ، والمُكَالَبَةُ عَلَيْهَا ، والاِسْتِكْثَارُ مِنَ القِنْيَةِ ، وادِّخَارُ الأَعْرَاضِ. وهَذَا الخُلُقُ مَكْرُوهٌ مِنْ جَمِيعِ النَّاسِ ، إلاَّ مِنَ المُلُوكِ. فَإِنَّ كَثْرَةَ الأَمْوَالِ والذَّخَائِرِ والأَعْرَاضِ تُعِينُ عَلى المُلْكِ ، وتُزَيِّنُ المُلُوكَ ، وتَزِيدُهُمْ هَيْبَةً في نُفُوسِ رَعِيَّتِهِمْ وأَعْوَانِهِمْ ، وأَعْدَائِهِمْ وأَضْدَادِهِمْ.

p. 71 ومِنْهَا التَّبَذُّلُ

24. وهُوَ اطِّرَاحُ الحِشْمَةِ ، وتَرْكُ التَّحَفُّظِ ، والإِكْثَارُ مِنَ الهَزْلِ واللَّهْوِ ؛ ومُخَالَطَةُ السُّفَهَاءِ ، وحُضُورُ مَجَالِسِ السُّخْفِ والهَزْلِ والفَوَاحِشِ ؛ والتَّفَوُّهُ بِالخَنى ، وذِكْرُ الأَعْرَاضِ ، والمَزْحُ ؛ والجُلُوسُ في الأَسْوَاقِ ، وعَلى قَوَارِعِ الطُّرُقِ ؛ والتَّكَسُّبُ بالمَعَايِشِ الزَّرِيَّةِ ، والتَّوَاضُعُ لِلسَّفَلَةِ. وهَذَا الخُلُقُ قَبِيحٌ بِجَمِيعِ النَّاسِ.

DEBAUCHERY

22. It is the abandonment of oneself to the appetites, being constantly involved with them, going to any length for pleasure, being addicted to it, committing lewd acts, and openly divulging them. In sum, it is dissipation in all the appetites. This moral quality is utterly abhorrent. It destroys shame, does away with self-respect, and rends the veil of decency.

GREED

23. It is avidity for the acquisition of money, for accumulating it, and for seeking it in any way, even if harsh treatment in acquiring it and frenzy for it are repugnant. It is also an excessive regard for possessions and for the hoarding of goods. This moral quality is abhorrent for everyone except for kings. An abundance of money, of stores, and of goods gives support to a reign; it puts kings in a favorable light, and it enhances them in terms of awe in the souls of their subjects, of their officials, of their enemies, and of their opponents.

PROFLIGACY

24. It is the discarding of shame, the abandonment of restraint. It is constantly engaging in joking and amusements; associating with foolish people; attending sessions of nonsense, banter, and lewdness. It is uttering obscenities, repeating inconsequential things, and jesting. It is sitting in the street markets and open roads, earning one's living by contemptible means, and being degraded to the lowest things. This moral quality is repugnant in all people.

ومِنْهَا السَّفَهُ

25. وهُوَ ضِدُّ الحِلْمِ. وهُوَ سُرْعَةُ الغَضَبِ، والطَّيْشُ مِنْ يَسِيرِ الأُمُورِ،
والمُبَادَرَةُ في البَطْشِ؛ والإيقَاعُ بالمُؤْذِي، والسَّرَفُ في العُقُوبَةِ؛ وإظْهَارُ الجَزَعِ مِنْ p. 72
أَدْنَى ضَرَرٍ؛ والسَّبُّ الفَاحِشُ. وهَذَا الخُلُقُ مُسْتَقْبَحٌ مِنْ كُلِّ أَحَدٍ، إلاَّ أَنَّهُ بالمُلُوكِ
والرُّؤَسَاءِ أَقْبَحُ.

ومِنْهَا الخُرْقُ

26. وهُوَ كَثْرَةُ الكَلامِ، والتَّحَرُّكُ مِنْ غَيْرِ حَاجَةٍ، وشِدَّةُ الضِّحْكِ، والمُبَادَرَةُ
إلى الأُمُورِ مِنْ غَيْرِ تَوَقُّفٍ، وسُرْعَةُ الجَوَابِ. وهذا الخُلُقُ مُستَقْبَحٌ مِنْ كلِّ أَحَدٍ،
وهُوَ بِأَهْلِ العِلْمِ وذَوِي النَّبَاهَةِ أَقْبَحُ. ومِنْ قَبِيلِ الخُرْقِ القِحَةُ. وهِيَ قِلَّةُ الاحْتِشَامِ
لِمَنْ يَجِبُ احْتِشَامُهُ، والمُجَاهَرَةُ بالجَوَابَاتِ الفَظَّةِ المُسْتَشْنَعَةِ. وهَذَا الخُلُقُ مَكْرُوهٌ، p. 73
وخَاصَّةً بِذَوِي الوَقَارِ.

ومِنْهَا العِشْقُ

27. وهُوَ إفْرَاطُ الحُبِّ، والسَّرَفُ فِيهِ. وهَذَا الخُلُقُ مَكْرُوهٌ عَلَى جَمِيعِ
الأَحْوَالِ، ومُسْتَقْبَحٌ. إلاَّ أَنَّ أَقْبَحَهُ وأَشَرَّهُ مَا كَانَ مَصْرُوفاً إلى طَلَبِ اللَّذَّةِ، واتِّبَاعِ
الشَّهْوَةِ الرَّدِيئَةِ. وقَدْ يَحْمِلُ هَذَا الخُلُقُ صَاحِبَهُ عَلَى الفُجُورِ، وارْتِكَابِ الفَوَاحِشِ،
وكَثْرَةِ التَّبَذُّلِ، وقِلَّةِ الحَيَاءِ؛ ويُكْسِبُهُ عَادَاتٍ رَدِيئَةً. وهُوَ بِكُلِّ أَحَدٍ قَبِيحٌ، إلاَّ أَنَّهُ
بالأَحْدَاثِ والمُتَرَفِّهِينَ والمُتَنَعِّمِينَ أَقَلُّ قُبْحاً.

FOLLY

25. It is the opposite of forbearance. It is being quick to anger, being reckless in small matters, rushing to violence, assaulting one's offender, being immoderate in meting out punishment, displaying impatience at the smallest injury, and engaging in obscene cursing. This moral quality is to be deemed repugnant for anyone but is most repugnant in kings and leaders.

LEVITY

26. It is too much talking, needless moving around, raucous laughter, rushing into things without hesitation, and haste in giving a reply. This moral quality is to be deemed repugnant for everyone. It is especially repugnant in people of knowledge and renown. A species of this folly is impudence. It is too little shame toward someone who should be respected, and the loud broadcasting of horrid, coarse replies. This moral quality is abhorrent, especially in modest people.

PASSION

27. It is immoderate love and intemperance in it. This moral quality is abhorrent in all cases and is to be deemed repugnant. However, the most repugnant and worst case of it is when it is directed to seeking pleasure and to the pursuit of an evil appetite. This moral quality may carry the one who possesses it to the point of debauchery, to the commission of lewd acts, to too much profligacy and too little shame. It will make him acquire bad habits. It is repugnant in everyone; but, in youths and those leading comfortable and luxurious lives, it is less repugnant.

p. 74 ومِنْهَا القَسَاوَةُ

28. وهُوَ خُلُقٌ مُرَكَّبٌ مِنَ البُغْضِ والشَّجَاعَةِ. والقَسَاوَةُ هِيَ التَّهَاوُنُ بِمَا
يَلْحَقُ الغَيْرَ مِنَ الأَلَمِ والأَذى. وهَذَا الخُلُقُ مَكْرُوهٌ مِنْ كُلِّ أَحَدٍ، إلاَّ مِنَ الجُنْدِ، وأَصْحَابِ
السِّلاحِ، والمُتَوَلِّينَ الحُرُوبَ. فَإِنَّ ذَلِكَ غَيْرُ مَكْرُوهٍ مِنْهُمْ، إذَا كَانَ في مَوْضِعِهِ.

ومِنْهَا الغَدْرُ

29. وهُوَ الرُّجُوعُ عَمَّا يَبْذُلُهُ الإِنْسَانُ مِنْ نَفْسِهِ، ويَضْمَنُ الوَفَاءَ بِهِ. وهَذَا
p. 75 الخُلُقُ مُسْتَقْبَحٌ، وإِنْ كَانَ لِصَاحِبِهِ فِيهِ مَصْلَحَةٌ ومَنْفَعَةٌ. وهُوَ بِالمُلُوكِ والرُّؤَسَاءِ أَقْبَحُ،
ولَهُمْ أَضَرُّ. فَإِنَّ مَنْ عُرِفَ مِنَ المُلُوكِ بِالغَدْرِ، لَمْ يَسْكُنْ إِلَيْهِ أَحَدٌ، ولَمْ يَثِقْ بِهِ إِنْسَانٌ.
وإِذَا لَمْ يُسْكَنْ إِلَيْهِ، فَسَدَ نِظَامُ مُلْكِهِ.

ومِنْهَا الخِيَانَةُ

30. وهِيَ الاسْتِبْدَادُ بِمَا يُؤْتَمَنُ الإِنْسَانُ عَلَيْهِ مِنَ الأَمْوَالِ والأَعْرَاضِ والحُرَمِ؛
وتَمَلُّكُ مَا يُسْتَوْدَعُ، ومُجَاحَدَةُ مُودِعِهِ. ومِنَ الخِيَانَةِ أَيْضاً طَيُّ الأَخْبَارِ، إِذَا نُدِبَ
p. 76 لِتَأْدِيَتِهَا؛ وتَحْرِيفُ الرَّسَائِلِ، إِذَا تَحَمَّلَهَا؛ وصَرْفُهَا عَنْ وُجُوهِهَا. وهَذَا الخُلُقُ، أَعْنِي
الخِيَانَةَ، مَكْرُوهٌ مِنْ جَمِيعِ النَّاسِ، يَثْلِمُ الجَاهَ، ويَقْطَعُ وُجُوهَ المَعَايِشِ.

HARSHNESS

28. It is a composite moral quality, made up of hatred and boldness. Harshness is indifference to the pain and suffering that afflicts someone else. This moral quality is abhorrent for everyone except for soldiers, those who carry weapons, and those who have the responsibility for war. For them it is not abhorrent when it is in its place.

PERFIDY

29. It is reneging on what a man will spend on his own accord, all the while guaranteeing the payment of it. This moral quality is to be deemed repugnant, even if there is some advantage and profit in it for the one possessing it. It is most repugnant in kings and leaders, and for them it is most harmful. No one relies on, and no man puts his trust in, any king known for perfidy. When he proves to be unreliable, the good order of his reign is vitiated.

DISHONESTY

30. It is arbitrarily disposing of the wealth, goods, or women to be safeguarded with which a man is entrusted. It is assuming ownership of what is deposited with one for safekeeping and denying the rights of the depositor. The concealment of accounts when one is appointed to render them is also part of dishonesty, as is distorting letters when one has assumed responsibility for them, and diverting them from their proper destinations. This moral quality—I mean dishonesty—is abhorrent for everyone. It sullies the reputation and cuts off the normal ways of life.

ومِنْهَا إفْشَاءُ السِّرِّ

31. وهَذَا الخُلُقُ مُرَكَّبٌ مِنَ الخُرْقِ والخِيَانَةِ. فَإِنَّهُ لَيْسَ بِوَقُورٍ مَنْ لَمْ يَضْبُطْ لِسَانَهُ، ولَمْ يَتَّسِعْ صَدْرُهُ لِحِفْظِ مَا يُسْتَسَرُّ بِهِ. والسِّرُّ إحْدَى الوَدَائِعِ، وإفْشَاؤُهُ نَقِيصَةٌ عَلَى صَاحِبِهِ، فَالمُفْشِي لِلسِّرِّ خَائِنٌ. وهَذَا الخُلُقُ قَبِيحٌ جِدّاً، وخَاصَّةً بِمَنْ يَصْحَبُ السَّلاطِينَ ويُدَاخِلُهُمْ. ومِنْ قَبِيلِ إفْشَاءِ السِّرِّ أَيْضاً النَّمِيمَةُ. وهُوَ أَنْ يُبَلِّغَ إنْسَانٌ إنْسَاناً
p. 77 عَنْ آخَرَ قَوْلاً مَكْرُوهاً. وهَذَا الخُلُقُ قَبِيحٌ جِدّاً، وإنْ لَمْ يُسْتَسَرَّ أَيْضاً بِمَا يَسْمَعُهُ أَوْ
يُبَلِّغُهُ. فَنَقْلُهُ إلَى مَنْ يَكْرَهُهُ قَبِيحٌ؛ لأَنَّ في ذَلِكَ إيقَاعَ وَحْشَةٍ بَيْنَ المُبَلِّغِ والمُبَلَّغِ عَنْهُ، وذَلِكَ غَايَةُ التَّشَرُّرِ.

ومِنْهَا الكِبْرُ

32. وهُوَ اسْتِعْظَامُ الإنْسَانِ نَفْسَهُ، واسْتِحْسَانُ مَا فِيهِ مِنَ الفَضَائِلِ، والاِسْتِهَانَةُ بِالنَّاسِ، واسْتِصْغَارُهُمْ، والتَّرَفُّعُ عَلَى مَنْ يَجِبُ التَّوَاضُعُ لَهُ. وهَذَا الخُلُقُ
p. 78 مَكْرُوهٌ، ضَارٌّ لِصَاحِبِهِ. لأَنَّ مَنْ أَعْجَبَتْهُ نَفْسُهُ، لَمْ يَسْتَزِدْ مِنِ اكْتِسَابِ الأَدَبِ؛ ومَنْ
لَمْ يَسْتَزِدْ، بَقِيَ عَلَى نَقْصِهِ. فَإِنَّ الإنْسَانَ لَيْسَ يَخْلُو مِنَ النَّقْصِ، وقَلَّمَا يَنْتَهِي إلى غَايَةِ الكَمَالِ. وأَيْضاً، فَإِنَّ الفِعْلَ يُبَغِّضُهُ إلى النَّاسِ، ومَنْ أَبْغَضَهُ النَّاسُ سَاءَتْ حَالُهُ.

ومِنْهَا العُبُوسُ

33. وهُوَ التَّقْطِيبُ عِنْدَ اللِّقَاءِ، وقِلَّةُ التَّبَسُّمِ، وإظْهَارُ الكَرَاهِيَّةِ. وهَذَا الخُلُقُ مُرَكَّبٌ مِنَ الكِبْرِ، وغِلَظِ الطَّبْعِ. فَإِنَّ قِلَّةَ البَشَاشَةِ هِيَ اسْتِهَانَةٌ بِالنَّاسِ، والاِسْتِهَانَةُ

DIVULGING SECRETS

31. This is a composite moral quality, being made up of levity and dishonesty. Whoever does not control his tongue is not modest, and he is not sagacious enough to keep what has been confided to him as a secret. A secret is one of those things given in trust; to divulge it is a fault against the interest of its owner. So the one divulging the secret is untrustworthy. This moral quality is exceedingly repugnant, especially in someone who associates with rulers and has access to them. Character defamation is of the same moral species as the divulging of secrets. It is when a man gives another man information of an abhorrent kind about someone else. This is an exceedingly repugnant moral quality, even if one has not been entrusted with a secret in connection with what he hears or the matter about which he gives information. To transmit it to someone who finds it abhorrent is repugnant because it brings about an estrangement between the one imparting the information and the one about whom the information is given. This is the utmost of wickedness.

ARROGANCE

32. It is a man's aggrandizement of himself by thinking well of the virtues that are in him while underrating other people and belittling them. It is also contempt for those before whom one must act humbly. This moral quality is abhorrent and harmful to the one who possesses it, because someone who admires himself too much does not try to acquire more refinement, and someone who does not try for more refinement stays with his deficiencies. Such a man is never free of shortcomings, and seldom does he arrive at the summit of perfection. Moreover, to do so would make him hateful to people, and anyone people hate is in a bad way.

SULLENNESS

33. It is scowling when meeting someone else. It is the want of a smile and the manifestation of antipathy. This is a composite moral quality, made up of arrogance and a certain coarseness of character. The want

بِالنّاسِ تَكُونُ مِنَ الإِعْجَابِ والكِبْرِ. وقِلَّةُ التَّبَسُّمِ، وخَاصَّةً عِنْدَ لِقَاءِ الإِخْوَانِ، تَكُونُ
p. 79 مِنْ غِلَظِ الطَّبْعِ. وهَذَا الخُلُقُ مُستَقْبَحٌ، وخَاصَّةً بِالرُّؤَسَاءِ والأَفَاضِلِ.

ومِنْهَا الكِذْبُ

34. وهُوَ الإِخْبَارُ عَنِ الشَّيْءِ، بِخِلافِ مَا هُوَ بِهِ. وهَذَا الخُلُقُ مَكْرُوهٌ، مَا
لَمْ يَكُنْ لِدَفْعِ مَضَرَّةٍ لاَ يُمْكِنُ أَنْ تُدْفَعَ إلاَّ بِهِ، أَوِ اجْتِنَاءِ نَفْعٍ لاَ غِنَى عَنْهُ، ولاَ يُوصَلُ إِلَيْهِ
إلاَّ بِهِ. فَإِنَّ الكِذْبَ عِنْدَ ذَلِكَ لَيْسَ بِمُسْتَقْبَحٍ، وإِنَّمَا يُسْتَقْبَحُ الكِذْبُ إِذَا كَانَ عَبَثاً،
p. 80 ولِنَفْعٍ يَسِيرٍ، لاَ خَطَرَ لَهُ، ولاَ يَفِي بِقَبَاحَةِ الكِذْبِ. والكِذْبُ يُقَبَّحُ بِالمُلُوكِ والرُّؤَسَاءِ
أَكْثَرَ، لأَنَّ اليَسِيرَ مِنَ النَّقْصِ يَشِينُهُمْ.

ومِنْهَا الخُبْثُ

35. وهُوَ إِضْمَارُ الشَّرِّ لِلْغَيْرِ، وإِظْهَارُ الخَيْرِ لَهُ؛ وَاسْتِعْمَالُ الغِيلَةِ والمكْرِ
والخَدِيعَةِ في المُعَامَلاتِ. وهَذَا الخُلُقُ مَكْرُوهٌ جِدّاً مِنْ جَمِيعِ النَّاسِ، إلاَّ مِنَ المُلُوكِ
والرُّؤَسَاءِ. فَإِنَّهُمْ إِلَيْهِ مُضْطَرُّونَ، واسْتِعْمَالُهُمْ إِيَّاهُ، مَعَ أَضْدَادِهِمْ وأَعْدَائِهِمْ، غَيْرُ
p. 81 مُسْتَقْبَحٍ؛ فَأَمَّا مَعَ أَوْلِيَائِهِمْ وأَصْحَابِهِمْ، فَإِنَّهُ غَيْرُ مُسْتَحْسَنٍ. ومِنْ قَبِيلِ الخُبْثِ الحِقْدُ.
وهُوَ إِضْمَارُ الشَّرِّ لِلْجَانِي، إذَا لَمْ يَتَمَكَّنْ مِنَ الاِنْتِقَامِ مِنْهُ، فَأَخْفَى تِلْكَ الأَحْقَادَ إِلَى
وَقْتِ إِمْكَانِ الفُرْصَةِ. وهَذَا الخُلُقُ مِنْ أَخْلاَقِ الأَشْرَارِ، وهُوِ مَذْمُومٌ جِدّاً.

of a friendly demeanor amounts to contempt for people, and contempt for people is part of being conceited and arrogant. The want of a smile, especially when meeting one's brothers, bespeaks a certain coarseness of character. Especially for leaders and the most prominent people, this moral quality is to be deemed repugnant.

LYING

34. It is giving information about something contrary to what is the case. This moral quality is abhorrent as long as it is not for the sake of repelling a harm that cannot be repelled except by this means, or, for reaping an indispensable benefit, which cannot be attained except by this means. Lying for this reason is not to be deemed repugnant. Lying is only to be deemed repugnant when it is to no avail, for a small gain which has no importance and which does not counterbalance the repugnance of lying. Lying is to be considered repugnant in kings and leaders most, because the slightest defect will bring them into disgrace.

MALEVOLENCE

35. It is harboring evil for someone else while making a display of good will toward him, and employing treachery, craftiness, and imposture in mutual relations. This moral quality is utterly abhorrent for everyone except kings and leaders. They are forced to it, and their employment of it with their adversaries and enemies is not to be deemed repugnant. But to use it with their friends and associates is not to be considered good. Resentment is of the same moral species as malevolence. It is harboring evil for the perpetrator of an offense when it is not possible to take revenge on him, and so one conceals these resentments until the time when the opportunity makes it possible. This is one of the worst moral qualities of evil people.

ومِنْهَا البُخْلُ

36. وهُوَ مَنْعُ المُسْتَرْفِدِ ، مَعَ القُدْرَةِ عَلَى رِفْدِهِ. وهَذَا الخُلُقُ مَكْرُوهٌ مِنْ جَمِيعِ
النَّاسِ ، إلاَّ أَنَّهُ مِنَ النِّسَاءِ أَقَلُّ كَرَاهِيَّةً ؛ بَلْ قَدْ يُسْتَحَبُّ مِنَ النِّسَاءِ البُخْلُ. فَأَمَّا سَائِرُ
النَّاسِ ، فَإِنَّ البُخْلَ يَشِينُهُمْ. وخَاصَّةً المُلُوكَ والعُظَمَاءَ ؛ فَإِنَّ البُخْلَ يُبْغَضُ مِنْهُمْ أَكْثَرَ مِمَّا p. 82
يُبْغَضُ مِنَ الرَّعِيَّةِ ، ويَقْدَحُ في مُلْكِهِمْ ؛ لأَنَّهُ يَقْطَعُ الأَطْمَاعَ مِنْهُمْ ، ويُبَغِّضُهُمْ إلى رَعِيَّتِهِمْ .

ومِنْهَا الجُبْنُ

37. وهُوَ الجَزَعُ عِنْدَ المَخَاوِفِ ، والإِحْجَامُ عَمَّا تُحْذَرُ عَاقِبَتُهُ ، ولاَ تُؤْمَنُ مَغَبَّتُهُ. وهَذَا الخُلُقُ مَكْرُوهٌ مِنْ جَمِيعِ النَّاسِ ، إلاَّ أَنَّهُ لِلْمُلُوكِ والجُنْدِ وأَصْحَابِ الحُرُوبِ أَضَرُّ .

ومِنْهَا الحَسَدُ

38. وهُوَ التَّأَلُّمُ بِمَا يَرَاهُ الإِنْسَانُ لِغَيْرِهِ مِنَ الخَيْرِ ، ومَا يَجِدُهُ فِيهِ مِنَ الفَضَائِلِ ؛
والاِجْتِهَادُ في إِعْدَامِ ذَلِكَ لِغَيْرِ مَا هُوَ لَهُ. وهَذَا الخُلُقُ مَكْرُوهٌ وقَبِيحٌ بِكُلِّ أَحَدٍ . p. 83

ومِنْهَا الجَزَعُ عِنْدَ الشِّدَّةِ

39. وهَذَا الخُلُقُ مُرَكَّبٌ مِنَ الخُرْقِ والجُبْنِ. وهو مُسْتَقْبَحٌ ، إذَا لَمْ يَكُنْ مُجْدِياً ولاَ مُفِيداً . فَأَمَّا إِظْهَارُ الجَزَعِ لِتَتَمَحَّلَ حِيلَةً بِذَلِكَ ، عِنْدَ الوُقُوعِ في الشِّدَّةِ ، أَوِ اسْتِغَاثَةِ مُغِيثٍ ، أَوِ اجْتِلاَبِ مُعِينٍ فِيمَا تُغْنِي فِيهِ المُعَاوَنَةُ ، فَغَيْرُ مَكْرُوهٍ ، ولاَ يُعَدُّ نَقِيصَةً .

NIGGARDLINESS

36. It is refusing to come to the aid of someone who asks for it when one has the capacity to aid him. This moral quality is abhorrent for everyone, but it is less abhorrent for women. Rather, niggardliness may even be preferable for women. As for the rest of the people, niggardliness disgraces them, especially kings and leaders. Niggardliness is loathsome for them much more than it is for their subjects; it is degrading in the exercise of their kingship because for them it cuts off ambition and makes them loathsome to their subjects.

COWARDICE

37. It is anxiety in the face of fearful things and a recoiling from anything in connection with which one is wary of the consequences, or one is unsure of the outcome. This moral quality is abhorrent for everyone, but it is most injurious for kings, soldiers, and combatants.

ENVY

38. It is the feeling of pain a man has when he sees something good belonging to someone else, or when he finds virtues in him. It is also the effort one makes to deprive that person of whatever one does not have oneself. This moral quality is abhorrent and repugnant for everyone.

ANXIETY IN THE FACE OF ADVERSITY

39. This is a composite moral quality, made up of levity and cowardice. It is to be deemed repugnant when it serves no useful or beneficial purpose. Being anxious for the purpose of cunningly seeking a way out of falling into adversity, or for the purpose of making an appeal for a helper, or for the purpose of procuring a supporter in a situation in which support would be of some benefit is not abhorrent, nor is it to be reckoned a defect.

ومِنْهَا صِغَرُ الهِمَّةِ

40. وهُوَ ضُعْفُ النَّفْسِ عَنْ طَلَبِ المَرَاتِبِ العَالِيَةِ، وقُصُورُ الأَمَلِ عَنْ بُلوغِ p. 84 الغَايَاتِ؛ واسْتِكْثَارُ اليَسِيرِ مِنَ الفَضَائِلِ، واسْتِعْظَامُ القَلِيلِ مِنَ العَطَايَا، والاِعْتِدَادُ بِهِ؛ والرِّضَى بِأَوْسَاطِ الأُمُورِ وأَصَاغِرِهَا. وهَذَا الخُلُقُ قَبِيحٌ بِكُلِّ أَحَدٍ، وهُوَ بِالمُلُوكِ أَقْبَحُ؛ بَلْ لَيْسَ بِمُسْتَحِقٍّ المُلْكَ مَنْ صَغُرَتْ هِمَّتُهُ.

ومِنْهَا الجَوْرُ

41. وهُوَ الخُرُوجُ عَنِ الاِعْتِدَالِ في جَمِيعِ الأُمُورِ، والسَّرَفُ والتَّقْصِيرُ؛ وأَخْذُ الأَمْوَالِ مِنْ غَيْرِ وَجْهِهَا، والمُطَالَبَةُ بِمَا لاَ يَجِبُ مِنَ الحُقُوقِ الوَاجِبَةِ؛ وفِعْلُ الأَشْيَاءِ في غَيْرِ مَوَاضِعِهَا، ولاَ أَوْقَاتِهَا، ولاَ عَلَى القَدْرِ الَّذِي يَجِبُ، ولاَ عَلَى الوَجْهِ الَّذِي يُسْتَحَبُّ.

p. 85 [في الأَخْلاَقِ الَّتِي تَكُونُ فَضِيلَةً أَوْ رَذِيلَة]

ومِنَ الأَخْلاَقِ مَا هُوَ في بَعْضِ النَّاسِ فَضِيلَةٌ، وفي بَعْضِهِمْ رَذِيلَةٌ.

فَمِنْهَا حُبُّ الكَرَامَةِ

42. وهُوَ أَنْ يُسَرَّ الإِنْسَانُ بِالتَّعْظِيمِ والتَّبْجِيلِ، والمُقَابَلَةِ بِالمَدْحِ والثَّنَاءِ الجَمِيلِ. وهَذَا الخُلُقُ مَحْمُودٌ في الأَحْدَاثِ والصِّبْيَانِ، لأَنَّ مَحَبَّةَ الكَرَامَةِ تَحُثُّهُمْ عَلَى اكْتِسَابِ

LACK OF AMBITION

40. It is an inability of the soul to seek the higher grades and a want of hope for attaining the utmost. It is thinking of the smallest of the virtues as too much, deeming the least of gifts as too great, thinking it to be inaccessible, and being content with mediocre and paltry concerns. This moral quality is repugnant for everyone; it is most repugnant for kings. Indeed, whoever lacks ambition is not even deserving of kingship.

INJUSTICE

41. It is deviating from the right proportion in all things, by way of excess or diminution. It is appropriating wealth in improper ways. It is laying claim to rights to which one has no due title. It is doing things in the wrong places and times, in an undue measure, and in some way other than the one to be preferred.

On moral qualities that are sometimes virtues and sometimes vices

Some moral qualities are virtues in some people but vices in others.

LOVE OF HONOR

42. It is that a man is made happy by the recognition of his greatness, by respect, by receiving praise and favorable commendation. This moral quality is commendable in youths and boys because the love of

الفَضَائِلِ. وذَلِكَ أَنَّ الحَدَثَ والصَّبِيَّ، إذَا مُدِحَ عَلَى فَضِيلَةٍ تُرَى فِيهِ، كَانَ ذَلِكَ دَاعِياً p. 86
لَهُ إلَى الازْدِيَادِ مِنَ الفَضَائِلِ فَأَمَّا الأَفَاضِلُ مِنَ النَّاسِ، فَإنَّ ذَلِكَ يُعَدُّ مِنْهُمْ نَقِيصَةً. لأَنَّ الإنْسَانَ، إنَّمَا يُمْدَحُ عَلَى الفَضِيلَةِ إذَا كَانَتْ مُسْتَغْرَبَةً مِنْهُ. وَإذَا كَانَ مِنْ أَهْلِ الفَضْلِ، فَلَيْسَ يَنْبَغِي أَنْ يُسْتَغْرَبَ مَا يَظْهَرُ مِنْهُ مِنَ الفَضَائِلِ. وكَذَلِكَ الإكْرَامُ والتَّبْجِيلُ، إنْ كَانَ زَائِداً عَلَى اسْتِحْقَاقِهِ، فَإنَّهُ يَجْرِي مَجْرَى المَلَقِ؛ والسُّرُورُ بِالمَلَقِ غَيْرُ مَحْمُودٍ، لأَنَّهُ مِنْ جِنْسِ الخَدِيعَةِ.

ومِنْهَا حُبُّ الزِّينَةِ

43. وهُوَ التَّصَنُّعُ بِحُسْنِ البِزَّةِ والمَرْكُوبِ والآلاتِ، وكَثْرَةِ الخَدَمِ والحَشَمِ.
وهَذَا مُسْتَحْسَنٌ مِنَ المُلُوكِ والعُظَمَاءِ، والأَحْدَاثِ والظُّرَفَاءِ، والمُتَنَعِّمِينَ، والنِّسَاءِ. p. 87
فَأَمَّا الرُّهْبَانُ، والزُّهَّادُ، والشُّيُوخُ، وأَهْلُ العِلْمِ، وخَاصَّةً الخُطَبَاءُ والوَاعِظُونَ ورُؤَسَاءُ الدِّينِ، فَإنَّ الزِّينَةَ والتَّصَنُّعَ مُسْتَقْبَحٌ مِنْهُمْ. والمُسْتَحْسَنُ مِنْهُمْ لِبْسُ الشَّعَرِ والخَشِنِ، والمَشْيُ والحَفَاءُ، ولُزُومُ الكَنَائِسِ والمَسَاجِدِ وغَيْرِهَا، وكَرَاهِيَّةُ التَّنَعُّمِ.

ومِنْهَا المُجَازَاةُ عَلَى المَدْحِ

44. وهُوَ مُجَازَاةُ مَنْ يَمْدَحُ الإنْسَانَ، ويَشْكُرُهُ في المَجَالِسِ والمَحَافِلِ.
وهَذَا الخُلُقُ مُسْتَحْسَنٌ مِنَ المُلُوكِ والرُّؤَسَاءِ. لأَنَّ ذَلِكَ يَدْعُو الَّذِي يَمْدَحُ الإنْسَانَ إلى مَدْحِهِ، ويُكْسِبُ المَمْدُوحَ ذِكْراً جَمِيلاً، يَبْقَى عَلَى الدَّهْرِ. ومِنْ فَضَائِلِ المُلُوكِ
والرُّؤَسَاءِ بَقَاءُ ذِكْرِهِمِ الجَمِيلِ. ومِنْ فَضَائِلِ المُلُوكِ والرُّؤَسَاءِ بَقَاءُ ذِكْرِهِمِ الجَمِيلِ. p. 88

honor prods them to acquire virtues. It is due to the fact that, when a youth or a boy is praised for a virtue that he evidently possesses, it prompts him to add to the number of his virtues. But [this moral quality] is to be reckoned a defect for mature people. The reason is that a man is to be praised for virtue only when it is deemed to be exceptional for him. If he is a person of virtue, it is inappropriate that the virtues perceptible in him be deemed exceptional. Therefore, showing him honor and respect, if it is in excess of his deserts, takes the course of flattery. Being happy with flattery is not commendable because it is a kind of deception.

LOVE OF POMP AND SPLENDOR

43. It is making a display of oneself with exquisite clothes, mounts, and appurtenances, along with a multitude of servants and attendants. It is to be considered good on the part of kings and leaders, youths, elegant people, those who live in luxury, and women. As for monks, ascetics, elders, and scholars—especially orators, preachers, and religious leaders—for them pomp and splendor and making a display of oneself are to be considered repugnant. What is to be considered good for them is clothing of hair and coarse material, traveling on foot, obscurity, attendance at churches and mosques and so forth, and an abhorrence for luxurious living.

PAYING FOR PRAISE

44. It is rewarding someone who praises a man and gives him thanks in public sessions and assemblies. This moral quality is to be deemed good for kings and leaders because it induces the one who praises a man to continue to praise him and to secure a good reputation for the praiseworthy person that will last for a long time. The permanence of their own good reputation is one of the virtues of kings and leaders.

فَأَمَّا مَحَبَّتُهُمْ سَمَاعَ المَدْحِ مِنَ المَادِحِ مُوَاجَهَةً، فَذَلِكَ غَيْرُ مُسْتَحَبٍّ. لِأَنَّهُ مِنْ جِنْسِ

المَلَقِ؛ وَحُبُّ المَلَقِ مَكْرُوهٌ، لِأَنَّهُ مِنْ قَبِيلِ الخَدِيعَةِ. فَأَمَّا إِيثَارُهُمُ انْتِشَارَ ذِكْرِهِمْ،

وَمَدْحَهُمْ وَتَدَاوُلَ النَّاسِ لَهُ، وَبَقَاءَهُ بَعْدَهُمْ، فَإِنَّ ذَلِكَ مَحْمُودٌ مِنْهُمْ. فَمُجَازَاةُ المَادِحِ

مُسْتَحْسَنَةٌ مِنَ المُلُوكِ، وَمَنْعُهُ مُسْتَقْبَحٌ وَضَارٌّ. لِأَنَّ ذَلِكَ يَدْعُو إِلَى ذَمِّهِمْ، وَذَمُّهُمْ

5   يَبْقَى أَيْضاً عَلَى الدَّهْرِ. فَيَنْشُرُ لَهُمْ ذِكْراً قَبِيحاً، وَذَلِكَ مَكْرُوهٌ لِلْمُلُوكِ وَالرُّؤَسَاءِ.

p. 89 فَأَمَّا أَصَاغِرُ النَّاسِ، فَمَحَبَّتُهُمْ جَزَاءَ المَادِحِ لَهُمْ غَيْرُ مُسْتَحْسَنٍ. لِأَنَّ المَادِحَ، إِذَا مَدَحَ

الدَّنِيءَ مِنَ النَّاسِ، فَإِنَّمَا يَخْدَعُهُ؛ فَإِذَا أَجَازَهُ، اعْتَقَدَ أَنَّهُ اسْتَنْفَذَ مِنْهُ تِلْكَ الجَائِزَةَ.

وَكَثِيرٌ مِنَ النَّاسِ، إِذَا مُدِحُوا بِمَا لَيْسَ فِيهِمْ، يُبَادِرُونَ إِلَى مُجَازَاةِ المَادِحِ؛ فَيَكُونُونَ قَدْ

وَضَعُوا الشَّيْءَ فِي غَيْرِ مَوْضِعِهِ. وَهُمْ إِذَا صَرَفُوا ذَلِكَ الشَّيْءَ إِلَى الضُّعَفَاءِ، وَأَهْلِ

10 المَسْكَنَةِ، كَانَ أَجْمَلَ بِهِمْ وَأَلْيَقَ.

وَمِنْهَا الزُّهْدُ

45. وَهُوَ قِلَّةُ الرَّغْبَةِ فِي الأَمْوَالِ وَالأَعْرَاضِ، وَالادِّخَارِ وَالقِنْيَةِ؛ وَإِيثَارُ

p. 90 القَنَاعَةِ بِمَا يُقِيمُ الرَّمَقَ؛ وَالاسْتِخْفَافُ بِالدُّنْيَا وَمَحَاسِنِهَا وَلَذَّاتِهَا؛ وَقِلَّةُ الاكْتِرَاثِ

15 بِالمَرَاتِبِ العَالِيَةِ؛ وَاسْتِصْغَارُ المُلُوكِ وَمَمَالِكِهِمْ وَأَرْبَابِ الأَمْوَالِ وَأَمْوَالِهِمْ. وَهَذَا

الخُلُقُ مُسْتَحْسَنٌ جِدّاً، وَلَكِنْ مِنَ العُلَمَاءِ، وَالرُّهْبَانِ، وَرُؤَسَاءِ الدِّينِ، وَالخُطَبَاءِ،

وَالوَاعِظِينَ، وَمَنْ يُرَغِّبُ النَّاسَ فِي المَعَادِ وَالبَقَاءِ بَعْدَ المَوْتِ. فَأَمَّا المُلُوكُ وَالعُظَمَاءُ،

فَإِنَّ ذَلِكَ غَيْرُ مُسْتَحْسَنٍ مِنْهُمْ، وَلَا لَائِقٍ بِهِمْ. لِأَنَّ المَلِكَ، إِذَا أَظْهَرَ الزُّهْدَ، فَقَدْ

صَارَ نَاقِصاً. لِأَنَّ مُلْكَهُ لَا يَتِمُّ إِلَّا بِاحْتِشَادِ الأَمْوَالِ وَالأَعْرَاضِ وَادِّخَارِهَا، لِيَذُبَّ

But the love of hearing the encomiast giving them praise face to face is undesirable because it is a species of flattery, and the love of flattery is abhorrent because it is a kind of deception. But the predilection for the wide diffusion of their reputation and of their praise, for people's passing it on, and for its continuation after them is commendable. So for kings to reward someone who gives praise is to be deemed good; for them to refuse it is to be deemed repugnant and wrong, for it would invite their disparagement, and their discredit would also last for a long time. It would also give them a widespread bad reputation. This is abhorrent for kings and leaders. As for lower-class people, their love for rewarding someone who gives them praise is not to be deemed good. If someone praises a lowly person, he only deceives him. And, when he is approved, he believes that he has deservedly gotten that approval. Many people, when they are praised for what is not in them, hurry to compensate the one giving the praise. But they will have deposited the amount in the wrong place. If they had disbursed that amount to the weak and to the poor people, it would have been better for them and more fitting.

RENUNCIATION

45. It is having little desire for money and goods, for accumulation and acquisition. It is choosing to be satisfied with what supports bare life, making light of this world and its goods and pleasures. It is paying little attention to the higher social orders, deeming kings and their kingdoms of small importance, along with the owners of money and their money. This moral quality is to be considered very good, but it is for scholars, monks, religious leaders, orators, preachers, and whoever gives people an interest in eternal life. It is not to be deemed good for kings and leaders, nor is it appropriate for them. For, when a king makes his practice of renunciation public, he becomes deficient. The reason is that his reign only achieves its full purpose with the collection of money and goods and the accumulation of them, so that he might defend

p. 91 بِهَا عَنْ مُلْكِهِ، ويَصُونَ بِهَا حَوْزَتَهُ، ويَفْتَقِدَ بِهَا رَعِيَّتَهُ؛ وذَلِكَ مُضَادٌّ لِلزُّهْدِ. فَإِنْ تَرَكَ الادِّخَارَ، بَطَلَ مُلْكُهُ، وصَارَ مَعْدُوداً في جُمْلَةِ النَّقِصِ مِنَ المُلُوكِ، الحَائِدِينَ عَنْ طَرِيقِ السِّيَاسَةِ.

his realm with them, conserve its assets, and come to the aid of his subjects. This is contrary to the practice of renunciation. So, if he abandons the accumulation [of goods], his reign becomes futile, and he will summarily be numbered among the most inadequate of the kings who deviate from the way of right government.

[القِسْمُ الرَّابِع] p. 92

[الارْتِيَاض بِمَكَارِمِ الأَخْلاَق]

[ضَرُورَةُ تَهْذِيبِ الأَخْلاَق]

1. فَهٰذِهِ الأَقْسَامُ الَّتِي ذَكَرْنَاهَا هِيَ أَخْلاَقُ جَمِيعِ النَّاسِ. أَمَّا المَحْمُودَةُ مِنْهَا، المَعْدُودَةُ فَضَائِلَ، فَقَلَّمَا تَجْتَمِعُ كُلُّهَا في إِنْسَانٍ وَاحِدٍ. وأَمَّا المَذْمُومَةُ مِنْهَا، المَعْدُودَةُ نَقَائِصَ ومَعَايِبَ، فَقَلَّمَا يُوجَدُ إِنْسَانٌ يَخْلُو مِنْ جَمِيعِهَا، حَتَّى لاَ يَكُونَ فِيهِ خُلُقٌ مَكْرُوهٌ، وخَاصَّةً مَنْ لَمْ يُرَوِّضْ نَفْسَهُ، ويُؤَدِّبْهَا. فَإِنَّ مَنْ لَمْ يَتَعَمَّلْ لِضَبْطِ نَفْسِهِ، p. 93 ويَتَفَقَّدْ عُيُوبَهُ، لَمْ يَخْلُ مِنْ عُيُوبٍ كَثِيرَةٍ، وإِنْ لَمْ يَحُسَّ بِهَا ولَمْ يَفْطُنْ لَهَا. وإِذَا كَانَ الأَمْرُ عَلَى مَا ذَكَرْنَا، كَانَ أَوْلَى الأُمُورِ بِالإِنْسَانِ أَنْ يَفْتَقِدَ أَخْلاَقَهُ؛ ويَتَأَمَّلَ عُيُوبَهُ، ويَجْتَهِدَ في إِصْلاَحِهَا ونَفْيِهَا عَنْ نَفْسِهِ؛ ويَتْبَعَ الأَخْلاَقَ المَحْمُودَةَ، ويَحْمِلَ نَفْسَهُ عَلَى اعْتِيَادِهَا والتَّخَلُّقِ بِهَا.

2. فَإِنَّ النَّاسَ، إِنَّمَا يَتَفَاضَلُونَ، عَلَى الحَقِيقَةِ، بِفَضَائِلِهِمْ، لاَ كَمَا يَعْتَقِدُ الجُهَّالُ والعَامَّةُ، أَنَّهُمْ يَتَفَاضَلُونَ بِأَحْوَالِهِمْ وأَمْوَالِهِمْ، وكَثْرَةِ الذَّخَائِرِ والأَعْرَاضِ.

Part Four

Practicing the noble moral qualities

The necessity of the reformation of morals

1. These traits we have mentioned are the moral qualities of people. The praiseworthy ones—those reckoned as virtues—seldom all come together in a single man. As for the blameworthy ones—those reckoned as defects and faults—seldom is a man found to be free of every one of them, to the point that there is no abhorrent moral quality left in him. This is especially the case if he is someone who does not train his soul and discipline it. Whoever does not take the trouble to control himself and to examine his faults is not free of many faults, even if he does not perceive them and does not advert to them. Since this is the case, the first concern for a man should be to examine his moral qualities, to consider his faults, to make an effort to mend them, and to remove them from his soul. He should also pursue commendable moral qualities, taking it upon himself to make them habitual and to be morally formed by them.

2. People will only really be distinguished in terms of their virtues, not, as ignorant and common people suppose, in terms of their status, their money, and the abundance of treasures and goods.

p. 94

3. فَإِنَّ أَكْثَرَ النَّاسِ، إِنَّمَا يَتَفَاخَرُونَ بِالذَّخَائِرِ وَالأَمْوَالِ وَالآلَاتِ، وَيُعَظِّمُونَ أَبَداً الأَغْنِيَاءَ وَذَوِي الأَمْوَالِ، وَلَا يَتَرَتَّبُ بَعْضُهُمْ عَلَى بَعْضٍ، إِلَّا بِكَثْرَةِ الأَمْوَالِ، أَوْ بِالجَاهِ المُكْتَسَبِ بِالمَالِ. وَلَيْسَ كَثْرَةُ الأَمْوَالِ مِمَّا يَتَفَاضَلُ بِهَا النَّاسُ، بَلْ كَثْرَةُ الأَمْوَالِ إِنَّمَا تَتَفَاضَلُ بِهَا أَحْوَالُ النَّاسِ. فَأَمَّا نُفُوسُهُمْ، فَلَيْسَتْ تَكُونُ أَفْضَلَ مِنْ نُفُوسِ غَيْرِهِمْ بِكَثْرَةِ الأَمْوَالِ. وَذَلِكَ أَنَّ الفَاجِرَ السَّفِيهَ، الجَاهِلَ الشِّرِّيرَ، وَإِنْ حَوَى أَمْوَالاً عَظِيمَةً، فَلَيْسَ يَكُونُ أَفْضَلَ مِنَ العَفِيفِ الحَكِيمِ، العَالِمِ الخَيِّرِ، وَإِنْ كَانَ فَقِيراً؛ بَلْ إِنَّمَا يَكُونُ بِكَثْرَةِ الأَمْوَالِ أَغْنَى مِنْهُ. فَأَمَّا الفَضْلُ، فَلَيْسَ يَكُونُ أَحَدٌ أَفْضَلَ مِنْ أَحَدٍ، إِلَّا بِكَثْرَةِ الفَضَائِلِ فَقَطْ.

p. 95

4. فَإِنِ اجْتَمَعَ لِلإِنْسَانِ، مَعَ الأَخْلَاقِ الجَمِيلَةِ وَالعَادَاتِ المُسْتَحْسَنَةِ، الغِنَى وَالثَّرْوَةُ، فَلَعَمْرِي إِنَّهُ يَكُونُ أَحْسَنَ حَالاً مِنَ الفَاضِلِ المُقْتَرِّ. لِأَنَّ مِنْ سَعَادَاتِ الإِنْسَانِ أَيْضاً، وَخَاصَّةً إِذَا كَانَ فَاضِلاً عَادِلاً عَفِيفاً، أَنْ يَصْرِفَ مَالَهُ فِي وُجُوهِهِ، وَيُنْفِقَهُ فِي حَقِّهِ، وَيَتَفَقَّدَ بِهِ مَنْ يُحِبُّ تَفَقُّدَهُ، وَيُسْعِفَ بِهِ أَهْلَ المَسْكَنَةِ، وَلَا يَقْعُدَ عَنْ حَقٍّ يَجِبُ عَلَيْهِ، وَلَا مَكْرُمَةٍ تَزِيدُ فِي مَحَاسِنِهِ.

p. 96

5. فَأَمَّا النَّاقِصُ الجَاهِلُ، السَّيِّئُ العَادَاتِ، فَإِنَّ الغِنَى رُبَّمَا زَادَهُ نَقْصاً، وَانْضَافَ إِلَى مَعَايِبِهِ. فَإِنَّهُ لَا يُعَدُّ بَخِيلاً مَنْ لَا مَالَ لَهُ، وَإِنْ كَانَ البُخْلُ فِي طَبْعِهِ. فَلَيْسَ يَظْهَرُ ذَلِكَ مِنْهُ. وَمَا لَمْ يَظْهَرْ ذَلِكَ مِنْهُ، فَلَيْسَ يُعَابُ بِهِ؛ لِأَنَّ الإِنْسَانَ إِنَّمَا يُعَابُ بِمَا يَظْهَرُ مِنْهُ. فَإِذَا كَانَ غَنِيّاً، ذَا مَالٍ وَيَسَارٍ، وَلَمْ يَجُدْ بِهِ، ظَهَرَ بُخْلُهُ، فَيَصِيرُ المَالُ جَالِباً عَلَيْهِ هَذَا العَيْبَ.

3. Most people boast only of treasures, money, and means. They always glorify the rich and those who have money. None of them will be subordinate to someone else except by reason of an abundance of money, or by reason of the rank acquired by means of money. But a lot of money is not that by which people will really be distinguished. Rather, a lot of money is only the means by which people vary in condition. The souls of the rich are not more virtuous than the souls of anyone else just by reason of a lot of money. That is because the silly libertine or the vicious ignoramus, even if he owns an enormous amount of money, will not be more virtuous than the wise, abstinent person or the beneficent savant who may be a poor man. Rather, by reason of a lot of money, he will only be richer than the other man is. As far as virtue is concerned, no one is more virtuous than anyone else except by reason of an abundance of virtues, and that is all.

4. If wealth and fortune come together for a man with superb moral qualities and well-esteemed habits, then, upon my life, he will be of a much higher condition than a destitute virtuous man. The reason is that it is also part of human happiness—especially when one is virtuous, just, and abstinent—to disburse one's money appropriately. He must spend it rightly, use it to help someone who wants the assistance, and aid poor people with it. He must not refrain from a claim that is incumbent upon him or from an honorable deed that would add to his good qualities.

5. Wealth sometimes increases the deficiency of an ignorant and deficient person of bad habits, and it is to be added to his faults. So someone who has no money is not reckoned to be niggardly, even if there is niggardliness in his nature, for it does not show in him. And, as long as it does not show in him, he is not blamed for it, because a man is blamed only for what shows in him. But if, when he has become rich, possessed of money and affluence, he is not generous with it, his niggardliness shows; and so the money is what brings the fault upon him.

p. 97 6. وأَيْضاً ، فَإِنَّ أَكْثَرَ الفُجُورِ والمَحْظُورَاتِ والشَّهَوَاتِ الرَّدِيئَةِ ، لَيْسَ تُنَالُ إِلاَّ
بِالأَمْوَالِ. فَالفَقِيرُ ، وإِنْ كَانَ في شِيمَتِهِ الفُجُورُ ، فَلَيْسَ يَكَادُ يَظْهَرُ ذَلِكَ مِنْهُ. فَإِذَا كَانَ
ذَا مَالٍ ، تَمَكَّنَ مِنْ شَهَوَاتِهِ ، فَتَظْهَرُ عُيُوبُهُ. فَقَدْ يَكُونُ الغِنَى مُكْسِباً لِصَاحِبِهِ عُيُوباً
ونَقَائِصَ ، وقَدْ يَكُونُ الفَقْرُ مُفِيداً لِصَاحِبِهِ فَضَائِلَ ومَحَاسِنَ. فَلَيْسَ تَتَفَاضَلُ النَّاسُ ،
عَلَى الحَقِيقَةِ ، بِالأَمْوَالِ والأَعْرَاضِ ، وإِنَّمَا يَتَفَاضَلُونَ بِالآدَابِ والمَحَاسِنِ الذَّاتِيَّةِ.

p. 98 7. فَحَقِيقٌ بِالإِنْسَانِ أَنْ يَسُوسَ نَفْسَهُ السِّيَاسَةَ المُسْتَحْسَنَةَ ، ويَسْلُكَ بِهَا
الطَّرِيقَةَ المَحْبُوبَةَ. فَإِنَّهُ بِذَلِكَ يَكُونُ مُحَبَّباً إِلى النَّاسِ ، مَقْبُولاً عِنْدَهُمْ ، مُعَظَّماً في
نُفُوسِهِمْ ، مُفَضَّلاً عَلَى غَيْرِهِ ، مُوَقَّراً عِنْدَ الرُّؤَسَاءِ والمُلُوكِ ، مَقْبُولَ القَوْلِ ، عَرِيضَ الجَاهِ.
وهَذِهِ خَيْرٌ مِنَ الرِّئَاسَةِ المُكْتَسَبَةِ بِالأَمْوَالِ ؛ لأَنَّ المَالَ قَدْ تَلْحَقُهُ الجَوَائِحُ. فَإِذَا فَارَقَ
صَاحِبَهُ ، سَقَطَتْ مَنْزِلَتُهُ مِنْ نُفُوسِ النَّاسِ ، وسَاوَى العَامَّةَ والسُّوقَةَ. لأَنَّهُ ، إِذَا رَأَسَ
بِالمَالِ ، فَالمُعَظِّمُ لَهُ هُوَ مَالُه ، لا نَفْسُهُ. فَإِذَا زَالَ ذَلِكَ المَالُ ، لَمْ يَبْقَ لَهُ شَيْءٌ يُعَظَّمُ مِنْ
p. 99 أَجْلِهِ. ولَيْسَ كَذَلِكَ الفَاضِلُ النَّفْسِ ، المُهَذَّبُ الأَخْلاَقِ. فَإِنَّ هَذَا رِئَاسَتُهُ بِفَضَائِلِهِ ،
وفَضَائِلُهُ غَيْرُ مُفَارِقَةٍ لَهُ. فَهُوَ رَئِيسٌ مَا دَامَ ، ومُعَظَّمٌ لِذَاتِهِ ، لا لِشَيْءٍ مِنْ خَارِجٍ.

8. ولأَنَّ الرَّاغِبَ في سِيَاسَةِ نَفْسِهِ ، المُؤْثِرَ تَهْذِيبَ أَخْلاَقِهِ ، إِذَا نُبِّهَ عَلَى
خُلُقٍ مَذْمُومٍ يَجِدُهُ في نَفْسِهِ وأَحَبَّ اجْتِنَابَهُ ، رُبَّمَا صَعُبَ عَلَيْهِ الانْتِقَالُ عَنْهُ مِنْ
p. 100 أَوَّلِ وَهْلَةٍ ، ورُبَّمَا لَمْ يَنَلِ التَّخَلُّصَ مِنْهُ ولَمْ يُطَاوِعْهُ طَبْعُهُ ، ورُبَّمَا اسْتَحْسَنَ أَيْضاً
خُلُقاً مَحْمُوداً لاَ يَجِدُهُ لِنَفْسِهِ ، وآثَرَ التَّخَلُّقَ بِهِ ، ولَمْ تَسْتَجِبْ لَهُ عَادَتُهُ ، ولَمْ يَصِلْ
إِلى مُرَادِهِ ، وَجَبَ أَنْ نَرْسُمَ ، لِلرَّاغِبِينَ في السِّيَاسَةِ المَحْمُودَةِ ، طُرُقاً يَتَدَرَّبُونَ بِهَا ،
ويَتَدَرَّجُونَ فِيهَا ، حَتَّى يَنْتَهُوا إِلى مُرَادِهِمْ ، مِنِ اعْتِيَادِ الأَخْلاَقِ الجَمِيلَةِ ، والانْطِبَاعِ

6. Furthermore, a good deal of debauchery, of what is prohibited, and of the viler appetites can only be indulged by means of money. So, even if debauchery is in the temperament of someone who is poor, it hardly shows in him. But, if he has money, he can afford his appetites, and so his faults show. Wealth, then, may be what procures faults and deficiencies for the one who has it, while poverty may be what gains virtues and good qualities for the one caught in it. So people really do not vary by means of money and goods; they vary only in terms of refinement and naturally good conduct.

7. The authentic thing for a man to do is to train his soul in good conduct and so to travel along the well-beloved way. He will then become lovable to men, will be well received in their company, will be extolled in their hearts, and will be given preference over others. He will also be honored in the company of leaders and kings; he will be a valued speaker and appreciated. This is much better than preeminence acquired by money, because calamities are often attached to money. So, when it is parted from its owner, his position declines in people's hearts, and he comes to be on a par with ordinary, common people. The reason is that, when someone enjoys preeminence because of money, what elevates him is his money, not his soul. And, when the money disappears, he has nothing to elevate him. Someone virtuous of soul, reformed of morals, is not like this. The preeminence of this sort of person is due to his virtues, and his virtues are not so readily parted from him. He is preeminent continuously, elevated by reason of his very essence, not by reason of something extrinsic.

8. When someone who wants to take control of himself, choosing to reform his morals, becomes aware of a blameworthy moral quality that he can find in himself and wants to avoid it, overcoming it is sometimes too difficult right away. Sometimes he does not succeed in getting rid of it, because his own nature does not obey him. In the same way, it is sometimes the case that he will find a certain commendable moral quality attractive that he cannot find in himself and would like to acquire it, but his customary practice is not worthy of it, and so he does not attain his wish. Therefore, we must sketch out for those who want to exercise a commendable degree of self-control some ways by which they might be trained and in which they might make progress. The point is to come eventually to their goal of making the good moral qualities habitual, to becoming naturally disposed

بِهَا ، وتَجَنُّبِ الأَخْلاَقِ القَبِيحَةِ ، والتَّفَرُّغِ مِنْهَا . فَنَذْكُرُ ، مِنْ أَجْلِ ذَلِكَ ، طَرِيقَ الارْتِيَاضِ بِالأَخْلاَقِ ، والتَّعَمُّلِ لاِعْتِيَادِهَا .

[تَرْوِيضُ النَّفْسِ الشَّهْوَانِيَّة] p. 101

9. وقَدْ ذَكَرْنَا فِيمَا تَقَدَّمَ ، أَنَّ سَبَبَ اخْتِلاَفِ الأَخْلاَقِ في النَّاسِ هُوَ اخْتِلاَفُ قُوَى النَّفْسِ الثَّلاَثِ فِيهِمْ ، وهِيَ الشَّهْوَانِيَّةُ ، والغَضَبِيَّةُ ، والنَّاطِقَةُ . وأَنَّ صَلاَحَ الأَخْلاَقِ هُوَ تَذْلِيلُ الشَّهْوَانِيَّةِ مِنْهَا والغَضَبِيَّةِ ؛ وتَمْيِيزُ عَادَاتِ النَّفْسِ النَّاطِقَةِ ، واسْتِعْمَالُ المَحْمُودِ مِنْ أَفْعَالِهَا . وطَرِيقُ التَّدَرُّجِ ، لاِسْتِعْمَالِ العَادَاتِ الجَمِيلَةِ ، والعُدُولِ عَنِ العَادَاتِ المُسْتَقْبَحَةِ ، هُوَ التَّدَرُّجُ في تَذْلِيلِ هَاتَيْنِ القُوَّتَيْنِ .

10. أَمَّا النَّفْسُ الشَّهْوَانِيَّةُ ، فَالطَّرِيقُ إلى قَمْعِهَا ، أَنْ يَتَذَكَّرَ الإِنْسَانُ ، في أَوْقَاتِ p. 102
شَهَوَاتِهِ ، وعِنْدَ شِدَّةِ القَرَمِ إلى لَذَّاتِهِ ، أَنَّهُ يُرِيدُ تَذْلِيلَ نَفْسِهِ الشَّهْوَانِيَّةِ ؛ فَيَعْدِلَ عَمَّا تَاقَتْ نَفْسُهُ إِلَيْهِ مِنَ الشَّهْوَةِ الرَّدِيئَةِ ، إلى مَا هُوَ مُسْتَحْسَنٌ مِنْ جِنْسِ تِلْكَ الشَّهْوَةِ ، ومُتَّفَقٌ عَلَى ارْتِضَائِهِ ، فَيَقْتَصِرَ عَلَيْهِ . فَإِنَّ بِذَلِكَ الفِعْلِ تَنْكَسِرُ شَهْوَتُهُ ، ثُمَّ يُعَلِّلُهَا ويُعِدُّهَا . فَإِنْ سَكَنَتْ ، . . . ؛ وإلاَّ ، عَاوَدَ الفِعْلَ مِنَ الوَجْهِ المُسْتَحْسَنِ . فَإِنَّهُ ، إذَا فَعَلَ ذَلِكَ وكَرَّرَ فِعْلَهُ ، كَفَّتِ النَّفْسُ . وإِذَا اسْتَمَرَّتْ عَلَى هَذِهِ الحَالِ ، أَلِفَتِ النَّفْسُ هَذِهِ العَادَةَ ، p. 103
وأَنِسَتْ بِهَا ، واسْتَوْحَشَتْ مِمَّا سِوَاهَا .

11. ويَنْبَغِي لِمَنْ أَرَادَ قَمْعَ نَفْسِهِ الشَّهْوَانِيَّةِ ، أَنْ يُكْثِرَ مِنْ مُجَالَسَةِ الزُّهَّادِ والرُّهْبَانِ والنُّسَّاكِ ، وأَهْلِ الوَرَعِ والوَاعِظِينَ ؛ ويُلاَزِمَ مَجَالِسَ الرُّؤَسَاءِ ، وأَهْلِ العِلْمِ . فَإِنَّ الرُّؤَسَاءَ وأَهْلَ العِلْمِ ، وخاصَّةً رُؤَسَاءَ الدِّينِ ، يُعَظِّمُونَ مَنْ كَانَ مَعْرُوفاً بِالعِفَّةِ ،

to them, to steer clear of the bad moral qualities, and to disengage from them. Therefore, we will recommend a program of training in the moral qualities and of seeking to make their practice habitual.

Training the appetitive soul

9. We have previously mentioned that the reason for the disparity of moral qualities among people is the disparity of the three powers of the soul in them: the appetitive, the irascible, and the rational. The right management of the moral qualities is to subjugate the appetitive and the irascible powers, to promote the habits of the rational soul, and to put the most commendable of its operations into effect. The way to make progress in putting good habits into effect and in abstaining from bad habits is to make progress in subjugating the aforementioned two powers.

10. The way to curb the appetitive soul is for a man to remember in times of desire, and at the moment of his vehement longing for pleasure, that he really wants to subjugate his appetitive soul. He should then turn his attention away from the vile appetite for which his soul yearns toward something more commendable for that species of appetite, consistent with his approval; and so he should confine himself to that. By this kind of action his appetite will be tamed; then he will be able to divert it and redirect it. It may subside, . . . if not, he will have to go back to acting in the most commendable way; and, when he does this repeatedly, the soul will eventually desist. If it perseveres in this state, the soul will accustom itself to this habit, get used to it, and develop an aversion for anything else.

11. Whoever wants to tame his appetitive soul must frequent the company of ascetics, monks, hermits, pious people, and preachers, in addition to attending the gatherings of leaders and scholars. Leaders and scholars, especially religious leaders, will extol whoever is known

p. 104 ويَسْتَزْرُونَ مَنْ كَانَ فَاجِراً مُتَهَتِّكاً. ومُلَازَمَتُهُ لِهَذِهِ المَجَالِسِ تَضْطَرُّهُ إلى التَّصَوُّنِ

والتَّعَفُّفِ والتَّجَمُّلِ لأُولَئِكَ، لِئَلّا يَسْتَزْرُوهُ، ويَغْضَبُوا مِنْهُ؛ ويَلْحَقَ بِرُتْبَةِ مَنْ يُعَظَّمُ في

المَحَافِلِ. ويَنْبَغِي لَهُ أَيْضاً أَنْ يُدِيمَ النَّظَرَ في كُتُبِ الأَخْلاقِ والسِّيَاسَةِ، وأَخْبَارِ الزُّهَّادِ

والرُّهْبَانِ والنُّسَّاكِ، وأَهْلِ الوَرَعِ. ويَجِبُ عَلَيْهِ أَنْ يَتَجَنَّبَ مَجَالِسَ الخُلَعَاءِ والسُّفَهَاءِ

5   والمُتَهَتِّكِينَ، ومَنْ يُكْثِرُ الهَزْلَ واللَّعِبَ.

12. وأَكْثَرُ مَا يَجِبُ عَلَيْهِ تَجَنُّبُهُ السُّكْرُ. فَإِنَّ السُّكْرَ مِنَ الشَّرَابِ يُثِيرُ نَفْسَهُ

الشَّهْوَانِيَّةَ ويُقَوِّيهَا، ويَحْمِلُهَا عَلَى التَّهَتُّكِ، وارْتِكَابِ الفَوَاحِشِ، والمُجَاهَرَةِ بِهَا. وذَلِكَ
p. 105

أَنَّ الإِنْسَانَ، إِنَّمَا يَرْتَدِعُ عَنِ القَبَائِحِ بِالعَقْلِ والتَّمْيِيزِ. فَإِذَا سَكِرَ، عَدِمَ ذَلِكَ الَّذِي

كَانَ يَرْدَعُهُ عَنِ الفِعْلِ القَبِيحِ، فَلَا يُبَالِي أَنْ يَرْتَكِبَ كُلَّ مَا كَانَ يَتَجَنَّبُ في صَحْوِهِ.

10 فَأَوْلَى الأَشْيَاءِ بِمَنْ طَلَبَ العِفَّةَ، هَجْرُ الشَّرَابِ بِالجُمْلَةِ. وإِنْ لَمْ يُمْكِنْهُ، فَلْيَقْتَصِرْ عَلَى

اليَسِيرِ مِنْهُ. ويَكُونُ في الخَلَوَاتِ، أَوْ مَعَ مَنْ لَا يَحْتَشِمُهُ؛ ويَتَجَنَّبُ مَجَالِسَ المُجَاهِرِينَ
p. 106

بِالشَّرَابِ والسُّكْرِ والخَلَاعَةِ. ولَا يَظُنَّنَّ أَنَّهُ، إِنْ حَضَرَ تِلْكَ المَجَالِسَ، واقْتَصَرَ عَلَى

اليَسِيرِ مِنَ الشَّرَابِ، لَمْ يَسْتَضِرَّ بِهِ، فَإِنَّ هَذَا غَلَطٌ. وذَلِكَ أَنَّ مَنْ يَحْضُرُ مَجَالِسَ

الشَّرَابِ، لَيْسَ تَنْقَادُ لَهُ نَفْسُهُ إلى القَنَاعَةِ بِيَسِيرِ الشَّرَابِ؛ بَلْ إِنْ [مَنْ] حَضَرَ مَجَالِسَ

15 الشَّرَابِ وكَانَ في غَايَةِ العِفَّةِ، تَارِكاً لِلشُّرْبِ، مُتَمَسِّكاً بِالوَرَعِ، حَمَلَتْهُ شَهْوَتُهُ عَلَى

التَّشَبُّهِ بِأَهْلِ المَجْلِسِ، وتَاقَتْ نَفْسُهُ إلى الفَتْكِ. ومَا أَكْثَرَ مَنْ فَعَلَ ذَلِكَ، وتَهَتَّكَ بَعْدَ

السَّتْرِ والصِّيَانَةِ. فَشَرُّ الأَحْوَالِ لِمَنْ طَلَبَ العِفَّةَ حُضُورُ مَجَالِسِ الشَّرَابِ، ومُخَالَطَةُ

أَهْلِهَا، والاسْتِكْثَارُ مِنْ مُعَاشَرَتِهِمْ.

for abstinence, and they will think little of anyone who is a shameless debauchee. One's attendance at these gatherings will oblige him to live chastely, to cultivate abstinence, and to make himself attractive to these people, so that they will not hold him in contempt or be angry with him. Then he might join the rank of those who are extolled in the assemblies. One must also be continually studying books on morality and deportment, as well as accounts of ascetics, monks, hermits, and pious people. And it is necessary to avoid the gatherings of foolish and dissolute people, and those who act disgracefully, as well as those who are constantly joking and playing.

12. Most of all, it is necessary to avoid intoxication. Intoxication from drink stimulates the appetitive soul, invigorates it, and induces it to act disgracefully, to commit lewd acts, and to engage in them openly. That is because man is only to be kept away from evil by means of the mind and the exercise of discrimination. When he is intoxicated, he is deprived of what used to hold him back from evil deeds, and so he is not conscious of doing everything he used to avoid in his sobriety. So, for someone who seeks abstinence the first thing to do is to refrain from drinking altogether. If that is not possible for him, then let him restrict himself to a little bit of it. Let him be alone, or with those of whom he will not be ashamed, and let him avoid gatherings of those who openly engage in drinking, intoxication, and dissipation. Let him not suppose that, if he attends these gatherings and limits himself to a little bit of drink, he will not be harmed by it. This is a mistake, because the soul of anyone who attends drinking parties is not going to obey him to the point of being content with a little bit of drink. Rather, if he attends drinking parties, having been most abstinent, refraining from drinking and holding fast to piety, his appetite will induce him to imitate the people at the party, and his soul will yearn for foolhardiness. So often people who do this come to disgrace after having been on guard and on the defensive. The worst situation for someone who seeks abstinence is attendance at drinking parties, associating with people who do attend, and frequenting their company.

p. 107 **13.** وَيَنْبَغِي لِمَنْ أَرَادَ قَمْعَ نَفْسِهِ الشَّهْوَانِيَّةِ أَنْ يُقِلَّ مِنِ اسْتِمَاعِ السَّمَاعِ، وَخَاصَّةً النِّسْوَانَ، والشَّابّاتِ مِنْهُنَّ، والمُتَصَنِّعَاتِ؛ فَإِنَّ لِلسَّمَاعِ قُوَّةً عَظِيمَةً في إِثَارَةِ الشَّهْوَةِ. فَإِذَا انْضَافَ إلى ذَلِكَ أَنْ تَكُونَ المُسْمِعَةُ مُشْتَهَاةً، مُتَعَمِّلَةً لاِسْتِمَالَةِ العُيُونِ إِلَيْهَا، اجْتَمَعَ عَلَى السَّامِعِ حَوَادِثُ كَثِيرَةٌ، فَرُبَّمَا لَمْ يَسْتَطِعْ دَفْعَ جَمِيعِهَا عَنْ نَفْسِهِ. والأَوْلَى لِمَنْ هَمَّ بِقَهْرِ الشَّهْوَةِ أَنْ يَتَجَنَّبَ السَّمَاعَ. وإِنْ لَمْ يَكُنْ لَهُ مِنْهُ بُدٌّ، ولَمْ تَسْتَجِبْ نَفْسُهُ إلى هَجْرِهِ بِالكُلِّيَّةِ، فَلْيَقْتَصِرْ عَلَى اسْتِمَاعِهِ مِنَ الرِّجَالِ، ومَنْ لاَ مَطْمَعَ لِلشَّهْوَةِ فِيهِ؛ والإقْلاَلُ مِنْهُ خَيْرٌ، وأَصْوَنُ لِلْمُتَعَفِّفِ.

p. 108 **14.** فَأَمَّا الطَّعَامُ، فَيَنْبَغِي أَنْ تَعْلَمَ أَنَّ غَايَتَهُ هُوَ الشِّبْعُ لِدَفْعِ أَلَمِ الجُوعِ. وفَاخِرُ طَعَامٍ ودَنِيئُهُ جَمِيعاً مُشْبِعَانِ؛ فَلَيْسَ لِلْمُبَالَغَةِ في تَجْوِيدِ الطَّعَامِ كَبِيرُ حَظٍّ. والأَوْلَى هُوَ التَّوَسُّطُ في أَنْوَاعِ المَآكِلِ، وأَنْ يَكُونَ مِنَ الجِنْسِ الَّذِي نَشَأَ عَلَيْهِ الإِنْسَانُ وَاعْتَادَهُ وأَلِفَهُ. عَلَى أَنَّ شَهْوَةَ الطَّعَامِ والنَّهَمَ فِيهِ، وإِنْ كَانَ مِنَ الأَخْلاَقِ الرَّدِيئَةِ، فَهُوَ أَسْهَلُهَا وأَهْوَنُهَا. ولَيْسَ يَكْتَسِبُ صَاحِبُهَا مِنَ العَارِ مَا تُكْسِبُهُ مَحَبَّةُ الشَّرَابِ، والمُبَاضَعَةُ، ومُعَاشَرَةُ النِّسْوَانِ، ومُصَاحَبَةُ الأَحْدَاثِ المُتَهَيِّئِينَ لِلْفَوَاحِشِ. فَإِنَّ ذَلِكَ في غَايَةِ القُبْحِ؛ p. 109 وشَهْوَةُ المَآكِلِ أَقَلُّ قُبْحاً مِنْهُ، وأَخَفُّ عَلَى فَاعِلِهِ؛ وهُوَ مَعَ ذَلِكَ قَبِيحٌ؛ والاِسْتِهْتَارُ بِهِ، وكَثْرَةُ النَّهَمِ والشَّرَهِ إِلَيْهِ، مَكْرُوهٌ. وطَرِيقُ التَّدَرُّجِ إلى الاِقْتِصَارِ في الطَّعَامِ هُوَ أَنْ يُبَادِرَ ذُو الشَّهْوَةِ إلى أَيِّ شَيْءٍ وَجَدَهُ مِنَ المَآكِلِ. فَإِنْ كَانَ المُشْتَهَى الَّذِي تَاقَتْ نَفْسُهُ إِلَيْهِ حُلْواً، فَإِلَى أَيِّ حَلاَوَةٍ وَجَدَهَا وإِنْ كَانَ غَيْرَ ذَلِكَ، فَإِلَى مَا شَابَهَهُ في الطَّعْمِ فَإِنَّهُ، إِذَا تَنَاوَلَ مِنَ الطَّعْمِ، فَإِنَّ شَهْوَتَهُ تَسْكُنُ ونَفْسَهُ تَكُفُّ.

13. Whoever wants to tame his appetitive soul must be seldom engaged in listening to music—especially that of women, and particularly the young and dressed-up among them—because music has a great power to arouse the appetite. If, added to that, the one making music is a desirable woman who goes to the trouble of attracting attention to herself, many stimuli will converge on the listener, and sometimes he will not be able to push all of them away from his soul. For one who intends to overcome an appetite, the very best thing to do is to avoid music altogether. If he has no way to escape it and his soul is not responsive to forgoing it completely, then let him reserve his listening to music performed by men, and by those in whom there is nothing appealing to the appetite. Having little to do with it is the best and safest thing for anyone who would practice abstinence.

14. As for food, we must understand that its purpose is satiety, to dispel the pain of hunger. The best and the worst foods are both filling, so there is little to be said for excessive refinements in food. The most important thing is to hold the middle course among the varieties of food, and to ensure that it be of the kind on which a man was brought up, to which he has grown accustomed, and with which he is thoroughly familiar. Nevertheless, even though the appetite for food and the ravenous hunger for it is one of the bad moral qualities, it is the mildest and the least of them. One possessed of it will not acquire the degree of shame that the love of drink will cause him to acquire, or the love of sexual intercourse, of associating with women, or of keeping company with youths ready for lewdness. That is the utmost of iniquity. The appetite for food is much less iniquitous and more insignificant for the one indulging it. Nevertheless, it is repulsive; and to be negligent of it, along with too much craving and greed for [food], is abhorrent. The way to make progress in limiting one's eating is for the person with a big appetite for food to make do with whatever food he finds. If the choice thing for which his soul yearns is a sweet thing, let it be for whatever sweet thing he finds. If it is something else, let it be for whatever resembles it in taste. If he gets just a taste, his appetite will abate and his soul will hold back.

p. 110 **15.** ويَنْبَغِي لِمَنْ أَحبَّ العِفَّةَ أَنْ يَكُونَ أَبداً مُتيَقِّظاً ، ذَاكِراً لِمَا يَلْحَقُ الفَاجِرَ
والنَّهِمَ والشَّرِهَ والمُتَهَتِّكَ ، مِنَ القَبَاحَةِ والعَارِ ؛ ويَجْعَلَ ذَلِكَ دَيْدَنَهُ وشِعَارَهُ. فَإِنَّ نَفْسَهُ
تُبْغِضُ الشَّهَوَاتِ الرَّدِيئَةَ ، وتَشْتَاقُ إِلَى التَّعَفُّفِ والقَنَاعَةِ ، وتَطْرَبُ عِنْدَ العُدُولِ عَنِ
الفَوَاحِشِ ، مَعَ القُدْرَةِ عَلَيْهَا ، وتَرْتَاحُ لِمَا يُنْشَرُ عَنْهَا ، ويَبْلُغُهَا عَنِ النَّاسِ مِنَ الثَّنَاءِ الجَمِيلِ
عَلَى صَاحِبِهَا .

16. فَهَذَا الَّذِي ذَكَرْنَا هُوَ طَرِيقٌ إِلَى رِيَاضَةِ النَّفْسِ الشَّهْوَانِيَّةِ ، وتَذْلِيلِهَا ،
وقَمْعِهَا . وهُوَ طَرِيقُ الارْتِيَاضِ بِالْعَادَاتِ المَحْمُودَةِ المَرْضِيَّةِ ، فِيمَا يَتَعَلَّقُ
بِالشَّهَوَاتِ واللَّذَّاتِ .

p. 111 [تَرْوِيضُ النَّفْسِ الغَضَبِيَّةِ]

17. فَأَمَّا النَّفْسُ الغَضَبِيَّةُ ، فَإِنَّ طَرِيقَ قَمْعِهَا وتَذْلِيلِهَا هُوَ أَنْ يَصْرِفَ الإِنْسَانُ
هِمَّتَهُ إِلَى تَفَقُّدِ السُّفَهَاءِ الَّذِينَ يُسْرِعُ إِلَيْهِمُ الغَضَبُ ، فِي أَوْقَاتِ طَيْشِهِمْ وحِدَّتِهِمْ ،
وتَسَفُّهِهِمْ عَلَى خُصُومِهِمْ ، وعُقُوبَتِهِمْ لِخَدَمِهِمْ وعَبِيدِهِمْ . فَإِنَّهُ يُشَاهِدُ مِنْهُمْ مَنْظَراً
p. 112 شَنِيعاً ، يَأْنَفُ مِنْهُ الخَاصُّ والعَامُّ . وأَنْ يَتَذَكَّرَ مَا شَاهَدَ مِنْهُمْ ، فِي أَوْقَاتِ غَضَبِهِ ، وعِنْدَ
جِنَايَاتِ خَدَمِهِ وعَبِيدِهِ ، وعِنْدَ ذُنُوبِ إِخْوَانِهِ وأَوِدَّائِهِ ، فِي جَمِيعِ مُحَاوَرَاتِهِ ومُعَامَلاَتِهِ .
فَإِنَّهُ ، إِذَا تَذَكَّرَ مَا كَانَ اسْتَقْبَحَهُ مِنَ السُّفَهَاءِ ، انْكَسَرَتْ بِذَلِكَ سَوْرَةُ غَضَبِهِ ، وأَحْجَمَ
عَمَّا يَهُمُّ بِالإِقْدَامِ عَلَيْهِ ، مِنَ السَّبِّ والوُثُوبِ . وإِنْ لَمْ يَكُفَّ بِالكُلِّيَّةِ ، قَصَّرَ ، ولَمْ يَنْتَهِ
إِلَى غَايَةِ الفُحْشِ .

15. Anyone who loves abstinence must always be vigilant and mindful of the repugnance and shame that attaches to the lewd person, the glutton, the greedy, and the shameless person. Let him make abstinence his practice and his distinguishing mark. Then his soul will come to detest bad appetites. It will long to practice abstinence and temperance; it will be delighted to abstain from debauchery, though having the power for it. It will be happy about anything that is said in public about it. People's favorable praise of its owner will redound to it.

16. What we have spoken of so far is a way to train the appetitive soul, to subdue it, and to tame it. It is the way to be trained in commendable, agreeable habits in anything connected with appetites and pleasures.

Taming the irascible soul

17. The way to tame and subdue the irascible soul is for a man to turn his attention to a consideration of the foolish people onto whom anger rushes in the moments of their heedlessness and impetuosity. He should consider their foolhardy actions against their opponents, and how they punish their own servants and slaves. He should observe their repulsive appearance, which people high and low disdain. Then, in all his own conversations and transactions, in his moments of anger, on the occasion of the offenses of his servants and his slaves, and on the occasion of the transgressions of his brothers and friends, he should call to mind what he has observed. If he calls to mind what he found to be repulsive on the part of the foolish people, his own vehemence and anger would abate because of it, and he would recoil from the abusive language and rash behavior in which he was intending to engage. And even if he does not hold back entirely, he will have cut it short, and he will not end up at the extremity of indecency.

18. وينبَغي ، لِمَنْ أَرَادَ أَنْ يَقْهَرَ نَفْسَهُ الغَضَبِيَّةَ ، أَنْ يَذْكُر (في أَوْقاتِ غَضَبِهِ
عَلى مَنْ يُؤْذِيهِ أَوْ يَجْني عَلَيْهِ) أَنَّهُ ، لَوْ كانَ هُوَ الجَانِي ، مَا الَّذي كانَ يَسْتَحِقُّ أَنْ يُقابَلَ
p. 113 عَلى جِنايَتِهِ؟ فَإِنَّهُ بِهَذا الفِعْلِ يَعْتَقِدُ أَنَّ دَرَكَ تِلْكَ الجِنايَةِ ، أَوْ أَرْشَ ذَلِكَ الأَذى ، يَسِيرٌ
جِدّاً . فَإِذَا اعْتَقَدَ ذَلِكَ ، كَانَتْ مُقَابَلَتُهُ لِلْجانِي والمُؤْذِي بِحَسَبِ اعْتِقادِهِ . فَلاَ يُسْرِفُ
في الاِنتِقَامِ ، ولاَ يَفْحُشُ في الغَضَبِ . فإذا فَعَلَ ذَلِكَ دائِماً ، وجَعَلَهُ دَيْدَناً ، وتَفَقَّدَ
مَعَايِبَ السُّفَهَاءِ ، ومَنْ يُسْرِعُ إِلَيْهِ الغَضَبُ ، لَمْ يَبْعُدْ أَنْ تَنْكَسِرَ نَفْسُهُ الغَضَبِيَّةُ ، وتَنْقادَ
لَهُ . فَإِذَا اسْتَمَرَّ عَلى ذَلِكَ مُدَّةً ، صار لَهُ خُلُقاً وعَادَةً .

p. 114 **19.** ويَنْبَغِي لِمَنْ يَرْغَبُ في تَذْلِيلِ نَفْسِهِ الغَضَبِيَّةِ أَنْ يَتَجَنَّبَ حَمْلَ السِّلاَحِ ،
وحُضُورَ مَوَاضِعِ الحُرُوبِ ومَقَامَاتِ الفِتَنِ ، ومُجَالَسَةَ الأَشْرَارِ ، ومُعَاشَرَةَ السُّفَهَاءِ ،
ومُخَالَطَةَ الشُّرَطِ . فَإِنَّ هَذِهِ المَوَاضِعَ تُكْسِبُ القَلْبَ قَسَاوَةً وغِلْظَةً ، وتُعْدِمُهُ الرَّأْفَةَ
والرَّحْمَةَ ، فَتَقْسُو لِذَلِكَ نَفْسُهُ الغَضَبِيَّةُ . فَإِذَا كَانَ يُرِيدُ تَذْلِيلَهَا وتَسْكِينَهَا ، وَجَبَ أَنْ
يَجْعَلَ مُجَالَسَتَهُ لأَهْلِ العِلْمِ ، وذَوِي الوَقَارِ ، والشُّيُوخِ والرُّؤَسَاءِ الأَفَاضِلِ ، ومَنْ يَقِلُّ
غَضَبُهُ ويَكْثُرُ حِلْمُهُ ووَقَارُهُ .

p. 115 **20.** ويَنْبَغِي لَهُ أَيْضاً أَنْ يَتَجَنَّبَ المُسْكِرَ مِنَ الشَّرَابِ . فَإِنَّ السُّكْرَ يُهَيِّجُ
النَّفْسَ الغَضَبِيَّةَ ، أَكْثَرَ مِمَّا يُهَيِّجُ النَّفْسَ الشَّهْوَانِيَّةَ . ولِذَلِكَ رُبَّمَا يُسْرِعُ إِلَى العَرْبَدَةِ ،
والوُثُوبِ عَلَى جُلَسَائِهِ ، والاِسْتِخْفَافِ بِهِمْ وسَبِّهِمْ وذِكْرِ أَعْرَاضِهِمْ ، بَعْدَ أَنْ كَانَ
يَتَحَنَّنُ عَلَيْهِمْ ويَتَوَدَّدُ إِلَيْهِمْ ، ولاَ يَكُونُ بَيْنَ الوَقْتَيْنِ إِلاَّ بِمِقْدَارِ مَا يَسْتَحْكِمُ بِهِ السُّكْرُ .
فَالسُّكْرُ مُثِيرُ القُوَّةِ الغَضَبِيَّةِ ، ومُقَوٍّ لَهَا . فَمَنْ أَرَادَ أَنْ يُسَكِّنَ نَفْسَهُ الغَضَبِيَّةَ ، فَلاَ بُدَّ

18. Anyone who wants to subdue his irascible soul must remember, in the moments of his anger against someone who is doing him wrong or offending him, what he himself would deserve in terms of recompense for his own offense, were he the offender. In doing this he will come to the conviction that the due recompense for the offense, or the right penalty for it, is exceedingly small. Since this is his conviction, his own reprisal against an offender and one who does him harm will be commensurate with his conviction, and he will not be excessive in taking revenge, nor will he be indecent in anger. If he does this continuously and makes a practice of it and carefully observes the faults of foolish people and those onto whom anger rushes quickly, it will not be difficult for his own irascible soul to be broken, and it will submit to him. And, if he persists in this practice for a period of time, it will become a habitual moral quality for him.

19. Whoever wants to subdue his irascible soul must avoid carrying weapons, attending fighting arenas and seditious meetings, keeping company with the wicked, being intimate with the foolish, and mixing with soldiers. These situations will make the heart acquire a certain hardness and coarseness, make it devoid of gentleness and mercy; and therefore the irascible soul will become harsh. If one wants to subdue it and to tame it, he will have to keep company with people of knowledge and dignity, elders, virtuous leaders and people whose anger is slight and whose gentleness and dignity are abundant.

20. He will also have to avoid intoxicating drinks. Intoxication stimulates the irascible soul much more than it stimulates the appetitive soul. For this reason, sometimes one is quick to be quarrelsome, to pounce onto one's associates, to treat them disdainfully, to revile them, and to insult their honor right after one has been treating them affectionately and seeking their friendship. Between the two moments, there only needs to be the interval of time it takes for intoxication to grow strong. Intoxication arouses the irascible power and invigorates it. So whoever wants to calm the irascible soul must inevitably avoid

مِنْ أَنْ يَتَجَنَّبَ السُّكْرَ. وإنْ تَمكَّنَ مِنْ هَجْرِ الشَّرَابِ البَتَّةَ، فَهُوَ أَصْلَحُ لِقَهْرِ النَّفْسِ الغَضَبِيَّةِ والشَّهْوَانِيَّةِ جَمِيعاً.

p. 116 **21.** ويَنْبَغِي لِمَنْ أَرَادَ تَذْلِيلَ قُوَّتَيْهِ الغَضَبِيَّةِ والشَّهْوَانِيَّةِ، أَنْ يَسْتَعْمِلَ، في جَمِيعِ مَا يَفْعَلُهُ، الفِكْرَ، ولاَ يُقْدِمَ عَلَى شَيْءٍ إلاَّ بَعْدَ أَنْ يَتَرَوَّى فِيهِ، ويَجْعَلَ الفِكْرَ واتِّبَاعَ الرَّأْيِ دَيْدَنَهُ وعَادَتَهُ. فَإنَّ الرَّأْيَ، وجُودَةَ الفِكْرَةِ، يُقَبِّحَانِ لَهُ السَّفَهَ، وسُرْعَةَ الغَضَبِ، والانْهِمَاكَ في الشَّهَوَاتِ، واتِّبَاعَ اللَّذَّاتِ. فَإذَا اسْتَقْبَحَ ذَلِكَ، أَحْجَمَ عَنْهُ، وعَدَلَ إلَى مَا يَقْتَضِيهِ الرَّأْيُ والفِكْرُ. وإنْ لَمْ يَرْتَدِعْ بِالْكُلِّيَّةِ، فَلاَ بُدَّ أَنْ يُؤَثِّرَ ذَلِكَ فِيهِ، فَيَقْتَصِرَ عَمَّا يُرِيدُ التَّسَرُّعَ فِيهِ.

p. 117

[تَقْوِيَةُ النَّفْسِ النَّاطِقَةِ]

22. ومَلاَكُ الأَمْرِ فِي تَهْذِيبِ الأَخْلاَقِ وضَبْطِ النَّفْسِ الشَّهْوَانِيَّةِ والنَّفْسِ الغَضَبِيَّةِ، هِيَ النَّفْسُ النَّاطِقَةُ. فَإنَّ بِهَذِهِ النَّفْسِ تَكُونُ جَمِيعُ السِّيَاسَاتِ. وهَذِهِ النَّفْسُ، إذَا كَانَتْ قَوِيَّةً مُتَمَكِّنَةً مِنْ صَاحِبِهَا، أَمْكَنَهُ أَنْ يَسُوسَ بِهَا قُوَّتَيْهِ البَاقِيَتَيْنِ، ويَكُفَّ عَنْ جَمِيعِ القَبَائِحِ، ويَتْبَعَ أَبَداً مَحَاسِنَ الأَخْلاَقِ. وإذَا لَمْ تَكُنْ هَذِهِ النَّفْسُ قَوِيَّةً فِي صَاحِبِهَا، كَانَتْ مَغْمُورَةً خَافِيَةً. فَأَوَّلُ مَا يَنْبَغِي أَنْ يَعْتَمِدَهُ فِي سِيَاسَةِ أَخْلاَقِهِ أَنْ يُرَوِّضَ هَذِهِ النَّفْسَ ويُقَوِّيهَا.

p. 118 **23.** وتَقْوِيَةُ هَذِهِ النَّفْسِ إنَّمَا تَكُونُ بِالعُلُومِ العَقْلِيَّةِ. فَإنَّهُ، إذَا نَظَرَ فِي العُلُومِ العَقْلِيَّةِ، ودَقَّقَ النَّظَرَ فِيهَا، ودَرَسَ كُتُبَ الأَخْلاَقِ والسِّيَاسَةِ، ودَاوَمَ عَلَيْهَا، تَيَقَّظَتْ نَفْسُهُ، وتَنَبَّهَتْ مِنْ شَهَوَاتِهَا، وانْتَعَشَتْ مِنْ خُمُولِهَا، وأَحَسَّتْ بِفَضَائِلِهَا، وأَنِفَتْ مِنْ

intoxication. If he manages to abstain from drink totally, then he will be much more fit to overcome the irascible soul and the appetitive soul together.

21. Whoever wants to subdue his irascible and appetitive powers must make use of critical thinking in everything he does, and he must not venture into anything until after he has reflected on it and undertaken to think critically and to follow considered opinion as his practice and habit. Considered opinion and sound thought will together censure folly and hasty anger as repugnant for him, along with a preoccupation with the appetites and the pursuit of pleasures. When he deems this sort of thing to be repugnant, he recoils from it and he turns to what considered opinion and critical thought would require. And even if he is not restrained completely, inevitably this practice will have an effect on him, and he will stop short of what impetuosity would crave.

Strengthening the rational soul

22. The basis of the enterprise to reform morals and to control the appetitive and the irascible souls is the rational soul. All the ways of behaving are in this soul. When this soul has a strong mastery over its owner, he is able by means of it to manage the remaining two faculties, to abstain from all repugnant things, and always to pursue good moral qualities. But, when this soul is not strong in its owner, it becomes submerged, concealed. So the first thing to which he must apply himself in the management of his moral qualities is to train this soul and to strengthen it.

23. The strengthening of this soul will come about only by means of the rational sciences. When one studies the rational sciences, refines his study of them, examines the books on morality and deportment, and lingers over them, his soul will awaken, take cognizance of its appetites, recover from its indolence, perceive its virtues, and reject

رَذَائِلِهَا . وذَلِكَ أَنَّ هَذِهِ النَّفْسَ إِنَّمَا تَضْعُفُ وتَخْفُتُ ، إِذَا عَدِمَتِ الفَضَائِلَ والمَنَاقِبَ ،
واسْتَوْلَتْ عَلَيْهَا الرَّذَائِلُ . فَإِذَا اقْتَنَتِ الفَضَائِلَ ، واكْتَسَبَتِ الآدَابَ ، تَيَقَّظَتْ مِنْ
غَشْيَتِهَا ، واسْتَفَاقَتْ مِنْ سُكْرِهَا ، وقَوِيَتْ بَعْدَ ضُعْفِهَا . وفَضَائِلُ هَذِهِ النَّفْسِ هِيَ p. 119
العُلُومُ العَقْلِيَّةُ ، وخَاصَّةً مَا دَقَّ مِنْهَا . فَإِذَا ارْتَاضَ الإِنْسَانُ بِالعُلُومِ العَقْلِيَّةِ ، شَرُفَتْ
نَفْسُهُ ، وعَظُمَتْ هِمَّتُهُ ، وقَوِيَ فِكْرُهُ ، وتَمَكَّنَ مِنْ نَفْسِهِ ، ومَلَكَ أَخْلاقَهُ ، وقَدَرَ
عَلَى إِصْلاحِهَا ، وانْقَادَ لَهُ طَبْعُهُ ، وسَهُلَ عَلَيْهِ تَهْذِيبُهُ ، وأَذْعَنَتْ لَهُ القُوَى الغَضَبِيَّةُ
والشَّهْوَانِيَّةُ ، وهَانَ عَلَيْهِ قَمْعُهَا وتَذْلِيلُهَا . فَأَوَّلُ مَا يَنْبَغِي أَنْ يَبْتَدِئَ بِهِ مَنْ يُحِبُّ أَخْلاقَهُ ،
النَظَرُ فِي كُتُبِ الأَخْلاقِ والسِّيَاسَاتِ ، ثُمَّ الارْتِيَاضُ بِعُلُومِ الحَقَائِقِ . فَإِنَّ أَشْرَفَ مَا
تَكُونُ النَّفْسُ [هُوَ] إِذَا أَدْرَكَتْ حَقَائِقَ الأُمُورِ ، وأَشْرَفَتْ عَلَى هَيْئَاتِ المَوْجُودَاتِ .
فَإِذَا شَرُفَتْ نَفْسُ الإِنْسَانِ ، وعَلَتْ هِمَّتُهُ ، تَرَقَّى إِلَى مَرَاتِبِ أَهْلِ الفَضْلِ .

24. ومِمَّا يُصْلِحُ النَّفْسَ النَّاطِقَةَ ويُقَوِّيهَا أَيْضاً مُجَالَسَةُ أَهْلِ العِلْمِ ومُخَالَطَتُهُمْ ، p. 120
والاقْتِدَاءُ بِأَخْلاقِهِمْ وعَادَاتِهِمْ ، وخَاصَّةً أَصْحَابِ عُلُومِ الحَقَائِقِ ، والمُتَيَقِّظِينَ مِنْهُمْ ،
المُسْتَعْمِلِينَ فِي جَمِيعِ أُمُورِهِمْ مَا تَقْتَضِيهِ عُلُومُهُمْ وتُوجِبُهُ عُقُولُهُمْ . فَأَمَّا تَمْيِيزُ عَادَاتِ
النَّفْسِ النَّاطِقَةِ ، واسْتِعْمَالُ مَا حَسُنَ فِيهَا ، واطِّرَاحُ مَا قَبُحَ ، فَذَلِكَ إِنَّمَا يُمْكِنُ ويَسْهُلُ
أَيْضاً إِذَا رَاضَ [الإِنْسَانُ] نَفْسَهُ النَّاطِقَةَ . فَإِنَّ النَّفْسَ النَّاطِقَةَ ، إِذَا ارْتَاضَتْ بِالعُلُومِ
الحَقِيقِيَّةِ ، وتَيَقَّظَتْ وتَشَرَّفَتْ ، أَنِفَتْ مِنَ العَادَاتِ المُسْتَقْبَحَةِ ، وتَنَزَّهَتْ عَنِ التَّدَنُّسِ
بِهَا ، فَيَهُونُ حِينَئِذٍ عَلَى صَاحِبِهَا تَجَنُّبُ مَا يَكْرَهُ مِنْ عَادَاتِهَا ، ويَغْلِبُ عَلَيْهِ اسْتِحْسَانُ p. 121
الأَخْلاقِ الجَمِيلَةِ ، والتَّخَلُّقُ بِهَا .

its vices. This soul grows weak and quiescent only when it lacks virtues and good qualities, and vices take possession of it. When it procures virtues and acquires refinement, it awakens from its faintness, recovers from its intoxication, and becomes reinvigorated after its debilitation. And the virtues of this soul are the rational sciences, especially the most refined of them. When a man schools himself in the rational sciences, his soul is ennobled, his resolution is immense, and his critical thinking is strong and it takes charge of his soul. It exercises control over his moral qualities and makes the decision to improve them. His natural disposition obeys him; to reform it becomes simple for him: The irascible and appetitive powers yield to him, and taming and subduing them becomes easy for him. Anyone who has a love for his own morals must start with the study of the books on morals and deportment, then proceed with schooling himself in the exact sciences. The soul is at its noblest when it attains true reality and surveys the dispositions of existing things. When the soul of a man is ennobled and his resolution is high, he advances into the ranks of the people of virtue.

24. To sit with people of knowledge, to frequent their company, and to emulate their moral qualities and habits will improve the rational soul and strengthen it. This is especially the case with the masters of the exact sciences and the most alert people. In all their affairs, they put into effect what their science demands and their intellects enjoin. As for discriminating among the habits of the rational soul, putting into effect the best of them and discarding what is repulsive, it is only possible—and even easy—when one exercises his rational soul. Then the rational soul, when it is exercised in the exact sciences, becomes alert and acts honorably. It disdains repulsive habits and transcends being contaminated by them. At that point it will be easy for its owner to avoid any of its habits that are abhorrent, while the active appreciation of the good moral qualities, and moral formation in them, will prevail in him.

25. وقَدْ تَبَيَّنَ مِنْ جَمِيعِ مَا ذَكَرْنَا أَنَّ طَرِيقَ الارْتِيَاضِ بِالأَخْلاقِ المَحْمُودَةِ، والتَصَنُّعِ لاِعْتِيَادِهَا، واتِّبَاعِ المَحْمُودِ المَرْضِيِّ مِنْهَا، واجْتِنَابِ المَذْمُومِ والمُسْتَقْبَحِ، وتَذْلِيلِ قُوَّةِ الشَّهْوَةِ الغَضَبِيَّةِ، وضَبْطِهَا وقَهْرِهَا، هُوَ إِصْلاَحُ النَّفْسِ النَّاطِقَةِ، وتَقْوِيَتُهَا، وتَحْلِيَتُهَا بِالْفَضَائِلِ والآدَابِ والمَحَاسِنِ. فَإِنَّ ذَلِكَ هُوَ آلَةُ السِّيَاسَةِ، ومَرْكَبُ الرِّيَاضَةِ.

26. ومَنْ لَمْ يَتَمَكَّنْ مِنِ اكْتِسَابِ العُلُومِ العَقْلِيَّةِ والإمْعَانِ فِيهَا، أَوْ تَعَذَّرَ عَلَيْهِ p. 122 ذَلِكَ، فَلْيَبْذُلْ جَهْدَهُ فِي تَدْقِيقِ الفِكْرِ، ومُجَاهَدَةِ النَّفْسِ، وتَمْيِيزِ مَا بَيْنَ عَادَتِهِ القَبِيحَةِ والجَمِيلَةِ. ويَنْظُرْ أَيُّهُمَا أَجْدَى عَلَيْهِ، وأَيُّهُمَا أَنْفَعُ لَهُ، وأَيُّهُمَا أَحْمَدُ عَاقِبَةً، وأَبْقَى عَلَى الأَيَّامِ. فَإِنَّهُ، إِذَا صَدَقَ نَفْسَهُ، وَجَدَ شَهَوَاتِهِ ولَذَّاتِهِ إِنَّمَا هِيَ مَلَذَّةٌ وَقْتَ اسْتِعْمَالِهَا فَقَطْ؛ فَأَمَّا بَعْدَ مُفَارَقَتِهَا، فَلَيْسَتْ بَاقِيَةً عَلَيْهِ ولاَ نَافِعَةً لَهُ. ويَجِدُ عَارَهَا وشَيْنَهَا بَاقِياً عَلَى الدَهْرِ، مُتَدَاوَلاً بَيْنَ النَّاسِ، يُعَابُ بِهِ ويُزْرَى عَلَيْهِ بِقُبْحِهِ. وكَذَلِكَ شِدَّةُ الغَضَبِ، p. 123 والتَسَرُّعُ إِلَى الاِنْتِقَامِ، والسَّبُّ، والفُحْشُ. فَإِذَا انْجَلَتْ غَمْرَتُهُ، وسَكَنَتْ سَوْرَتُهُ، تَأَمَّلَ أَمْرَهُ، ورَأَى مَا فَعَلَهُ، وجَدَهُ قَبِيحاً، ولَمْ يَجِدْهُ مُجْدِياً ولاَ مُفِيداً. وقَدْ صَارَ مَا فَعَلَهُ عِنْدَ الغَضَبِ نَقِيصَةً يُوسَمُ بِهَا، ومَعَرَّةً يُسَبُّ بِهَا. ورُبَّمَا ارْتَكَبَ فِي الغَضَبِ جِنَايَاتٍ، يُعَاقَبُ عَلَيْهَا ويُؤَدَّبُ مِنْ أَجْلِهَا.

27. وكَذَلِكَ العَادَاتُ المَكْرُوهَةُ مِنْ عَادَاتِ النَّفْسِ النَّاطِقَةِ أَيْضاً، يَجِدُهَا غَيْرَ نَافِعَةٍ ولاَ مُجْدِيَةٍ. ذَلِكَ أَنَّ الحَسَدَ والحِقْدَ والخُبْثَ، وأَمْثَالَ هَذِهِ، لاَ يَنْتَفِعُ بِهَا صَاحِبُهَا. p. 124 وإِنِ انْتَفَعَ بِالخُبْثِ والشَّرِّ، فَشَرُّ مَنْفَعَةٍ؛ ومَعَ ذَلِكَ هُوَ ضَارٌّ لَهُ. فَإِنَّ مَنْ تَشَرَّرَ، قَصَدَهُ النَّاسُ بِالشَّرِّ؛ واسْتَعَدُّوا لأَذِيَّتِهِ، وتَعَمَّلُوا لِلإِضْرَارِ بِهِ؛ وتَوَقَّوْهُ، واحْتَرَزُوا مِنْهُ؛ وكَرِهُوا

25. From all that we have said so far, it is clear that to improve the rational soul, to empower it and to embellish it with virtues, refinement, and good deeds is the way to put the commendable moral qualities into practice and to make them habitual. It is also the way to pursue the most agreeably commendable of them, to avoid what is objectionable and repulsive, to subdue the power of irascible desire, to control it, and to overcome it. It is a tool for self-management, a vehicle of practice.

26. Whoever does not have the ability to acquire the rational sciences and to apply himself assiduously to them, or for whom they are too difficult, should make an effort to refine [his] critical thinking, to struggle with [his] soul, and to discriminate between his good and bad habits. He should look to see which of them is the most productive for him, which of them is the most beneficial to him, and which of them in the end is the most commendable and the most enduring for the future. If he is honest with himself, he will find his appetites and his pleasures to be pleasurable only for the time of their indulgence and no more. After he has disengaged from them, their enjoyment does not endure for him, nor are they beneficial for him. He will find their shame and dishonor enduring for a long time and being broadcast among the people, while he will be blamed and scolded for his ignominy. So, too, with intense anger, the rush to vengeance, abusiveness, and indecency. When one's exuberance dissipates and his vehemence subsides and he considers his situation and sees what he has done, he finds it repulsive. He does not find it productive or advantageous. Sometimes what he has done in anger becomes a defect with which he will be stigmatized and a blemish for which he will be reviled. Sometimes he commits crimes in anger for which he will be punished and because of which he will be disciplined.

27. Similarly, with the abhorrent habits of the rational soul, one will find them unprofitable and unproductive. That is because envy, resentment, malevolence and the like yield no benefit for the one who is possessed of them. And, even if he does get some benefit from malevolence and evil, it is an evil benefit, and simultaneously it will do him harm. People look with an evil intent on anyone who does evil. They are willing to harm him, they take pains to do violence to him, they are wary of him, they are on their guard against him, they detest

نَفْعَهُ ، وقَصَّرُوا عَلَيْهِ وَجُوهَ الخَيْرِ ، واجْتَهَدُوا فِي ذَلِكَ. وَمَا أَسْوَأَ حَالَ مَنْ هَذِهْ صِفَتُهُ ! فَمُسْتَعْمِلُ الشَّرِّ والخُبْثِ سَيِّئُ الحَالِ، يَضُرُّهُ شَرُّهُ أَكْثَرَ مِمَّا يَنْفَعُهُ. فَإِذَا حَاسَبَ الإِنْسَانُ نَفْسَهُ ، وأَجَالَ فِكْرَهُ وتَمْيِيزَهُ ، عَلِمَ أَنَّ الضَّرَرَ فِي مَسَاوِئِ الأَخْلاقِ أَكْثَرُ مِنَ النفْعِ بِهَا ، p. 125
وأَنَّ الَّذِي يَعُدُّهُ مِنْهَا نَفْعاً ، فَلَيْسَ هُوَ بِنَفْعٍ ، عَلَى الحَقِيقَةِ ، وهُوَ يَسِيرٌ جِدّاً ، غَيْرُ بَاقٍ ولاَ مُسْتَمِرٍّ. فَإِنَّ هَذَا اليَسِيرَ ، الَّذِي يَعُدُّهُ نَفْعاً ، لاَ يَفِي بِالضَّرَرِ الكَثِيرِ والعَارِ الدَّائِمِ المُتَّصِلِ. ويَعْلَمُ أَيْضاً أَنَّ الشَّرَّ والخُبْثَ يَجْلِبَانِ عَلَيْهِ الشَّرَّ ، ويُوحِشَانِ مِنْهُ النَّاسَ. فَإِذَا أَدَامَ ذَلِكَ ، وأَكْثَرَ مِنْهُ ، قَوِيَ فِي نَفْسِهِ اتِّبَاعُ مَحَاسِنِ الأَخْلاقِ ، وسَهُلَ عَلَيْهِ اطِّرَاحُ مَسَاوِئِهَا وَمقَابِحِهَا ، وغَلَبَ عَلَيْهِ الخَيْرُ والسَّدَادُ ، وفَزِعَ مِنَ العَيْبِ والعَارِ. فَإِذَا فَعَلَ ذَلِكَ دَائِماً ، لَمْ يَلْبَثْ أَنْ تَصْلُحَ أَخْلاقُهُ ، وتَحْسُنَ طَرِيقَتُهُ ، وتُهَذَّبَ شَمَائِلُهُ ، ويَلْحَقَ بِرُتْبَةِ أَهْلِ الفَضْلِ ، ويَتَمَيَّزَ عَنْ أَهْلِ الدَّنَسِ والنَّقْصِ.

28. ويَنْبَغِي لِمَنْ أَرَادَ سِيَاسَةَ أَخْلاقِهِ أَنْ يَجْعَلَ غَرَضَهُ ، مِنْ كُلِّ فَضِيلَةٍ ، p. 126
غَايَتَهَا ونِهَايَتَهَا ، ولاَ يَقْنَعَ مِنْهَا بِمَا دُونَ الغَايَةِ ، ولاَ يَرْضَى إِلاَّ بِأَعْلَى دَرَجَةٍ. فَإِنَّهُ ، إِذَا جَعَلَ ذَلِكَ غَرَضَهُ ، كَانَ حَرِيّاً أَنْ يَتَوَسَّطَ فِي الفَضَائِلِ ، ويَبْلُغَ فِيهَا رُتْبَةً مَرْضِيَّةً إِنْ فَاتَتْهُ الدَّرَجَةُ العَالِيَةُ. فَأَمَّا إِنْ قَنِعَ بِالتَّوَسُّطِ ، لَمْ يَأْمَنْ أَنْ يُقَصِّرَ عَنْ بُلُوغِهِ ، فَيَبْقَى فِي أَدْوَنِ المَرَاتِبِ ، ويَفُوتُهُ المَطْلُوبُ ، ولاَ يَطْمَعُ أَبَداً فِي التَّمَامِ.

his well-being, they check any goodwill toward him, and they work hard at it. How horrible is the situation of anyone of this description! The condition of the one who engages in iniquity and malevolence is bad; his wrongdoing harms him so much more than it benefits him. When a man calls himself to account and puts to work his critical thinking and his powers of discrimination, he comes to understand that the harm in bad moral action is much greater than the benefit of it. Any part of it he reckoned to be a benefit is in reality not a benefit; it is very slight, neither lasting nor enduring. And this slight bit that he reckoned to be a benefit will not cover the cost of the abundant harm and the shame connected with it. He will also come to understand that iniquity and malevolence will together bring evil upon him, and they will make people stay away from him. When one persists in this [train of thought] and engages in it frequently, the pursuit of good moral action will be strengthened in his soul, and the discarding of evil and repulsive moral qualities will become easier for him. What is good and right will triumph over him and he will be terrified of whatever is blameworthy or shameful. When one does this continually, it will not be long before his moral qualities will be improving, his way will come right, his character will be reformed, and he will attain the rank of the people of virtue. He will be set apart from the people of faults and defilement.

28. Whoever wants to manage his moral qualities must fix his goal for each virtue at its utmost limit, and he must not be satisfied with anything below the acme, nor must he be pleased with any but the highest rank. If he fixes this as his goal, even if the highest rank does elude him, he will be fit to hold the middle ground in the virtues and to attain an agreeable rank in them. As for being satisfied with holding the middle ground, he would not then be secure against falling short of it. He would remain on the lower levels. The goal to be sought would slip by him, and he would never aspire to fulfillment.

p. 127 [خَاتِمَةُ القِسْمِ الرَّابِعِ]

29. فَهَذَا الَّذِي ذَكَرْنَا هُوَ طَرِيقُ الارْتِيَاضِ بِمَكَارِمِ الأَخْلاَقِ، ومَنْهَجُ التَّدَرُّجِ فِي مَحْمُودِ العَادَاتِ. فَإِذَا أَخَذَ الإِنْسَانُ نَفْسَهُ بِهِ، وأَكْثَرَ مُرَاعَاتَهُ وتَعَهَّدَهُ، صَارَتْ لَهُ الفَضَائِلُ دَيْدَناً والمَحَاسِنُ خُلُقاً وطَبْعاً.

Epilogue

29. What we have set forth is the way to put the noblest moral qualities into practice, and the procedure for making progress in the most commendable of habits. If a man commits himself to it, is constant in his observance of it, and pledges himself to it, the virtues will become habitual practice for him, and good works second nature.

[القِسْمُ الخَامِس] p. 128

[بُلوغُ الإنْسانِ إلى الكمال]

[أَوْصَافُ الإنْسَانِ التَّامِّ]

1. وقَدْ بَقِيَ عَلَيْنَا أَنْ نَذْكُرَ أَوْصَافَ الإنْسَانِ التَّامِّ، الجَامِعِ لِمَحَاسِنِ الأَخْلاَقِ، وطَرِيقَتَهُ الَّتِي يَصِلُ بِهَا إلَى التَّمام. فَنَقُولُ:

2. إنَّ الإنْسَانَ التَّامَّ هُوَ الَّذِي لَمْ تَفُتْهُ فَضِيلَةٌ، ولَمْ تَشِنْهُ رَذِيلَةٌ. وهَذَا الحَدُّ قَلَّمَا يَنْتَهِي إلَيْهِ إنْسَانٌ. وإذَا انْتَهَى الإنْسَانُ إلَى هَذَا الحَدِّ، كَانَ بِالمَلاَئِكَةِ أَشْبَهَ مِنْهُ p. 129 بِالنَّاسِ. فَإنَّ الإنْسَانَ مَضْرُوبٌ بِأَنْوَاعِ النَّقْصِ، مُسْتَوْلٍ عَلَيْه وعَلَى طَبْعِهِ ضُرُوبُ الشَّرِّ. فَقَلَّمَا يَخْلُصُ مِنْ جَمِيعِهَا، حَتَّى تَسْلَمَ نَفْسُهُ مِنْ كُلِّ عَيْبٍ ومَنْقَصَةٍ، وتُحِيطَ بِكُلِّ فَضِيلَةٍ ومَنْقَبَةٍ. إلاَّ أَنَّ التَّمَامَ، وإنْ كَانَ عَزِيزاً بَعِيدَ التَّنَاوُلِ، فَإنَّهُ ممكِنٌ. وهُوَ غَايَةُ مَا يَنْتَهِي إلَيْهِ الإنْسَانُ، ونِهَايَةُ مَا هُوَ مُتَهَيِّئٌ لَهُ. فَإذَا صَدَقَتْ عَزِيمَةُ الإنْسَانِ، وأَعْطَى الاجْتِهَادَ حَقَّهُ، كَانَ قَمِيناً بِأَنْ يَنْتَهِيَ إلَى غَايَتِهِ الَّتِي هُوَ مُتَهَيِّئٌ لَهَا، ويَصِلَ إلَى بُغْيَتِهِ الَّتِي تَسْمُو نَفْسُهُ إلَيْهَا.

Part Five

Man's attainment of perfection

Description of the complete man

1. It remains for us to speak of the attributes of the complete man, including good moral action, and the way by which one comes to fulfillment. So we say as follows:

2. The complete man is the one whom virtue does not bypass, whom vice does not disfigure. A man seldom ends up at this point. But, when a man does finally come to this point, it is the angels he resembles more than he resembles men. A man who is battered by various kinds of deficiency is someone over whom varieties of evil prevail, and they prevail over his nature, too. Seldom can he escape from all of them to the point that his soul will be free of every fault and defect and comprise every virtue and advantage. Nevertheless, fulfillment, even if it is difficult and far to reach, is possible. It is the utmost at which a man may arrive, the ultimate end for which he is to prepare himself. When a man's determination is true and he gives the effort its due, he will be fit to come ultimately to the goal for which he is preparing himself and to attain the object of the desire to which his soul aspires.

p. 130 3. فَأَمَّا تَفْصِيلُ أَوْصَافِ الإِنْسَانِ التَّامِّ، فَهُوَ أَنْ يَكُونَ مُتَفَقِّداً لِجَمِيعِ أَخْلاَقِهِ، مُتَيَقِّظاً لِجَمِيعِ مَعَايِبِهِ، مُتَحَرِّزاً مِنْ دُخُولِ نَقْصٍ عَلَيْهِ، مُسْتَعْمِلاً لِكُلِّ فَضِيلَةٍ، ومُجْتَهِداً فِي بُلُوغِ الغَايَةِ، عَاشِقاً لِصُورَةِ الكَمَالِ، مُسْتَلِذّاً لِمَحَاسِنِ الأَخْلاَقِ، مُتَيَقِّظاً فِي الأَصْلِ، مُتَبَغِّضاً لِمَذْمُومِ العَادَاتِ، مُعْتَنِياً بِتَهْذِيبِ نَفْسِهِ، غَيْرَ مُسْتَكْثِرٍ لِمَا يَقْتَنِيهِ مِنَ الفَضَائِلِ، مُسْتَعْظِماً لِلْيَسِيرِ مِنَ الرَّذَائِلِ، مُسْتَصْغِراً لِلرُّتْبَةِ العُلْيَا، مُسْتَحْقِراً لِلْغَايَةِ القُصْوَى، يَرَى التَّمَامَ دُونَ مَحَلِّهِ، والكَمَالَ أَقَلَّ أَوْصَافِهِ.

p. 131 4. فَأَمَّا الطَّرِيقَةُ الَّتِي تُوصِلُهُ إِلَى التَّمَامِ، وتَحْفَظُ عَلَيْهِ الكَمَالَ، فَهِيَ أَنْ يَصرِفَ عِنَايَتَهُ إِلَى النَّظَرِ فِي العُلُومِ الحَقِيقِيَّةِ، ويَجْعَلَ غَرَضَهُ الإِحَاطَةَ بِمَاهِيَّاتِ الأُمُورِ المَوْجُودَةِ، وكَشْفَ عِلَلِهَا وأَسْبَابِهَا، وتَفَقُّدَ غَايَاتِهَا ونِهَايَاتِهَا. ولاَ يَقِفُ عِنْدَ غَايَةٍ مِنْ عَمَلِهِ، إِلاَّ ورَنَا بِطَرْفِهِ إِلَى مَا فَوْقَ تِلْكَ الغَايَةِ. ويَجْعَلُ شِعَارَهُ لَيْلَهُ ونَهَارَهُ قِرَاءَةَ كُتُبِ الأَخْلاَقِ، وتَصَفُّحَ كُتُبِ السِّيَرِ والسِّيَاسَاتِ، وأَخْذَ نَفْسِهِ باسْتِعمَالِ مَا أَمَرَ أَهلُ p. 132 الفَضْلِ باسْتِعمَالِهِ، وأَشَارَ المُتَقَدِّمُونَ مِنَ الحُكَمَاءِ بِاعْتِيَادِهِ. ويَشْدُو أَيْضاً طَرَفاً مِنْ أَدَبِ اللِّسَانِ والبَلاَغَةِ، ويَتَحَلَّى بِشَيْءٍ مِنَ الفَصَاحَةِ والخَطَابَةِ. ويَغْشَى أَبَداً مَجَالِسَ أَهْلِ العِلْمِ والحِكْمَةِ، ويُعَاشِرُ دَائِماً أَهْلَ الوَقَارِ والعِفَّةِ. هَذَا إِنْ كَانَ رَعِيَّةً وسُوقَةً. فَإِنْ كَانَ مَلِكاً أَوْ رَئِيساً، فَيَنْبَغِي أَنْ يَجْعَلَ جُلَسَاءَهُ ومُنَادِمِيهِ، وحَاشِيَتَهُ والمُطِيفِينَ بِهِ، كُلَّ مَنْ كَانَ مَعْرُوفاً بِالسَّرْوِ والسَّدَادِ، مَوْصُوفاً بِالأَدَبِ والوَقَارِ، مُخَصَّصاً بِالْعِلْمِ والحِكْمَةِ، مُتَحَقِّقاً بِالفَهْمِ والفِطْنَةِ؛ ويَقْرُبَ مَجَالِسَ أَهْلِ العِلْمِ ويَبْسُطَهُمْ، ويُكْثِرَ مُجَالَسَتَهُمْ والأُنْسَ بِهِمْ؛ ويَجْعَلَ تَفَرُّجَهُ وتَفَكُّهَهُ مُذَاكَرَتَهُمْ فِي العِلْمِ وفُنُونِهِ، وسِيَاسَةِ المُلْكِ ورُسُومِهِ، وأَخْبَارِ الحُكَمَاءِ وأَخْلاَقِهِمْ، وسِيَرِ المُلُوكِ الأَخْيَارِ وعَادَاتِهِمْ.

3. As for an itemized statement of the attributes of the complete man, it is as follows: He will be someone watchful over all his moral qualities, attentive to all his faults, and wary of the intrusion of any defect. He will be ready to put every virtue into action, assiduous to reach the goal, passionate for the image of perfection. He will be disposed to find pleasure in good moral actions. He will be radically alert, inimical to blameworthy habits, and solicitous to reform himself. He will be disinclined to overestimate the virtues he will have acquired but inclined to regard the least of the vices as grave. He will be disposed to regard high rank as of small value and will be scornful of the farthest goal. He will consider fulfillment beneath his station and perfection the least of his attributes.

4. The way that will bring one to fulfillment and sustain him in perfection is for him to direct his attention to the study of the "exact sciences." It is to make it his goal to grasp the quiddities of existing things, to disclose their causes and occasions, and to search out their final ends and purposes. He shall not pause in his labor at any particular end without giving some consideration to what is beyond that end. He shall make it his badge of honor, night and day, to read books on morals, to scrutinize books of biographies and of policies. He shall devote himself to implementing what virtuous people have bidden to be implemented and what the sages who have gone before have advised to be made habitual. He shall also acquire a modicum of the discipline of grammar and rhetoric and be endowed with a measure of eloquence and oratorical felicity. He shall always frequent the sessions of scholars and sages and continually associate with modest and abstinent people—this if he is an ordinary citizen or commoner. If one is a king or a leader, he must take as his comrades, as his boon companions, as his entourage, and as those who will be around him, all who are known for nobility and level-headedness. They are to be characterized by refinement and dignity, singled out for knowledge and wisdom, and proven in understanding and perspicacity. One must also frequent gatherings of scholars. He should enlarge them and increase their meetings, as well as the goodwill among them. He must make it his own pleasure and delight to take counsel with them about knowledge and its special fields, about the conduct of kingship and its ceremonies, about the histories of wise men and their moral qualities, and about the biographies of the best kings and their habits.

p. 133 5. وينْبَغِي لِلإنْسَانِ التَّامِّ، ولِمَنْ طَلَبَ التَّمَامَ أَيْضاً، أَنْ يَجْعَلَ لِشَهَوَاتِهِ ولَذَّاتِهِ
قَانُوناً رَاتِباً، يَقْصِدُ فِيهِ الاعْتِدَالَ، ويَتَجَنَّبُ السَّرَفَ والإفْرَاطَ، ويَعْتَمِدُ مِنَ الشَّهَوَاتِ
واللَّذَّاتِ المُعْتَدِلَةِ مَا كَانَ مِنَ الوُجُوهِ المُرْتَضَاةِ المُسْتَحْسَنَةِ، ويَأْخُذُ نَفْسَهُ بِذَلِكَ، ويَحْصُرُ
عَلَيْهَا الطَّمَعَ في لَذَّةٍ مَكْرُوهَةٍ، أَوْ شَهْوَةٍ مُسْرِفَةٍ. ويَهْجُرُ أَصْحَابَ اللَّذَّاتِ ومُعَاشَرَتَهُمْ،
ويَنْقَبِضُ عَنِ الخُلَعَاءِ ومُخَالَطَتِهِمْ. ويُشْعِرُ نَفْسَهُ أَنَّ الشَّهْوَةَ عَدُوٌّ مُكَاشِحٌ، وخَصْمٌ
p. 134 مُكَافِحٌ، يُرِيدُ أَبَداً ضَرَرَهُ وأَذِيَّتَهُ، ويَعْتَمِدُ شَيْنَهُ وفَضِيحَتَهُ. فَيُنَاصِبُ شَهْوَتَهُ بِالعَدَاوَةِ،
ويُكَاشِفُهَا بِالمُعَانَدَةِ؛ ويَقْمَعُ أَبَداً سَوْرَتَهَا، ويَكْسِرُ دَائِماً حِدَّتَهَا، ويَقْهَرُ دَائِماً سَطْوَتَهَا؛
ويُذَلِّلُ عَلَى التَّدْرِيجِ عِزَّهَا، ويُسَكِّنُ عَلَى التَّرْتِيبِ فَوْرَهَا. فَإِنَّهُ، إذَا فَعَلَ ذَلِكَ، كَانَ
خَلِيقاً أَنْ يَمْلِكَ نَفْسَهُ، وتَنْقَادَ لَهُ شَهْوَتُهُ، ويَنْطَبِعَ بِالعِفَّةِ، ويَأْلَفَ حُسْنَ السِّيرَةِ. ومَتَى
p. 135 أَرْخَى لِشَهْوَتِهِ عِنَانَهَا، وسَمَحَ لَهَا في مُرَادِهَا، وأَهْمَلَ سِيَاسَتَهَا ومُرَاعَاتَهَا، اسْتَطَالَتْ
وشَمَخَتْ، ولَمْ تَلْبَثْ أَنْ تُوهِنَ صَاحِبَهَا، وتَقُودَهُ وتَحْمِلَهُ عَلَى مَا يَسُوءُهُ ويَغُرُّهُ.
فَيَصِيرُ بِذَلِكَ بَعِيداً مِنَ التَّمَامِ، غَيْرَ طَامِعٍ في الكَمَالِ.

6. ويَنْبَغِي لِمَنْ يَطْلُبُ التَّمَامَ أَنْ يَعْلَمَ أَنَّهُ لا سَبِيلَ لَهُ إلَى بُلُوغِ غَرَضِهِ، مَا
دَامَتِ اللَّذَّةُ عِنْدَه مُسْتَحْسَنَةً، والشَّهْوَةُ مُسْتَحَبَّةً. وهَذِهِ الحَالُ صَعْبَةٌ جِدّاً، مُتَعَسِّرَةٌ
p. 136 عَلَى طَالِبِهَا، بَعِيدَةُ المَأْخَذِ. وهِيَ عَلَى المُلُوكِ والرُّؤَسَاءِ أَصْعَبُ وأَبْعَدُ. لأَنَّ المُلُوكَ
والرُّؤَسَاءَ أَقْدَرُ عَلَى اللَّذَّاتِ، وأَشَدُّ تَمَكُّناً؛ والشَّهَوَاتُ واللَّذَّاتُ لَدَيْهِمْ مُعَرَّضَةٌ، ولَهُمْ
سَجِيَّةٌ وعَادَةٌ. فَمُفَارَقَتُهَا عَلَيْهِمْ مُتَعَذِّرَةٌ، وإعْرَاضُهُمْ عَنْهَا كَالشَّيْءِ المُمْتَنِعِ، خَاصَّةً
لِمَنْ قَدْ نَشَأَ عَلَى الانْهِمَاكِ فِيهَا، والتَّوَفُّرِ عَلَيْهَا. إلاَّ أَنَّ المُلُوكَ، وإنْ كَانُوا أَقْدَرَ
عَلَى اللَّذَّاتِ، وأَكْثَرَ اعْتِيَاداً لَهَا، كَمَا مَرَّ، فَهُمْ أَعْظَمُ هِمَماً وأَعَزُّ نُفُوساً. والمُحَصِّلُ

5. The complete man, and also anyone who seeks fulfillment, must establish a solid rule for his appetites and pleasures by means of which he will strive for balance. He will avoid dissipation and excess. In his moderate appetites and pleasures he will aim for what is appropriately agreeable. In this way he will take charge of his soul, hold it back from craving any abhorrent pleasure or excessive appetite. He will dissociate himself from pleasure seekers and their company, and he will shut himself off from the dissolute and their society. He will put himself on notice that appetite is a malevolent enemy and a combative adversary which always wants to do him harm and injury and intends to degrade and dishonor him. So he will oppose his appetite aggressively. He will stubbornly expose it, he will always curb its vehemence, he will continually blunt its keenness, and he will continually repulse its attack. He will subdue its force by degrees, and he will settle its seething methodically. When he does this, he will be equipped to rule his soul, and his appetite will yield to him. He will become naturally disposed to abstinence, and he will become accustomed to a good way of life. But, whenever he loosens the rein on his appetite, allows it to pursue its own purposes, and neglects its management and supervision, it will become overbearing and arrogant. It will not be slow to weaken its owner, to guide him and to carry him off to what will do him harm and delude him. He will then wind up far away from fulfillment, no longer even wishing for perfection.

6. Whoever seeks fulfillment must know that there is no way for him to reach his goal as long as pleasure seems good to him and appetite desirable. The position is exceedingly difficult, very trying for the one who seeks it, and distant to approach. It is most difficult and most distant for kings and leaders. The fact is that kings and leaders have the most means for pleasure, and they are the strongest in terms of power. Appetites and pleasures are easily available to them. They have both the natural disposition and the habit. For them to disengage themselves is impractical; for them to relinquish these things is like something impossible. This is especially the case for someone who has grown up involved with them and with enthusiasm for them. Nevertheless, even though kings have the most means for pleasure and they are the most likely to become habituated to it, as has been said, they also have the highest ambitions and the strongest souls. The most successful

مِنْهُمْ، إذَا سَمَتْ نَفْسُهُ إلَى التَّمَامِ الإنْسَانِيِّ، واشْتَاقَتْ إلَى الرِّئَاسَةِ الحَقِيقِيَّةِ، عَلِمَ أَنَّ المَلِكَ أَحَقُّ بِأَنْ يَكُونَ أَتَمَّ أَهْلِ زَمَانِهِ، وأَفْضَلَ مِنْ أَعْوَانِهِ ورَعِيَّتِهِ، فَيَهُونَ عَلَيْهِ مُفَارَقَةُ الشَّهَوَاتِ الرَّدِيئَةِ، وهَجْرُ اللَّذَّاتِ الدَّنِيئَةِ.

p. 137

[قَانُونُ الكَرَمِ والجُودِ]

7. ويَنْبَغِي لِمَنْ رَغِبَ فِي سِيَاسَةِ أَخْلَاقِهِ، وأَحَبَّ أَنْ يَسْلُكَ طَرِيقَ الاِعْتِدَالِ فِي شَهَوَاتِهِ، أَنْ يَجْعَلَ لَهُ قَانُوناً يَقْتَصِرُ عَلَيْهِ، فِي المَآكِلِ والمَشَارِبِ، مَعْرُوفاً بِالكَرَمِ. وهُوَ أَنْ لاَ يَسْتَبِدَّ بِالمَأْكَلِ والمَشْرَبِ وَحْدَهُ. بَلْ يَقْصِدَ أَنْ يُشْرِكَ، فِي مَا لَهُ مِنْ ذَلِكَ، إِخْوَانَهُ وأَوِدَّاءَهُ، إِنْ كَانَ رَعِيَّةً وسُوقَةً. وإِنْ كَانَ مَلِكاً أَوْ رَئِيساً، فَيَجْمَعَ عَلَيْهِ حَاشِيَتَهُ ونُدَمَاءَهُ، ويَعُمَّ بِهِ أَصْحَابَهُ وأَعْوَانَهُ، ويَتَفَقَّدُ بِفَضَلَاتِهِ أَهْلَ الفَقْرِ والمَسْكَنَةِ، p. 138 وخَاصَّةً مَنْ سَبَقَتْ لَهُ مَعْرِفَةٌ، أَوْ تَقَدَّمَتْ لَهُ حُرْمَةٌ. ويَصْرِفُ إِلَى ذَلِكَ حَظًّا مِنْ عِنَايَتِهِ؛ فَإِنَّ اعْتِدَادَ هَؤُلَاءِ بِمَا يَصِلُ إِلَيْهِمْ مِنْ بِرِّهِ أَكْثَرُ مِنِ اعْتِدَادِ حَاشِيَتِهِ وأَصْحَابِهِ. ولْيُظْهِرْ لِمَنْ يَجْتَمِعُ عَلَى مَائِدَتِهِ وعَلَى طَعَامِهِ وشَرَابِهِ، مِنْ إِخْوَانِهِ وأَصْدِقَائِهِ ورَعِيَّتِهِ ونُدَمَائِهِ، إِنْ كَانَ مَلِكاً أَوْ رَئِيساً، أَنَّ جَمْعَهُ لَهُمْ لِلأُنْسِ بِهِمْ، والسُّرُورِ بِمُعَاشَرَتِهِمْ، لاَ لِيُكْرِمَهُمْ بِطَعَامِهِ وشَرَابِهِ، ولاَ أَنَّ بِذَلِكَ قَدْراً يَعْتَدُّ بِهِ. ولْيَحْتَرِزْ كُلَّ الاِحْتِرَازِ مِنْ أَنْ يَبْدُوَ مِنْهُ امْتِنَانٌ بِالطَّعَامِ والشَّرَابِ، أَوْ تَبَجُّحٌ بِهِ. فَإِنَّ ذَلِكَ يَزْرِي بِفَاعِلِهِ ويَغُضُّ مِنْهُ، ويُوحِشُ مَنْ يَغْشَاهُ، ويَقْطَعُهُمْ عَنْهُ. وقَدْ يُسْتَحْسَنُ مِنَ الإِنْسَانِ أَيْضاً، إِذَا كَانَ مُقِلاًّ، p. 139 أَنْ يُؤَاسِيَ بِطَعَامِهِ إِخْوَانَهُ، وإِنْ كَانَ مُحْتَاجاً إِلَيْهِ. ويُسْتَحْسَنُ مِنْهُ أَيْضاً أَنْ يُؤَاسِيَ

of them, when his soul aspires to human fulfillment and yearns for authentic sovereignty, knows that a king is the most worthy to become the most complete person of his time, more virtuous than his officers and subjects. So it should be easy for him to disengage from evil appetites and to forgo vile pleasures.

The rule of high-mindedness and generosity

7. Whoever wishes to govern his moral qualities and wants to travel on the way of moderation in his appetites must make for himself a rule according to which he will restrict himself in eating and drinking, as one known for generosity. He will not monopolize food and drink for himself alone. Rather, he will strive to give a share of what he has of it to his relatives and friends, if he is a subject and a commoner. If he is a king or a leader, he will assemble for it his entourage and his boon companions, and he will include his associates and his officials. With the leftovers he will visit the people of poverty and misery, especially those of previous acquaintance or earlier esteem. To them he will direct a portion of his solicitude. In return for what comes to them of his magnanimity, the regard of these people will be so much more than the regard of his entourage and his associates. If he is a king or a leader, he will make it clear to those of his relatives, friends, subjects and servants who gather at his table for his food and drink that his gathering of them is due to friendship with them and joy in their company. It is not for the purpose of honoring them with his food and drink, nor to pay them some special regard. And let him take every precaution lest there appear to be any show of favor with the food and drink or any boasting about it. That would be to bring disparagement to the one doing it, to diminish him, to make those who frequent his company uneasy, and to cut them off from him. It is also to be deemed good for a man, even if he possesses little, to share his food with his relatives, although he is himself in need of it. And it is to be deemed good too for him to share it

بِهِ الفُقَرَاءَ والضُّعَفَاءَ . وقَدْ يُسْتَحْسَنُ أَيْضاً أَكْثَرَ مِنْ ذَلِكَ : أَنْ يُؤْثِرَ الإِنْسَانُ بطَعَامِهِ
وشَرَابِهِ غَيْرَهُ ، وإِنْ كَانَ شَدِيدَ الاِضْطِرَارِ إِلَيْهِ ، وكَانَ لاَ يَقْدِرُ عَلَى غَيْرِهِ .

8. ويَنْبَغِي أَيْضاً لِمَنْ طَلَبَ السِّيَاسَةَ التَّامَّةَ أَنْ يَسْتَهِينَ بِالمَالِ ويَحْتَقِرَهُ ، ويَنْظُرَ
إِلَيْهِ بِالعَيْنِ الَّتِي يَسْتَحِقُّهَا . فَإِنَّ المَالَ إِنَّمَا يُرَادُ لِغَيْرِهِ ، ولَيْسَ هُوَ مَطْلُوباً لِذَاتِهِ . فَإِنَّهُ في
نَفْسِهِ غَيْرُ نَافِعٍ ، وإِنَّمَا الاِنْتِفَاعُ بِالأَعْرَاضِ الَّتِي تُنَالُ بِهِ . فَالمَالُ آلَةٌ تُنَالُ بِهَا الأَعْرَاضُ ؛
فَلاَ يَجِبُ أَنْ يُعْتَقَدَ أَنَّ اقْتِنَاءَهُ وادِّخَارَهُ مُفِيدٌ . فَإِنَّهُ ، إِذَا ادُّخِرَ وحُرِسَ ، لَمْ يَنَلْ صَاحِبُهُ p. 140
شَيْئاً مِنَ الأَعْرَاضِ الَّتِي هُوَ بِالحَقِيقَةِ مُحْتَاجٌ إِلَيْهَا . فَالمَالُ هُوَ مَطْلُوبٌ لِغَيْرِهِ .

9. ويَنْبَغِي لِسَدِيدِ الرَّأْيِ ، العَالِي الهِمَّةِ ، أَنْ يَزِنَهُ بِوَزْنِهِ ؛ فَيَكْسِبُهُ مِنْ وَجْهِهِ ،
ويُفَرِّقُهُ في وُجُوهِهِ . ويَكُونُ مَعَ ذَلِكَ غَيْرَ مُتَوَانٍ في اكْتِسَابِهِ ، ولاَ مُفْتَرٍ في طَلَبِهِ .
لأَنَّ عَدَمَ المَالِ يَضْطَرُّهُ إِلَى التَّوَاضُعِ لِمَنْ هُوَ دُونَهُ ، إِذَا وَجَدَ عِنْدَهُ حَاجَتَهُ ؛ ووُجُودَ
المَالِ يُغْنِيهِ عَمَّنْ هُوَ فَوْقَهُ ، وإِنْ دَنَتْ مَنْزِلَتُهُ . ويَكُونُ أَيْضاً غَيْرَ مُدَّخِرِهِ ، ولاَ مُتَمَسِّكٍ
بِهِ ؛ بَلْ يَصْرِفُهُ في حَاجَاتِهِ ، ويُنْفِقُهُ في مُهِمَّاتِهِ . ويَقْصِدُ الاِعْتِدَالَ في تَفْرِيقِهِ ، ويَحْذَرُ p. 141
مِنَ السَّرَفِ والتَّبْذِيرِ في تَخْرِيجِهِ . ولاَ يَمْنَعُ حَقّاً يَجِبُ عَلَيْهِ ، ولاَ يَصْرِفُهُ في شَيْءٍ لاَ
يُحَبُّ ولاَ يُشْكَرُ عَلَيْهِ .

10. وإِذَا فَرَغَ مِنْ حَاجَاتِهِ ، واسْتَكْفَى مِنْ نَفَقَاتِهِ ، وسَدَّ جَمِيعَ خَلَلِهِ ، عَادَ
إِلَى النَّظَرِ في أَمْرِهِ . فَإِنْ كَانَ بَقِيَ مِنْ مَالِهِ بَقِيَّةٌ فَاضِلَةٌ عَنْ مُهِمِّ أَغْرَاضِهِ ، أَخْرَجَ مِنْهَا
قِسْطاً ، فَجَعَلَهُ عِدَّةً يَسْتَظْهِرُ بِهَا لِشِدَّةٍ ويُعِدُّهَا لِنَائِبَةٍ . ثُمَّ عَمَدَ إِلَى البَاقِي ، فَفَرَّقَهُ
في ذَوِي الحَاجَةِ ، مِنْ أَهْلِهِ وأَقَارِبِهِ وإِخْوَانِهِ وأَهْلِ مَوَدَّتِهِ . وجَعَلَ فِيهِ قِسْطاً لِلضُّعَفَاءِ
والمَسَاكِينِ ، وأَهْلِ الفَاقَةِ المَسْتُورِينَ . ويَجْعَلُ اهْتِمَامَهُ بِإِفْضَالِهِ وبِرِّهِ أَكْثَرَ مِن اهْتِمَامِهِ p. 142

with the poor and the weak. Even more than that, it is also to be deemed good for a man to prefer to give someone else his food and drink, even though he has a great need for it and he will not be able to get anything else.

8. It is also necessary for anyone who seeks complete self-control to disdain money, to scorn it, and to look upon it according to its deserts. Money is only to be wanted for the sake of something else; it is not to be sought for its own sake. In itself it is worthless; the worth is in the goods that are obtained by means of it. Money is a tool by means of which goods are obtained. So one must not believe that procuring it and hoarding it is advantageous. If it is hoarded and safeguarded, its owner does not obtain any of the goods he really needs. So money is to be sought for the sake of something else.

9. The right-thinking, high-minded person must balance it by its own weight, so that he will acquire it in the right way and dispense it for the right reasons. As a result, he will be anything but negligent in acquiring it, but he also will not be a wrongdoer in seeking it. Whereas the lack of money would oblige him to behave humbly toward those who are below him whenever he finds himself in need of them, the availability of money will free him from those who are above him, even though his own station is a lowly one. He will become a non-hoarder also, and he will not hold onto it. Rather, he will spend it for his needs and disburse it for his requirements. He will aim for moderation in distributing it; he will be cautious of extravagance and of waste in disbursing it. He will not refuse a claim that is obligatory for him, nor will he divert [money] for something undesirable or for which he would not be thanked.

10. When he has attended to his needs and has been sparing in his expenses and has settled his claims, he will go back to review his situation. And if there is anything remaining of his money—left over from his most important concerns—he will set aside a portion of it. He will make it an amount to which he can have recourse in misfortune, and he will make adjustments to it according to need. Then he will turn his attention to what is left, and he will disperse it among the needy of his people, his neighbors, his relatives, and his friends. He will designate a portion of it for the weak, the poor, and the poverty-stricken—those who are overlooked. He will be solicitous to do favors and show kindness, much more so than to take care of his

بِضَرُورِيَّاتِهِ، فَإِنَّ الضَّرُورِيَّاتِ تَقُودُهُ كَرْهاً إِلَيْهَا. والبِرُّ والنَوَافِلُ، مَتَى لَمْ يَهْتَمَّ بِهَا ويُشْعِرْ نَفْسَهُ الْتِزَامَهَا، لَمْ يَسْهُلْ عَلَيْهِ فِعْلُهَا. لأَنَّ ضُعْفَ النَّفْسِ، وسُوءَ الظَّنِّ يَصْرِفَانِهِ عَنْهَا. وإِنْ لَمْ يَكُنْ لَهُ جَاذِبٌ مِنْ نَفْسِهِ، ودَاعٍ قَوِيٌّ مِنْ هِمَّتِهِ، لَمْ يُقْدِمْ عَلَيْهَا، وغَلَبَ عَلَيْهِ التَّوَانِي. فَإِذَا تَوَانَى عَنِ البِرِّ والتَّفَضُّلِ، كَانَ شَحِيحاً ضَنِيناً بَخِيلاً دَنِيئاً، ولَيْسَ بِتَامٍّ. بَلْ لَيْسَ بِالحَقِيقَةِ إِنْسَانٌ مَنْ لَمْ يَكُنْ لَهُ بِرٌّ يُعْرَفُ، ولَمْ تُنْشَرْ عَنْهُ أَفْعَالٌ تُوصَفُ. هَذَا إِنْ كَانَ مِنْ أَوْسَاطِ النَّاسِ.

p. 143 **11.** فَأَمَّا المُلُوكُ والرُؤَسَاءُ، فَإِنَّهُمْ أَحَقُّ بِهَذِهِ السِّيَاسَةِ، ويَجِبُ أَنْ يَكُونُوا
بِذَلِكَ أَشَدَّ عِنَايَةً. فَيَجْبُوا الأَمْوَالَ مِنْ حَقِّهَا ووَاجِبَاتِهَا، ويَصْرِفُوا مِنْهَا فِي نَفَقَاتِهِمْ
ومَؤُونَاتِهِمْ، وأَرْزَاقِ جُنْدِهِمْ وأَصْحَابِهِمْ، قَدْرَ الكِفَايَةِ، مِنْ غَيْرِ سَرَفٍ ولاَ تَقْتِيرٍ.
ويُعِدُّوا مِنْهُ شَطْراً لِخَوْفِ عَاقِبَةٍ؛ ويَصْرِفُوا البَاقِيَ فِي طُرُقِ الكَرَمِ والجُودِ، ووُجُوهِ
الخَيْرِ والبِرِّ. فَيُعْطُوا أَهْلَ العِلْمِ عَلَى طَبَقَاتِهِمْ، ويَجْعَلُوا لَهُمْ رَوَاتِبَ مِنْ خَوَاصِّ أَمْوَالِهِمْ،
ويَدْفَعُوا لِمَنْ هُوَ مُثَابِرٌ عَلَى العِلْمِ والأَدَبِ. ويَبَرُّوا الضُّعَفَاءَ والمَسَاكِينَ، ويَتَفَقَّدُوا
p. 144 الغُرَبَاءَ والمُنْقَطِعِينَ. ويَهْتَمُّوا بِالزُّهَّادِ النُّسُكِ، ويَخُصُّوهُمْ بِقِسْطٍ مِنْ أَفْضَالِهِمْ وأَنْعَامِهِمْ.
ويَعْتَنُوا بِالصَّغِيرِ والكَبِيرِ مِنْ رَعِيَّتِهِمْ، ويُنْفِقُوا فِي مَصَالِحِهِمْ شَطْراً مِنْ أَمْوَالِهِمْ. فَإِنَّ
المُلُوكَ أَوْلَى بِالكَرَمِ مِنَ الرَّعِيَّةِ، وأَحَقُّ بِالجُودِ مِنَ العَامَّةِ.

12. وقَدْ يُسْتَحْسَنُ أَيْضاً مِنَ المُقِلِّينَ أَوِ المُقَتِّرِينَ المُؤَاسَاةُ بِالمَالِ والإِيثَارُ بِهِ،
وإِنْ كَانُوا مُحْتَاجِينَ إِلَيْهِ. وكُلَّمَا كَانَتْ حَاجَاتُهُمْ أَشَدَّ، كَانَ ذَلِكَ الفِعْلُ أَحْسَنَ.
وهَذِهِ الحَالُ تُسْتَحْسَنُ، إِذَا رَأَى الرَّجُلُ أَخاً مِنْ إِخْوَانِهِ، أَوْ صَدِيقاً مِنْ أَصْدِقَائِهِ
p. 145 يَخْتَصُّ بِهِ، قَدْ دَعَتْهُ الحَاجَةُ إِلَى مَا لاَ يَقْدِرُ عَلَيْهِ لإِصْلاَحِ شَيْءٍ مِنْ شَأْنِهِ، أَوْ لِدَفْعِ

own necessities; for necessities will attract his attention whether he likes it or not. When one is not solicitous, and does not lay an obligation on oneself to show kindness or works of supererogation, to do so is not easy for him because weakness of the soul and wrong thinking distract him. If, on the part of his soul, he has nothing to induce him and, on the part of his determination, no strong prompter, he will not take the risk, and indifference will overcome him. And, if he becomes indifferent to bestowing acts of kindness and to practicing virtue, he will become stingy, grudging, greedy, mean, and imperfect. The fact is that a man in the true sense is not one to whom no act of kindness is credited, nor is he someone of whom no laudable actions are publicly known. This is the situation if he is of the middle class of people.

11. As for kings and leaders, they are the most fit for this line of conduct, and they must be the ones most strenuously concerned with it. They should raise money rightfully and dutifully and they should pay it out for their own expenses and supplies, for provisions for their army and their associates, in sufficient measure, without extravagance or niggardliness. They should set aside a portion for fear of the future, and they should pay out the rest in liberal, generous ways, in a kindly, beneficent fashion. They should give to scholars according to their classes, they should assign them salaries from their own private monies, and they should reward anyone who perseveres in knowledge and refinement. They should deal kindly with the weak and the poor, and they should search out the strangers and the alienated. They should be solicitous for ascetics and devout people, and they should allot them proportionately a share of their goods and their flocks. They should be solicitous of the young and the old among their subjects, and they should pay for their requirements with a portion of their monies. Kings are more suited for liberality than their subjects, and they are more apt to be generous than the common people are.

12. Even for the destitute or the parsimonious, it is good to share money with others—to prefer to do so, even if they are themselves in need of it. The stronger their need is, the better is the good work. This condition is considered good when a man sees one of his brothers, or one of his friends who is special to him, whom need calls to an [expenditure] he cannot afford to settle some affair of his own or to avert a

مِحْنَةٍ نَزَلَتْ بِهِ، وكَانَ هُوَ قَادِراً عَلَى ذَلِكَ القَدْرِ مِنَ المَالِ؛ فَيَبْتَدِئُ بِإسْعافِهِ، عَفْواً، مِنْ غَيْرِ مَسْأَلَةٍ. فَإِنْ فَعَلَ هَذَا الفِعْلَ مَعَ الغَرِيبِ الَّذِي لاَ يَعْرِفُهُ، ولَمْ تَسْبِقْ لَهُ حُرْمَةٌ ولاَ مَوَدَّةٌ، كَانَ جَمِيلاً مُسْتَحْسَناً.

[الحِلْمُ ومَحَبَّةُ النَّاسِ أَجْمَعِين]

13. ويَنْبَغِي لِمُحِبِّ الكَمالِ أَنْ يُشْعِرَ نَفْسَهُ أَنَّ الغَضْبَانَ بِمَنْزِلَةِ البَهَائِمِ
p. 146 والسِّبَاعِ، يَفْعَلُ مَا يَفْعَلُهُ مِنْ غَيْرِ عِلْمٍ ولاَ رَوِيَّةٍ. فَإِنْ جَرَى بَيْنَهُ وبَيْنَ غَيْرِهِ مُحَاوَرَةٌ،
أَدَّتْ إِلَى أَنْ يُغْضِبَ خَصْمَهُ، ويُسَفِّهِ عَلَيْهِ، اِعْتَقَدَ فِيهِ أَنَّهُ، فِي تِلْكَ الحَالِ، بِمَنْزِلَةِ
البَهَائِمِ والسِّبَاعِ، فَيُمْسِكُ عَنْ مُقَابَلَتِهِ، ويُحْجِمُ عَنِ الاِقْتِصَاصِ مِنْهُ. لأَنَّهُ يَعْلَمُ أَنَّ
الكَلْبَ لَوْ نَبَحَ عَلَيْهِ، لَمْ يَكُنْ يَسْتَجِيزُ مُقَابَلَتَهُ عَلَى نَبْحِهِ. وكَذَلِكَ البَهِيمَةُ لَوْ رَمَحَتْهُ،
لَمْ يُسْتَحْسَنْ عُقُوبَتُهَا، لأَنَّهَا غَيْرُ عَالِمَةٍ بِمَا تَصْنَعُهُ. إِلاَّ أَنْ يَكُونَ جَاهِلاً سَفِيهاً. فَإِنَّ
مِنَ السُّفَهَاءِ مَنْ يَغْضَبُ عَلَى البَهِيمَةِ إِذَا رَمَحَتْهُ، ويُوجِعُهَا ضَرْباً إِذَا أَذَتْهُ. ورُبَّمَا
عَثَرَ السَّفِيهُ، فَشَتَمَ مَوْضِعَ عَثْرَتِهِ، ورَفَسَهُ بِرِجْلِهِ. فَأَمَّا الحَلِيمُ الوَقُورُ، فَلاَ يَسْتَحْسِنُ
p. 147 شَيْئاً مِنْ ذَلِكَ. وإِذَا اسْتَشْعَرَ مِنْ خَصْمِهِ أَنَّه بِمَنْزِلَةِ البَهَائِمِ، صَارَ هَذَا الاِسْتِشْعَارُ
مِنْهُ طَرِيقاً إِلَى ضَبْطِ النَّفْسِ الغَضَبِيَّةِ وزَمِّهَا. فَإِنْ آذَاهُ مُؤْذٍ بِغَيْرِ سَبَبٍ فَيُؤَدِّي ذَلِكَ
الأَذَى إِلَى حَالٍ تُغْضِبُهُ، أَنِفَ أَيْضاً مِنَ الغَضَبِ، مَعَ اسْتِشْعَارِهِ أَنَّ الغَضْبَانَ والبَهِيمَةَ
سَوَاءٌ؛ فَيَعْدِلُ حِينَئِذٍ إِلَى مُقَابَلَةِ مُؤْذِيهِ بِجَمِيلِ مَا يَقْتَضِيهِ الرَّأْيُ، مِنْ حَيْثُ لاَ يَظْهَرُ
فِيهِ غَضَبٌ ولاَ سَفَهٌ.

misfortune that afflicts him. If he has the monetary means to afford it, he will spontaneously spring to offer assistance without question. If he does this same thing for a stranger, with whom he is not acquainted and for whom there is no prior esteem or love, it is truly a beautifully good deed.

Patience and the love of all men

13. One who loves perfection must take notice of the fact that an angry person is on the level of the animals and the predators; he does what he does without knowledge or deliberation. If, then, one [who loves perfection] gets into an argument with someone else, leading up to the point that he infuriates his adversary and that person abuses him, he will believe that, in this situation, that person is on the level of the animals and the predators. So he will stand back from replying in kind and shrink from retaliating against him, because he knows that, if a dog barks at him, he will not think it is a good idea to confront him on account of his barking. In the same way, were an animal to kick him, he would not think it worthwhile to punish it, because it would not know what it was doing. To do otherwise would be to be foolishly ignorant. There are fools who will get angry at an animal when it kicks them, and they will deal it a painful blow whenever it hurts them. Sometimes a fool stumbles, and he heaps abuse on the place where he stumbled and he kicks at it with his foot. But the gentle, modest man would not think anything of that sort is good. So, when he perceives that his adversary is on the level of the animals, that perception becomes for him a way to exercise control over his own irascible soul and to subdue it. If someone harms him without cause and that harm reaches the point of infuriating him, he will nevertheless despise anger, as a result of his awareness that the angry man and the animal are on a par. So he will, at that moment, turn to confront his assailant with the kind of graceful action which good judgment requires, in which, as a consequence, neither anger nor folly will appear.

14. وَيَنْبَغِي لِمُحِبِّ الكَمَالِ أَيْضاً أَنْ يُعَوِّدَ نَفْسَهُ مَحَبَّةَ النَّاسِ أَجْمَعَ، وَالتَّوَدُّدَ إِلَيْهِمْ، وَالتَّحَنُّنَ عَلَيْهِمْ، وَالرَّأْفَةَ، وَالرَّحْمَةَ لَهُمْ. فَإِنَّ النَّاسَ قَبِيلٌ وَاحِدٌ، مُتَنَاسِبُونَ، تَجْمَعُهُمُ الإِنْسَانِيَّةُ. وَحِلْيَةُ القُوَّةِ الإِلَهِيَّةِ هِيَ فِي جَمِيعِهِمْ، وَفِي كُلِّ وَاحِدٍ مِنْهُمْ؛ وَهِيَ النَّفْسُ العَاقِلَةُ. وَبِهَذِهِ النَّفْسِ صَارَ الإِنْسَانُ إِنْسَاناً، وَهِيَ أَشْرَفُ جُزْئَيِ الإِنْسَانِ اللَّذَيْنِ هُمَا النَّفْسُ وَالجَسَدُ. فَالإِنْسَانُ بِالحَقِيقَةِ هُوَ النَّفْسُ العَاقِلَةُ، وَهِيَ جَوْهَرٌ وَاحِدٌ فِي جَمِيعِ النَّاسِ. وَالنَّاسُ كُلُّهُمْ، بِالحَقِيقَةِ شَيْءٌ وَاحِدٌ، وَبِالأَشْخَاصِ كَثِيرُونَ. وَإِذَا كَانَتْ نُفُوسُهُمْ وَاحِدَةً، وَالمَوَدَّةُ إِنَّمَا تَكُونُ بِالنَّفْسِ، فَوَاجِبٌ أَنْ يَكُونُوا كُلُّهُمْ مُتَحَابِّينَ مُتَوَادِّينَ.

15. وَذَلِكَ فِي النَّاسِ طَبِيعَةٌ، لَوْ لَمْ تَقُدْهُمُ النَّفْسُ الغَضَبِيَّةُ. فَإِنَّ هَذِهِ النَّفْسَ تُحِبُّ لِصَاحِبِهَا التَّرَؤُّسَ، فَتَقُودُ صَاحِبَهَا إِلَى الكِبْرِ وَالإِعْجَابِ، وَالتَّسَلُّطِ عَلَى المُسْتَضْعَفِ، وَاسْتِضْغَارِ الفَقِيرِ، وَحَسَدِ الغَنِيِّ وَذِي الفَضْلِ؛ فَتُسَبِّبُ مِنْ أَجْلِ هَذِهِ الأَسْبَابِ العَدَاوَاتِ، وَتَتَأَكَّدُ البَغْضَاءُ بَيْنَهُمْ. فَإِذَا ضَبَطَ الإِنْسَانُ نَفْسَهُ الغَضَبِيَّةَ، وَانْقَادَ لِنَفْسِهِ العَاقِلَةِ، صَارَ لَهُ النَّاسُ كُلُّهُمْ أَحْبَاباً وَإِخْوَاناً. وَإِذَا أَعْمَلَ الإِنْسَانُ فِكْرَهُ، رَأَى أَنَّ ذَلِكَ وَاجِبٌ. لِأَنَّ النَّاسَ إِمَّا أَنْ يَكُونُوا فُضَلَاءَ، أَوْ نُقَصَاءَ. فَالفُضَلَاءُ يَجِبُ عَلَيْهِ مَحَبَّتُهُمْ لِمَوْضِعِ فَضْلِهِمْ، النُّقَصَاءُ يَجِبُ عَلَيْهِ رَحْمَتُهُمْ لِمَوْضِعِ نَقْصِهِمْ. فَبِحَقٍّ يَجِبُ لِمُحِبِّ الكَمَالِ أَنْ يَكُونَ مُحِبّاً لِجَمِيعِ النَّاسِ، مُتَحَنِّناً عَلَيْهِمْ، رَؤُوفاً بِهِمْ. وَخَاصَّةً المَلِكُ وَالرَّئِيسُ. فَإِنَّ المَلِكَ لَيْسَ يَكُونُ مَلِكاً، مَا لَمْ يَكُنْ مُحِبّاً لِرَعِيَّتِهِ رَؤُوفاً بِهِمْ. وَذَلِكَ أَنَّ المَلِكَ وَرَعِيَّتَهُ، بِمَنْزِلَةِ رَبِّ الدَّارِ وَأَهْلِ دَارِهِ. وَمَا أَقْبَحَ رَبَّ الدَّارِ أَنْ يُبْغِضَ أَهْلَ دَارِهِ، وَلَا يَتَحَنَّنَ عَلَيْهِمْ، وَلَا يُحِبَّ مَصَالِحَهُمْ.

p. 148
p. 149
p. 150

14. One who loves perfection must also make it a habit to love people generally, to treat them with affection, to act sympathetically toward them, and to be gentle and compassionate with them. Men are a single tribe, related to one another; humanity unites them. The adornment of the divine power is in all of them and in each one of them, and it is the rational soul. By means of this soul, man becomes man. It is the nobler of the two parts of man, which are the soul and the body. So man in his true being is the rational soul, and it is a single substance in all men. All men in their true being are a single thing, but they are many in persons. Since their souls are one, and love is only in the soul, all of them must then show affection for one another and love one another.

15. This is a natural disposition in men as long as the irascible soul does not lead them on. This soul presses its owner to dominate, and it leads its owner to display pride, to behave arrogantly, to exercise control over anyone who is thought to be weak, to belittle the poor, and to be envious of the rich and well-favored. For these reasons it gives rise to enmities, and mutual hatred is strengthened. If a man controls his irascible soul and follows the lead of his rational soul, all people become friends and brothers to him. When a man puts his critical thinking to work, he sees that this is necessary. While people are either excellent or deficient, he must love the excellent ones for the sake of their excellent qualities and he must have compassion on the deficient ones for the sake of their deficiency. And the lover of perfection must certainly be a lover of all people, having compassion on them and being merciful to them—and this is especially true of a king and a leader. A king will not be a king as long as he is not a lover of his subjects, being compassionate toward them. That is because a king and his subjects are like the master of a household and the people of his household. How disgraceful it would be for the master of a household to loathe the people of his household and not to have compassion for them, nor to want their best interests!

16. وَيَنْبَغِي لِمُحِبِّ الكَمالِ أَنْ يَجْعَلَ هِمَّتَه فِعْلَ الخَيْرِ مَعَ جَمِيعِ النَّاسِ، وإِنْفَاقَ مَا يَفْضُلُ مِنْ مَالِهِ في مَا يُبْقِي لَهُ الذِّكْرَ الجَمِيلَ بَعْدَ مَوْتِه؛ وَيَتَحَرَّزَ مِنْ فِعْلِ الشَّرِّ. فَإِنَّهُ، إِذَا حَاسَبَ نَفْسَهُ، عَلِمَ أَنَّ مَنْ يَفْعَلُ الشَّرَّ، فَإِنَّمَا يَفْعَلُهُ لِخَيْرٍ يَعْتَقِدُ أَنَّهُ يَصِلُ إِلَيْهِ بِذَلِكَ الشَّرِّ؛ وَرُبَّمَا كَانَ غَالِطاً، وَرُبَّمَا كَانَ مُصِيباً. وَإِذَا عُلِمَ أَنَّ الأَمْرَ عَلَى هَذِهِ الصِّفَةِ، p. 151
كَانَ وَاجِباً أَنْ يَطْلُبَ الخَيْرَ الَّذِي يَرُومُه، مِنْ طَرِيقٍ غَيْرِ طَرِيقِ التَّشَرُّرِ، إِذَا كَانَ هُوَ الغَرَضَ المَطْلُوبَ، لاَ فِعْلُ الشَّرِّ. فَأَمَّا إِنْ كَانَ تَشَرُّرُهُ لِشِفَاءِ غَيْظٍ يَلْحَقُهُ، فَلْيَعْلَمْ أَنَّهُ، إِذَا سَكَنَ غَيْظُهُ، وَجَدَ ذَلِكَ المَقْصُودَ بِالشَّرِّ غَيْرَ مُسْتَحِقٍّ لِذَلِكَ الفِعْلِ. فَفِعْلُ الشَّرِّ قَبِيحٌ، وَخَاصَّةً بِمَنْ قَدْ جَمَعَ الفَضَائِلَ. إِلاَّ أَنْ يَكُونَ ذَلِكَ الشَّرُّ تَأْدِيباً عَلَى جُرْمٍ، أَوِ اقْتِصَاصاً مِنْ جَانٍ. لأَنَّ هَذِهِ الحَالَ مُسْتَحَبَّةٌ مَحْمُودَةٌ، بَلْ لاَ تُعَدُّ شَرّاً. لأَنَّ ذَلِكَ p. 152
الشَّرَّ إِنَّمَا يَصِلُ إِلَى الجَانِي فَقَطْ، وَيَكُونُ مِنْهُ نَفْعٌ عَامٌّ لِجَمِيعِ النَّاسِ، بِأَنْ يَرْتَدِعَ بِهِ أَمْثَالُهُ مِنَ الجُنَاةِ، فَتَكُونُ المَنْفَعَةُ فِيهِ أَكْثَرَ. فَمِنْ أَجْلِ ذَلِكَ لاَ يُعَدُّ شَرّاً.

17. وَإِذَا اعْتَمَدَ الإِنْسَانُ فِعْلَ الخَيْرِ وَأَلِفَهُ، وَتَجَنَّبَ الشَّرَّ وَاسْتَوْحَشَ مِنْهُ، أَنِفَ مِنَ الأَخْلاَقِ المَكْرُوهَةِ الَّتِي تُعَدُّ شَرّاً، كَالحَسَدِ، وَالحِقْدِ، وَالخُبْثِ، وَالخَدِيعَةِ، وَالنَّمِيمَةِ، وَالغِيبَةِ، وَالوَقِيعَةِ، وَأَمْثَالِ هَذِهِ العَادَاتِ. وَإِذَا فَكَّرَ العَاقِلُ المُحَصِّلُ فِيهَا، عَلِمَ أَنَّهَا غَيْرُ مُجْدِيَةٍ عَلَيْهِ نَفْعاً، وَهِيَ مَعَ ذَلِكَ تَشِينُهُ وَتُقَبِّحُ صُورَتَهُ. وَإِذَا كَانَ مُحِبّاً لِلتَّمَامِ، مُسْتَشْرِفاً لِلْكَمَالِ، كَانَ وَاجِباً عَلَيْهِ تَجَنُّبُ هَذِهِ الأَخْلاَقِ.

16. The lover of perfection must make it his resolve to do well by all people, to spend his surplus money on whatever will preserve for him a good reputation after his death, and to be on his guard against evildoing. When he takes account of himself, he knows that whoever does something evil does it only for the sake of a good that he believes will come to him by reason of that evil action. Sometimes he misses the mark; sometimes he hits the target. Since one knows that this is the case, he must seek the good he craves by means of a way other than the way of doing evil, since that is the goal to be sought and not the doing of evil. However, if his evildoing is for the sake of curing an exasperation that has come over him, he should understand that, if and when his exasperation subsides, he will find out that what was intended by the evil action was not actually due to that action. Doing evil is repugnant, especially in someone who has already accumulated virtues, unless the evil action is by way of a punishment for an offense or an exaction of vengeance on a delinquent. This course of action is to be recommended; it is praiseworthy. Indeed, it is not to be reckoned an evil. Evil in this case only redounds to the delinquent, while the general benefit deriving from it belongs to all the people. The reason is that, by this means, delinquents like him are held in check. The advantage in it is greater, and for this reason it is not really to be reckoned an evil.

17. If a man intends to do what is good and becomes accustomed to it, and if he avoids evil and develops an aversion for it, he will scorn the abhorrent moral qualities that are reckoned to be evil. Such qualities are envy, resentment, imposture, malevolence, defamation of character, slander, calumny, and other such habits. When a reasonable, deductive man thinks critically about them, he will understand that they are not going to yield him any benefit and that, moreover, they will disfigure him and make his image repugnant. If he is a lover of fulfillment, aspiring to perfection, it will be incumbent upon him to avoid these moral qualities.

p. 153 [المَلِكُ التَّامُّ]

18. ويَنْبَغِي لِمُحِبِّ الكَمالِ أَنْ يَعْتَقِدَ أَنَّهُ لَيسَ شَيْءٌ مِنَ العُيُوبِ والقَبائِحِ خَافِياً عَنِ النَّاسِ، وإِنِ اجْتَهَدَ صَاحِبُهَا في سَتْرِهَا. فَلاَ تَطْمَعُ نَفسُهُ في ارْتِكابِ فِعْلٍ قَبيحٍ، يَظُنُّ أَنَّهُ يَتَكَتَّمُ عَنِ النَّاسِ حَتَّى لا يَقِفَ عَلَيْهِ أَحَدٌ. ويَجِبُ أَنْ يَعْلَمَ أَنَّ النَّاسَ
p. 154 بِالطَّبْعِ مُوَكَّلُونَ بِتَتَبُّعِ عُيُوبِ النَّاسِ، وتَعْيِيرِهِمْ بِهَا. وذَلِكَ في النَّاسِ غَرِيزَةٌ. والسَّبَبُ فِيهِ أَنَّ الإِنْسَانَ، مَا لَمْ يَبْلُغِ التَّمَامَ، فَلَيْسَ يَخْلُو مِنْ تَقْصِيرٍ يُعابُ بِهِ. ويَسُوءُهُ أَنْ يَكونَ غَيْرُهُ أَفْضَلَ مِنْهُ. فَهُوَ يُسَرُّ أَنْ يَكُونَ النَّاسُ كُلُّهُمْ نُقَصَاءَ، لِيُساوُوهُ في النَّقْصِ، ويَحِلُّوا دُونَهُ. فَهُوَ أَبَداً يَتَتَبَّعُ مَعَايِبَ النَّاسِ ويُعَيِّرُهُمْ بِهَا، لِيُرِيَ النَّاسَ أَنَّهُ أَفْضَلُ مِمَّنْ فِيهِ ذَلِكَ العَيْبُ. ويُشْعِرُ نَفْسَهُ أَيْضاً ذَلِكَ، لِتَطِيبَ بِمَا فِيهَا مِنَ العَيْبِ. فَلَيْسَ شَيْءٌ مِنَ العُيُوبِ بِخَافٍ عَنِ النَّاسِ، وإِنِ اعْتَمَدَ سَتْرَهُ.

19. وقَدْ يَظُنُّ كَثِيرٌ مِنَ المُلُوكِ والرُّؤَسَاءِ أَنَّ عُيُوبَهُمْ مَسْتُورَةٌ عَنِ النَّاسِ، غَيْرُ
p. 155 بَادِيَةٍ. وذَلِكَ لِمَوْضِعِ هَيْبَتِهِمْ، وعِظَمِ سَطْوَتِهِمْ. ويَسْتَشْعِرُونَ أَنَّ حَاشِيَتَهُمْ وخَوَاصَّهُمْ لا يَجْسُرُونَ عَلَى إِظْهَارِ أَسْرَارِهِمْ، إِنْ وَقَفُوا عَلَى شَيْءٍ مِنْهَا. وهَذَا نِهَايَةُ الغَلَطِ. لأَنَّ خَوَاصَّ المَلِكِ وحَاشِيَتَهُ، كَمَا أَنَّهُمْ عِنْدَهُ ثِقَاتٌ أُمَنَاءُ، كَذَلِكَ لِكُلِّ وَاحِدٍ مِنْهُمْ خَاصَّةٌ وثِقَةٌ، يَخْرُجُ إِلَيْهِ بِأَسْرَارِهِ. والَّذِي لا يَسْتُرُ الإِنْسَانُ عَنْهُ أَسْرَارَ نَفْسِهِ، فَمُحَالٌ أَنْ يَسْتُرَ عَنْهُ أَسْرَارَ غَيْرِهِ. وهَذِهِ الحَالُ طَرِيقٌ إِلَى انْتِشَارِ مَعَايِبِ المُلُوكِ، الَّذِينَ يَظُنُّونَ أَنَّهَا مَسْتُورَةٌ. والعِلَّةُ في ظَنِّهِمْ أَنَّ عُيُوبَهُمْ مَسْتُورَةٌ هُوَ أَنَّهُمْ لاَ يَسْمَعُونَ أَحَداً يَذْكُرُهَا، ولا
p. 156 أَحَداً يَتَنَصَّحُ إِلَيْهِمْ بِهَا؛ فَيَظُنُّونَ أَنَّهَا خَفِيَّةٌ. فَإِذَا أَحَبَّ الإِنْسَانُ أَنْ يَعْلَمَ أَنَّ عُيُوبَهُ غَيْرُ خَافِيَةٍ، فَلْيَعُدْ إِلَى نَفْسِهِ، ويَنْظُرْ هَلْ يَعْرِفُ لأَحَدٍ عَيْباً كَانَ يَسْتُرُهُ ويُخْفِيهِ. فَإِنَّهُ يَجِدُ

The perfect king

18. Whoever loves perfection must believe that no faults or abominable qualities are hidden from people, even if the one who possesses them goes to great pains to conceal them. So his soul should not desire to commit an abominable deed which he supposes he will be able to hide from people to the point that no one will notice it. He must understand that people by nature are commissioned to keep track of people's faults and to reprove them for them. It is an instinct in people. And the reason for it is that as long as a man has not reached fulfillment, he is not free of a deficiency for which he can be blamed. And it grieves him that anyone else should become more virtuous than he is. So he is delighted that all people are deficient and that they will either be equal to him in deficiency or fall below him. And he is always keeping track of people's faults and blaming them for them so that he might show people that he is more virtuous than those in whom there is this or that fault. He will also keep himself informed so that he might take delight in the faultfinding. So no fault is hidden from people, even if one intends to conceal it.

19. Many kings and leaders often suppose that their faults are hidden from the people and that they are unobservable. That is due to their position of prestige and the magnitude of their authority. They are under the misapprehension that their entourage and their favorites will not venture to expose their secrets, if they come to know anything of them. This is completely wrong. The fact is that although a king's favorites and his entourage are trustworthy and loyal to him, each one of them also has a favorite and a confidant of his own to whom he goes with his own secrets. It is impossible that one should hide someone else's secrets from someone from whom one does not hide one's own secrets. This predicament is the reason why the publication of the faults of kings becomes widespread, while they suppose they are hidden. The reason they think their faults are hidden is that they do not hear anyone mentioning them nor anyone giving them advice about them, so they think that they are concealed. But, if a man wants to know that his faults are not concealed, let him turn his attention to himself to see whether he knows of anyone who has a fault that he hides and conceals.

لِلنَّاسِ عِنْدَه عُيُوباً كَثِيرَةً، قَدِ اجْتَهَدُوا في سَتْرِهَا، وحَرَصُوا عَلَى صَوْنِهَا. ومِنْهُمْ
مَنْ يَظُنُّ أَنَّهَا خَفِيَّةٌ، ومِنْهُمْ مَنْ يَعْلَمُ أَنَّهَا قَدِ انْتَشَرَتْ بَعْدَ السَّتْرِ. فَإِذَا عَلِمَ أَنَّهُ عَارِفٌ
بِأَسْرَارِ كَثِيرٍ مِنَ النَّاسِ كَانَتْ مَسْتُورَةً، فَالوَاجِبُ أَنْ يَعْتَقِدَ أَنَّ عَيْبَهُ غَيْرُ خَافٍ ولاَ
مُنْكَتِمٍ، وأَنَّ النَّاسَ يَعْرِفُونَ مِنْ عُيُوبِهِ أَكْثَرَ مِمَّا يَعْرِفُ مِنْ عُيُوبِهِمْ.

p. 157 **20.** فَيَنْبَغِي لِمُحِبِّ الكَمَالِ أَنْ يَعْتَقِدَ أَنَّ عُيُوبَهُ ظَاهِرَةٌ، وإِنِ اجْتَهَدَ في
إِخْفَائِهَا. ولَيْسَ بِتَامٍّ مَنْ عُرِفَ لَهُ عَيْبٌ. ولاَ طَرِيقَ إِلَى التَّمَامِ، إِلاَّ بِاجْتِنَابِ العُيُوبِ
بِالكُلِّيَّةِ، والتَّمَسُّكِ بِالفَضَائِلِ في سَائِرِ الأُمُورِ. وهَذِهِ الرُّتْبَةُ غَايَةُ تَمَامِ الإِنسَانِيَّةِ، ونِهَايَةُ
الفَضِيلَةِ البَشَرِيَّةِ. ووَاجِبٌ عَلَى كُلِّ إِنْسَانٍ الاِجْتِهَادُ في بُلُوغِهَا، وَاسْتِفْرَاغُ الوُسْعِ في
الوُصُولِ إِلَيْهَا. لأَنَّ التَّمَامَ مَطْلُوبٌ لِذَاتِهِ، والنَّقْصَ مَكْرُوهٌ لِعَيْبِهِ.

p. 158 **21.** وأَحَقُّ النَّاسِ بِطَلَبِ هَذِهِ المَرْتَبَةِ، وأَوْلاَهُمْ بِالتَّجَمُّلِ لِبُلُوغِ هَذِهِ المَنْزِلَةِ،
المُلُوكُ والرُّؤَسَاءُ. لأَنَّ المُلُوكَ والرُّؤَسَاءَ أَشْرَفُ النَّاسِ، وأَعْظَمُهُمْ قَدْراً. ومَا أَقْبَحَ
بِالشَّرِيفِ العَظِيمِ القَدْرِ أَنْ يَكُونَ نَاقِصاً! فَالمُلُوكُ إِذاً يَنْبَغِي أَنْ يَكُونُوا أَشَدَّ النَّاسِ
حِرْصاً عَلَى بُلُوغِ الكَمَالِ. لأَنَّ الكَامِلَ مِنَ النَّاسِ، الجَامِعَ لِلْفَضَائِلِ، مُتَوَثِّبٌ بِالطَّبْعِ
عَلَى النَّاقِصِ مِنَ النَّاسِ. فَالإِنْسَانُ التَّامُّ رَئِيسٌ بِالطَّبْعِ. وإِذَا كَانَ المَلِكُ تَامّاً، جَامِعاً
لِمَحَاسِنِ الأَخْلاَقِ، مُحِيطاً بِجَمِيعِ المَنَاقِبِ، كَانَ مَلِكاً بِالطَّبْعِ. وإِذَا كَانَ نَاقِصاً كَانَ
p. 159 مَلِكاً بِالقَهْرِ. ومَا أَوْلَى بِالمَلِكِ أَنْ يَرْغَبَ في الرِّئَاسَةِ الحَقِيقِيَّةِ، لاَ الَّتِي تَكُونُ بِالقَهْرِ؛
والشَّرَفِ الذَّاتِيِّ، لاَ مَا هُوَ بِالوَضْعِ.

22. فَالوَاجِبُ أَنْ يَصْرِفَ المَلِكُ هِمَّتَهُ إِلَى اكْتِسَابِ الفَضَائِلِ، وَاقْتِنَاءِ
المَحَاسِنِ؛ ويَطْلُبَ الغَايَةَ مِنَ المَكَارِمِ، ويَسْتَصْغِرَ الكَبِيرَ مِنْهَا، حَتَّى يَحُوزَ جَمِيعَهَا؛

He will find out that the people around him have many faults that they make every effort to conceal, and that they are bent on safeguarding them. Some of them suppose that their faults are hidden; some of them know that they may become publicly known after having been kept secret. So, since he knows that he is aware of many other people's secrets that are to be kept concealed, he must believe that his own fault is neither hidden nor kept secret and that people will be aware of his faults much more than he is aware of their faults.

20. Whoever loves perfection must believe that his faults are apparent, even if he makes every effort to conceal them. Whoever is known to have a fault is not a complete man, and there is no way to fulfillment except by avoiding faults altogether and by holding fast to virtues in all situations. This degree is the apogee of human fulfillment and the utmost of human virtue. To exert the effort to achieve it is incumbent on every man, just as it is incumbent to exhaust one's means to arrive at it. Fulfillment is to be sought for its own sake, and deficiency is to be abhorred precisely because of its defectiveness.

21. Kings and leaders are the people most fit to seek this high grade, and they are the ones most apt to improve themselves sufficiently to achieve this level. The reason is that kings and leaders are the noblest of people and the greatest of them in terms of worth. How repugnant it would be for a great nobleman of worth to be deficient! Therefore, kings must be the most strongly determined of all people to achieve perfection. The reason is that the most perfect person, one who comprises all the virtues, has a natural advantage over the most deficient person. The complete man is a leader by nature. If a king is fulfilled, embodying good moral qualities, including all the virtuous traits, he is a king by nature. If he is deficient, he is a king by force. What is most appropriate for a king is that he should want authentic sovereignty, which does not come about by force, and also personal nobility, which is not the result of imposition.

22. A king must be determined to acquire virtues and to gain good qualities. He must seek the highest noble traits. He must deem the greatest of them a small matter until he gets possession of all of them.

ولاَ يَرضَى بِالنِّهَايَةِ، حَتَّى يَزِيدَ عَلَيْهَا . فَإِنَّهُ إِنْ رَضِيَ بِرُتْبَةٍ فَوْقَهَا رُتْبَةٌ، لَمْ يَصِرْ
p. 160 أَبداً إِلَى التَّمَامِ؛ وإِنَّ أَبْعَدَ النَّاسِ مِنَ التَّمَامِ مَنْ رَضِيَ لِنَفْسِهِ بِالنُّقْصَانِ. فَإِذَا طَلَبَ
المَلِكُ الكَمالَ، فَأَوَّلُ مَا يَجِبُ أَنْ يَعْتَادَهُ عِظَمُ الهِمَّةِ؛ فَإِنَّ عِظَمَ الهِمَّةِ تُصَغِّرُ في عَيْنَيْهِ
كُلَّ رَذِيلَةٍ، وتُحَسِّنُ لَهُ كُلَّ فَضِيلَةٍ. وإِذَا عَظُمَتْ هِمَّةُ المَلِكِ، سَلِمَ مِنَ الإِعْجَابِ
بِمُلْكِهِ، ورَأَى نَفْسَهُ وهِمَّتَهُ أَعْظَمَ قَدْراً مِنْ أَنْ يَسْتَكْثِرَ ذَلِكَ المُلْكَ. وإِذَا احْتَقَرَ
المَلِكُ مُلْكَهُ، الَّذِي بِهِ عِزُّهُ وعَظَمَتُهُ، طَلَبَ لِنَفْسِهِ مَا يُعَظِّمُهَا بِالحَقِيقَةِ، ولَيْسَ تُعَظَّمُ
النَّفْسُ إِلاَّ بِالفَضَائِلِ.

23. ثُمَّ يَنْبَغِي لَهُ أَنْ يَكْرَهَ المَلَقَ، ويُبْغِضَ المُتَمَلِّقِينَ، ويَنْهَاهُمْ عَنْ تَلَقِّيهِ بِهِ.
p. 161 ومَلاَكُ أَمْرِهِ أَنْ يَتَعَرَّفَ عُيُوبَهُ، حَتَّى يُمْكِنَهُ تَوَقِّيهَا، والتَّحَرُّزُ مِنْهَا وهَذَا أَبداً في المُلُوكِ
صَعْبٌ، لأَنَّ الإِنْسَانَ بِالطَّبْعِ يَخْفَى عَلَيْهِ كَثِيرٌ مِنْ عُيُوبِهِ؛ فَالَّذِي يَخْفَى عَلَى المُلُوكِ
أَكْثَرُ، لإِعْجَابِهِمْ بِمَحَاسِنِهِمْ، وعِظَمِ مَرْتَبَتِهِمْ. وأَيْضاً فَإِنَّ الرَّعِيَّةَ والسُّوقَةَ يُبَكِّتُونَ
بِعُيُوبِهِمْ ويُعَيِّرُونَ بِهَا، فَهُمْ يَعْرِفُونَهَا. والمُلُوكُ لاَ يَجْسُرُ أَحَدٌ عَلَى تَبْكِيتِهِمْ، ولاَ يُقْدِمُ
أَحَدٌ عَلَى نُصْحِهِمْ وتَبْكِيتِهِمْ عَلَى عُيُوبِهِمْ. لأَنَّ النَّاسَ أَجْمَعَ يَقْصِدُونَ التَّقَرُّبَ إِلَى
المُلُوكِ وتَمَلُّقَهُمْ، فَلاَ يَقُولُونَ لَهُمْ إِلاَّ مَا يُحِبُّونَ، لِيَنَالُوا الحُظْوَةَ عِنْدَهُمْ. فَعُيُوبُ المُلُوكِ
أَبداً خَفِيَّةٌ عَنْهُمْ.

p. 162 **24.** ويَنْبَغِي لِلْمَلِكِ، إِذَا أَحَبَّ أَنْ يَتَنَزَّهَ مِنَ العُيُوبِ ويَتَطَهَّرَ مِنْ دَنَسِهَا، أَنْ
يَتَقَدَّمَ إِلَى خَوَاصِّهِ وثِقَاتِهِ، ومَنْ كَانَ يَسْكُنُ إِلَى عَقْلِهِ وفِطْنَتِهِ، مِنْ خَدَمِهِ وحَاشِيَتِهِ؛
فَيَأْمُرُهُمْ أَنْ يَتَفَقَّدُوا عُيُوبَهُ ونَقَائِصَهُ، ويُطْلِعُوهُ عَلَيْهَا، ويُعْلِمُوهُ بِهَا. ويَنْبَغِي لَهُ أَنْ
يَتَلَقَّى مَنْ يَهْدِي إِلَيْهِ شَيْئاً مِنْ عُيُوبِهِ، بِالبِشْرِ والقَبُولِ، ويُظْهِرُ لَهُ الفَرَحَ والسُّرُورَ، بِمَا

He should not be content with the end until he exceeds it. If he is content with one grade when there is a grade above it, he will never arrive at perfection. The man farthest from fulfillment is the one who is content with the deficiency his soul possesses. If a king seeks perfection, the first thing necessary is that high ambition become habitual for him, because high ambition will demean every vice in his eyes and present every virtue to him in a favorable light. If a king is highly ambitious, he is safe from complacency about his kingship. He will see himself and his ambition as of much greater worth than thinking too highly of that kingship. If a king scorns his own kingship, wherein is his might and majesty, he will seek for his own soul what will truly make it great; and a soul is only made great by means of virtues.

23. Then he must abhor flattery, loathe flatterers, and forbid them to receive him with it. The foundation of his authority is that he be aware of his own faults, so that it will be possible for him to be on guard against them and to defend himself against them. This is always a difficulty for kings, because by nature most of a man's faults are hidden from him; and most of all are they hidden from kings because of their complacency about their good deeds and the grandeur of their rank. Also, while subjects and commoners are censured for their faults and are reproached for them, that they acknowledge them, no one ventures to reproach kings, nor does anyone dare to give them advice or to reproach them for their faults. The reason is that everybody aspires to curry favor with kings and to flatter them, so they will not say to them anything other than what they will like so that they might gain a favorable position with them. So the faults of kings are always hidden from them.

24. If a king wants to become free of faults and to be cleansed of their defilement, he must approach his favorites and his confidants and those of his servants and of his entourage on whose mind and thinking he relies. He must bid them to examine his faults and deficiencies, to disclose them to him, and to inform him about them. He must receive someone who guides him to any of his faults with joy and cordiality, and he must show him delight and pleasure for what

أَطْلَعَهُ عَلَيْهِ. بَلِ المُسْتَحْسَنُ مِنْهُ أَنْ يُجِيزَ الَّذِي يُوقِفُهُ عَلَى عُيُوبِهِ أَكْثَرَ مِمَّا يُجِيزُ
المَادِحَ عَلَى المَدْحِ والثَّنَاءِ الجَمِيلِ، ويَشْكُرَ مَنْ يُنَبِّهُهُ عَلَى نَقْصِهِ، ويَتَحَمَّلَ لَوْمَتَه عَلَى
فِعْلِهِ. فإِنَّهُ إِذَا لَزِمَ هَذِهِ الطَّرِيقَةَ، وعُرِفَ بِهَا، يُسْرِعُ أَصْحَابُهُ وخَوَاصُّهُ إِلَى تَنْبِيهِهِ عَلَى p. 163
عُيُوبِهِ. وإِذَا نُبِّهَ عَلَى مَا فِيهِ مِنَ النَّقْصِ، أَنِفَ مِنْهُ، واسْتَشْعَرَ أَنَّ أُولَئِكَ سَيُعَيِّرُونَهُ
بِهِ، ويُصَغِّرُونَهُ مِنْ أَجْلِهِ. فَيَلْزَمُهُ حِينَئِذٍ أَنْ يَأْخُذَ نَفْسَهُ بِالتَّنَزُّهِ مِنَ العُيُوبِ، ويَقْهَرَهَا
عَلَى التَخَلُّصِ مِنْ دَنَسِهَا.

25. فَإِذَا فَعَلَ ذَلِكَ، وتَوَفَّرَ عَلَى اقْتِنَاءِ الفَضَائِلِ، وأَلْزَمَ نَفْسَهُ التَّخَلُّقَ
بِالمَحَاسِنِ، ولَمْ يَرْضَ مِنْ مَنْقَبَةٍ إِلاَّ بِغَايَتِهَا، ولَمْ يَقِفْ عِنْدَ فَضِيلَةٍ إِلاَّ وطَلَبَ الزِّيَادَةَ
عَلَيْهَا، وَاجْتَهَدَ فِيمَا يُحْسِنُ سِيَاسَةَ نَفْسِهِ عَاجِلاً، ويُبْقِي لَهُ الذِّكْرَ الجَمِيلَ آجِلاً، لَمْ p. 164
يَلْبَثْ أَنْ يَبْلُغَ الغَايَةَ مِنَ التَّمَامِ، ويَرْتَقِيَ إِلَى النِّهَايَةِ مِنَ الكَمَالِ، فَيَحُوزَ السَّعَادَةَ الإِنْسَانِيَّةَ،
والرِّئَاسَةَ الحَقِيقِيَّةَ؛ ويَبْقَى لَهُ حُسْنُ الثَّنَاءِ مُؤَبَّداً، وجَمِيلُ الذِّكْرِ مُخَلَّداً.

[خَاتِمَةُ الكِتَاب]

26. فَقَدْ أَتَيْنَا عَلَى صِفَةِ الإِنْسَانِ التَّامِّ، الجَامِعِ لِمَحَاسِنِ الأَخْلاقِ؛ والطَّرِيقَةِ
الَّتِي تُؤَدِّيهِ إِلَى هَذِهِ الرُّتْبَةِ، وتَحْفَظُ عَلَيْهِ هَذِهِ المَنْزِلَةَ. وقَدَّمْنَا مَا يَجِبُ تَقْدِيمُهُ مِنْ
سِيَاسَةِ الأَخْلاقِ وتَهْذِيبِ النُفُوسِ. فَمَا أَوْلَى مَنْ نَظَرَ فِي هَذَا القَوْلِ وتَصَفَّحَهُ، وفَهِمَ p. 165
مَضْمُونَهُ وتَدَبَّرَهُ، أَنْ يَأْخُذَ عَلَى نَفْسِهِ بِاسْتِعْمَالِ مَا بَيْنَ فُصُولِهِ، ويَسُوسَ أَخْلاقَهُ

he has disclosed to him. Even better than that would be for him to give more privilege to someone who notifies him of his faults than he gives to an encomiast for glorifying him and giving him praise. He should thank anyone who informs him of his deficiency and tolerate his criticism of his actions. If he persists in this practice and becomes known for it, his associates and his favorites will be quick to notify him of his faults. And, when he has been notified of some deficiency in himself, he will show disdain for it. He will realize that those people will reproach him for it, and they will belittle him because of it. And so it will behoove him then to engage himself in getting free of faults and to force his soul to become free from their defilement.

25. If he does this and spares no trouble to acquire the virtues, if he obliges his soul to be formed by doing good deeds and then rests content only with the highest degree of good qualities, if he does not stand still with a virtue but seeks to grow in it, and exerts every effort to improve his conduct in this life and to leave behind him a good reputation hereafter, then he will not be long in achieving the apogee of fulfillment and in advancing to the utmost of perfection. And so he will attain human happiness and authentic aristocracy. Great renown will be his, as well as a good reputation forever.

Conclusion of the text

26. We have now completed the description of the perfect man who comprises the good moral qualities, as well as the description of the way that conducts him to this rank and maintains him on this level. We prefaced it with what must come first in terms of the governance of the moral qualities and the reformation of souls. So it now well behooves anyone who looks into this discussion, studies it, understands its purport, and thinks about it to engage himself in putting into practice what is in its several sections. It behooves him to conduct his moral life

بِالتَّطَرُّقِ إلَى الّذِي فُنِّنَ في تَضَاعِيفِهِ، ويَجْتَهِدَ كلَّ الاجْتِهَادِ في تَكْمِيلِ نَفْسِهِ، ويَسْتَفْرِغَ غَايَةَ الوُسْعِ في طَلَبِ تَمَامِهِ. فَمَا أَقْبَحَ النَّقْصَ بِالقَادِرِ عَلَى التَّمَامِ، والعَجْزَ مِنْ المُسْتَعِدِّ لِنَيْلِ الكَمَالِ.

27. وهَذَا حِينَ نَخْتِمُ القَوْلَ في تَهْذِيبِ الأَخْلاقِ. والمَجْدُ لِوَاهِبِ العَقْلِ دَائِماً أَبَداً. آمِينْ.

in such a way as to gain access to what is set out in its contents, to make every effort to perfect himself, and to exert himself to the utmost of his capacity in seeking his fulfillment. How repugnant is deficiency in someone with the potential for perfection, and weakness on the part of someone well prepared to attain fulfillment!

27. This is the point at which we conclude the discussion on the reformation of morals. Praised be the One who endows the intellect always and forever. Amen.

Bibliography

Abel, Armand. *Abū ᶜĪsā Muḥammad b. Hārūn al-Warrāq, Le livre pour la réfutation des trois sectes chrétiennes.* Bruxelles: Mimeo, 1949.

Abrahamov, Binyamin. *Islamic Theology: Traditionalism and Rationalism.* Edinburgh: Edinburgh University Press, 1998.

Arkoun, Mohammed. *L'humanisme arabe au IVᵉ/Xᵉ siècle: Miskawayh, philosophe et historien.* 2d ed. Études musulmanes 12. Paris: Vrin, 1982.

———, trans. *Miskawayh (320/21–420), Traité d'éthique.* 2d ed. Damas: Institut Français de Damas, 1988.

Barṣaum, Mar Severius Afram. "Jaḥjā ibn ᶜAdī's Treatise on Character Training." *American Journal of Semitic Languages and Literature* 45 (1928): 1–129.

Braun, Oskar. "Briefe des Katholikos Timotheos I." *Oriens christianus* 2 (1902): 1–32.

Brock, Sebastian P. "The 'Nestorian' Church: A Lamentable Misnomer." *Bulletin of the John Rylands University Library of Manchester* 78 (1996): 23–35.

———. "The Syriac Commentary Tradition." Pages 3–18 in *Glosses and Commentaries on Aristotelian Logical Texts: The Syriac, Arabic and Medieval Latin Traditions.* Edited by Charles Burnett. London: Warburg Institute, 1993.

———. "Two Letters of the Patriarch Timothy from the Late Eighth Century on Translations from Greek." *Arabic Sciences and Philosophy* 9 (1999): 233–46.

Brown, H. V. B. "Avicenna and the Christian Philosophers in Baghdad." Pages 35–48 in *Islamic Philosophy and the Classical Tradition: Essays Presented by His Friends and Pupils to Richard Walzer on His Seventieth Birthday.* Edited by S. M. Stern, Albert H. Hourani, and Vivian Brown. Columbia: University of South Carolina Press, 1972.

Colpe, Carsten. "Anpassung des Manichäismus an den Islam (Abū ᶜĪsā al-Warrāq)." *Zeitschrift der deutschen morgenländischen Gesellschaft* 109 (1959): 82–91.

Dodge, Bayard, ed. and trans. *The Fihrist of al-Nadīm: A Tenth-Century Survey of Muslim Culture.* 2 vols. New York: Columbia University Press, 1970.

Druart, Thérèse-Anne. "Al-Fārābī, Ethics, and First Intelligibles." *Documenti e studi sulla tradizione filosofica medievale* 8 (1997): 403–23.

———. "Al-Kindi's Ethics." *Review of Metaphysics* 47 (1993): 329–57.

———. "The Ethics of al-Razi (865–925?)." *Medieval Philosophy and Theology* 6 (1997): 47–71.

———. "Philosophical Consolation in Christianity and Islam: Boethius and al-Kindi." *Topoi* 19 (2000): 25–34.

———. "La philosophie morale arabe et l'antiquité tardive." *Bulletin d'études orientales de l'Institut Français de Damas* 48 (1996): 183–87.

Endress, Gerhard. "The Debate between Arabic Grammar and Greek Logic in Classical Islamic Thought." *Journal for the History of Arabic Science* [Aleppo] 1 (1977): 320–23, 339–51.

———. "The Defense of Reason: The Plea for Philosophy in the Religious Community." *Zeitschrift für Geschichte der arabisch-islamischen Wissenschaften* 6 (1990): 1–49.

———. "Grammatik und Logik: Arabische Philologie und griechische Philosophie im Widerstreit." Pages 163–299 in *Sprachphilosophie in Antike und Mittelalter.* Edited by Burkhard Mojsisch. Bochumer Studien zur Philosophie 3. Amsterdam: Gruner, 1986.

———. *The Works of Yaḥyā ibn ᶜAdī: An Analytical Inventory.* Wiesbaden: Dr. Ludwig Reichert Verlag, 1977.

———. "Yaḥyā ibn ᶜAdī: Maqāla fī tabyīn al-faṣl bayna ṣināᶜat al-manṭiq al-falsafī wa al-naḥw al-ᶜarabī." *Journal for the History of Arabic Science* [Aleppo] 2 (1978): 181–93.

Ess, Josef van. *Theologie und Gesellschaft im 2. und 3. Jahrhundert Hidschra: Eine Geschichte des religiösen Denkens im frühen Islam.* 6 vols. Berlin: de Gruyter, 1991–97.

Fakhry, Majid. "Aspects de la pensée morale de Yaḥyā ibn ᶜAdī." *Annales de philosophie de l'Université Saint-Joseph* 6 (1985): 121–30.

———. *A History of Islamic Philosophy.* 2d ed. Studies in Oriental Culture 5. New York: Columbia University Press, 1983.

Fiey, J. M. "Tagrît: Esquisse d'histoire chrétienne." *L'Orient syrien* 8 (1963): 289–342. Repr. in *Communautés syriaques en Iran et Irak dès origines à 1552.* Variorum Reprints Collected Studies Series 106. London: Variorum Reprints, 1979.

Frank, Richard M. *Beings and Their Attributes: The Teaching of the Basrian School of the Muᶜtazila in the Classical Period.* Albany: State University of New York Press, 1978.

———. "Reason and Revealed Law: A Sample of Parallels and Divergences in Kalâm and Falsafa." Pages 123–38 in *Recherches d'Islamologie: Recueil d'articles offerts à G. Anawati et L. Gardet par leurs collègues et amis.* Bibliothèque philosophique de Louvain 26. Louvain: Peeters, 1977.

———. "The Science of Kalām." *Arabic Sciences and Philosophy* 2 (1992): 9–37.

Graf, Georg. *Geschichte der christlichen arabischen Literatur.* 5 vols. Studi e testi 118, 133, 146, 147, 172. Vatican City: Biblioteca Apostolica Vaticana, 1944–53.

———. *Die Philosophie und Gotteslehre des Jaḥjâ ibn ʿAdî und späterer Autoren: Skizzen nach meist ungedruckten Quellen.* Münster: Aschendorffschen Buchhandlung, 1910.

———. *Die Schriften des Jacobiten Ḥabīb ibn Ḫidma Abū Rāʾiṭa.* Corpus scriptorum christianorum orientalium 130–31. Louvain: Peeters, 1951.

Griffith, Sidney H. "The Apologetic Treatise of Nonnus of Nisibis." *ARAM* 3 (1991): 115–38.

———. *The Beginnings of Christian Theology in Arabic: Muslim-Christian Encounters in the Early Islamic Period.* Variorum Reprints Collected Studies Series 746. Aldershot, Eng.: Ashgate, 2002.

———. " 'Melkites', 'Jacobites' and the Christological Controversies in Arabic in Third/Ninth-Century Syria." Pages 9–55 in *Syrian Christians under Islam: The First Thousand Years.* Edited by David Thomas. Leiden: Brill, 2001.

———. "The Muslim Philosopher al-Kindi and His Christian Readers: Three Arab Christian Texts on 'The Dissipation of Sorrows.' " *Bulletin of the John Rylands University Library of Manchester* 78 (1996): 111–27.

———. "Reflections on the Biography of Theodore Abū Qurrah." *Parole de l'Orient* 18 (1993): 143–70.

Gutas, Dimitri. *Avicenna and the Aristotelian Tradition.* Leiden: Brill, 1988.

———. *Greek Thought, Arabic Culture: The Graeco-Arabic Translation Movement in Baghdad and Early ʿAbbasid Society (2nd–4th/8th–10th Centuries).* London: Routledge, 1998.

———. "Paul the Persian on the Classification of the Parts of Aristotle's Philosophy: A Milestone between Alexandria and Bagdad." *Der Islam* 60 (1983): 231–67.

Haddad, Cyrille. *ʿIsa ibn Zurʿa: Philosophe arabe et apologiste chrétien.* Beirut: Dar al-Kalima, 1971.

Hadot, Pierre. *Philosophy as a Way of Life.* Oxford: Blackwell, 1995.

Hatem, Jad. "Fī ʾanna al-malika lā yastaṭīʿu anna yakūna insānan tāmman." *Al-Machriq* 66 (1992): 161–77.

———. "Que le roi ne peut être un homme parfait selon Yāḥyā ibn ʿAdī." *Annales de philosophie de l'Université Saint-Joseph* 6 (1985): 89–104.

Holmberg, Bo. "Notes on a Treatise on the Unity and Trinity of God Attributed to Yaḥyā ibn ʿAdī." Pages 235–45 in *Actes du deuxième congrès international d'études arabes chrétiennes (Oosterhesselen, septembre 1984).* Edited by Khalil Samir [Samir Khalil Samir]. Orientalia christiana analecta 226. Rome: Pont. Institutum Studiorum Orientalium, 1986.

Hugonnard-Roche, Henri. "L'intermédiaire syriaque dans la transmission de la philosophie grecque à l'arabe: Le cas de l'*Organon* d'Aristote." *Arabic Sciences and Philosophy* 1 (1991): 187–209.

———. "Notes sur Sergius de Rešʿainā, traducteur du grec en syriaque et commentateur d'Aristote." Pages 121–43 in *The Ancient Tradition in Christian and Islamic Hellenism.* Edited by Gerhard Endress and Remke Kruk. CNWS Publications 50. Leiden: Research School CNWS, 1997.

———. "Les traductions du grec au syriaque et du syriaque à l'arabe (à propos de l'*Organon* d'Aristote)." Pages 131–47 in *Rencontres de cultures dans la philosophie médiévale: Traductions et traducteurs de l'antiquité tardive au XIVe siècle*. Edited by Jacqueline Hamesse and Marta Fattori. Louvain-la-Neuve: Université Catholique de Louvain, 1990.

Ibn Abī Uṣaybiʿah, Aḥmad ibn al-Qāsim. *Kitab ʿuyūn al-anbaʾ fī ṭabaqāt al-aṭibbāʾ*. Edited by August Müller. 2 vols. Cairo & Köningsberg: n.p., 1882–84.

Keating, Sandra Toenies. "Dialogue between Muslims and Christians in the Early 9th Century: The Example of Ḥabīb ibn Khidmah Abū Rāʾiṭah al-Takrītī's Theology of the Trinity." Ph.D. diss., The Catholic University of America, 2001.

Khalil, Samir [Samir Khalil Samir]. "Nouveaux renseignements sur le *Tahḏīb al-aḫlāq* de Yaḥyā ibn ʿAdī et sur le 'Taymūr aḫlāq 290.'" *Arabica* 26 (1979): 158–78.

———. "Yaḥyā ibn ʿAdī (893–974)." *Bulletin d'arabe chrétien* 3 (1979): 45–63.

Kraemer, Joel L. *Humanism in the Renaissance of Islam: The Cultural Revival during the Buyid Age*. Leiden: Brill, 1986.

Kraus, Paul, ed. *Kitāb al-akhlāq li-Gālīnūs*. Majallat kulliyat al-adāb 5. Dirāsāt fī tāʾrīkh al-tarjama fī al-islām 1. Cairo: Fuad I University, 1937.

Kussaim, Samir Khalil [Samir Khalil Samir]. *Yaḥyā ibn ʿAdī (893–974): Tahdhīb al-aḫlāq*. Beirut: CEDRAC, 1994.

Landron, Bénédicte. "Les chrétiens arabes et les disciplines philosophiques." *Proche-Orient chrétien* 36 (1986): 23–45.

———. *Chrétiens et musulmans en Irak: Attitudes nestoriennes vis-à-vis de l'Islam*. Études chrétiennes arabes. Paris: Cariscript, 1994.

Madelung, Wilferd. "Abū ʿĪsā al-Warrāq über die Bardesaniten, Marcioniten und Kantäer." Pages 210–24 in *Studien zur Geschichte und Kultur des Vorderen Orients: Festschrift für Berthold Spuler*. Edited by Hans R. Roemer and Albrecht Noth. Leiden: Brill, 1981. Repr. in *Religious Schools and Sects in Medieval Islam*. Variorum Reprints Collected Studies Series 213. London: Variorum Reprints, 1985.

Mahdi, Muhsin S. *Alfarabi and the Foundation of Islamic Political Philosophy*. Chicago: University of Chicago Press, 2001.

———. "Language and Logic in Classical Islam." Pages 51–83 in *Logic in Classical Islamic Culture*. Edited by G. E. von Grunebaum. Wiesbaden: Harrassowitz, 1970.

Margoliouth, D. S. "The Discussion between Abū Bishr Mattā and Abū Saʿīd al-Sīrāfī." *Journal of the Royal Asiatic Society* (1905): 79–129.

Massignon, Louis. "La politique islamo-chrétienne des scribes nestoriens de Deir Qunna à la cour de Bagdad au IXe siècle de notre ère." *Vivre et penser* 2 (1942): 7–14. Repr. pages 250–57 in vol. 1 of *Opera Minora*. Edited by Youakim Moubarac. 3 vols. Beirut: Dar al-Maaref, 1963.

Mattock, J. N. "A Translation of the Arabic Epitome of Galen's Book Περὶ Ἠθῶν." Pages 235–60 in *Islamic Philosophy and the Classical Tradition:*

Essays Presented by His Friends and Pupils to Richard Walzer on His Seventieth Birthday. Edited by S. M. Stern, Albert H. Hourani, and Vivian Brown. Columbia: University of South Carolina Press, 1972.

Mistrih, Vincent. "Traité sur la continence de Yaḥyā ibn ᶜAdī, édition critique." *Studia orientalia christiana. Collectanea* 16 (1981): 1–137.

Mottahedeh, Roy. *Loyalty and Leadership in an Early Islamic Society*. Rev. ed. London: Tauris, 2001.

Netton, Ian Richard. *Al-Fārābī and His School*. Richmond, Eng.: Curzon, 1992.

Périer, Augustin. "Un traité de Yahyâ ben ᶜAdî: Défense du dogme de la trinité contre les objections d'al-Kindî." *Revue de l'Orient chrétien*, 3d ser., 2 (1920–21): 3–21.

———. *Yaḥyā ben ᶜAdî: Un philosophe arabe chrétien du Xᵉ siècle*. Paris: Gabalda & Geuthner, 1920.

Peters, F. E. *Aristotle and the Arabs: The Aristotelian Tradition in Islam*. New York: New York University Press, 1968.

———. *Greek Philosophical Terms: A Historical Lexicon*. New York: New York University Press, 1967.

Pines, Shlomo. "La 'philosophie orientale' d'Avicenne et sa polémique contre les Bagdadiens." *Archives d'histoire doctrinale et littéraire du moyen-âge* 27 (1952): 5–37.

Pines, Shlomo, and Michael Schwarz. "Yaḥyā ibn ᶜAdī's Refutation of the Doctrine of Acquisition *(iktisāb)*." Pages 49–94 in *Studia orientalia memoriae D. H. Baneth dedicata*. Jerusalem: Magnes Press, Hebrew University of Jerusalem, 1979.

Platti, Emilio. *Abū ᶜĪsā al-Warrāq, Yaḥyā ibn ᶜAdī: De l'incarnation*. Corpus scriptorum christianorum orientalium 490–91. Louvain: Peeters, 1987.

———. "Une compilation théologique de Yaḥyā ibn ᶜAdī par al-Ṣafī ibn al-ᶜAssāl." *Mélanges de l'Institut Dominicain d'Études Orientales du Caire* 13 (1977): 291–303.

———. "Une cosmologie chrétienne." *Mélanges de l'Institut Dominicain d'Études Orientales du Caire* 15 (1982): 75–118.

———. "Deux manuscrits théologiques de Yaḥyā b. ᶜAdī." *Mélanges de l'Institut Dominicain d'Études Orientales du Caire* 12 (1974): 217–29.

———. "La doctrine des chrétiens d'après Abū ᶜĪsā al-Warrāq dans son traité sur la Trinité." *Mélanges de l'Institut Dominicain d'Études Orientales du Caire* 20 (1991): 7–30.

———. *La grande polémique antinestorienne (et la discussion avec Muhammad al-Misri)*. Corpus scriptorum christianorum orientalium 427–28. Louvain: Peeters, 1981.

———. "Intellect et révélation chez Ibn ᶜAdī: Lecture d'une page d'un petit traité." Pages 229–34 in *Actes du deuxième congrès international d'études arabes chrétiennes (Oosterhesselen, septembre 1984)*. Edited by Khalil Samir [Samir Khalil Samir]. Orientalia christiana analecta 226. Rome: Pont. Institutum Studiorum Orientalium, 1986.

———. "Les objections de Abū ᶜĪsā al-Warrāq concernant l'incarnation et les réponses de Yaḥyā ibn ᶜAdī." *Quaderni di studi arabi* 5–6 (1987–88): 661–66.

———. "Yaḥyā b. ᶜAdī and His Refutation of al-Warrāq's Treatise on the Trinity in Relation to His Other Works." Pages 172–91 in *Christian Arabic Apologetics during the Abbasid Period (750–1258)*. Edited by Samir Khalil Samir and Jørgen S. Nielsen. Studies in the History of Religions 63. Leiden: Brill, 1994.

———. "Yahyā b. ᶜAdī, philosophe et théologien." *Mélanges de l'Institut Dominicain d'Études Orientales du Caire* 14 (1980): 167–84.

———. *Yaḥyā ibn ᶜAdī, théologien chrétien et philosophe arabe: Sa théologie de l'Incarnation.* Orientalia lovaniensia analecta 14. Leuven: Katholieke Universiteit Leuven, Departement Oriëntalistiek, 1983.

Rissanen, Seppo. *Theological Encounter of Oriental Christians with Islam during Early Abbasid Rule.* Åbo: Åbo Akademi University Press, 1993.

Rosenthal, Franz. *The Classical Heritage in Islam.* London: Routledge & Kegan Paul, 1975.

Saliba, George. "Competition and the Transmission of the Foreign Sciences: Ḥunayn at the Abbasid Court." *Bulletin of the Royal Institute for Inter-Faith Studies* 2 (2000): 85–101.

Samir, Khalil [Samir Khalil Samir]. "Rôle des chrétiens dans les renaissances arabes." *Annales de philosophie de l'Université Saint-Joseph* 6 (1985): 1–31.

———. "Le *Tahḏīb al-aḫlāq* de Yaḥyā b. ᶜAdī (m. 974) attribué à Ǧāḥiẓ et à Ibn al-ᶜArabī." *Arabica* 21 (1974): 111–38.

———. *Le traité de l'unité de Yaḥyā ibn ᶜAdī (893–974): Étude et édition critique.* Patrimoine arabe chrétien. Jounieh, Lebanon: Librairie St. Paul, 1980.

al-Takriti, Naji. *Yaḥyā ibn ᶜAdī: A Critical Edition and Study of His* Tahdhīb al-akhlāq. Beirut: Oueidat, 1978.

Thomas, David. "Abū ᶜĪsā al-Warrāq and the History of Religions." *Journal of Semitic Studies* 41 (1996): 275–90.

———. *Anti-Christian Polemic in Early Islam: Abū ᶜĪsā al-Warrāq's "Against the Trinity."* University of Cambridge Oriental Publications 45. Cambridge: Cambridge University Press, 1992.

Thomson, Robert W. "*Vardapet* in the Early Armenian Church." *Muséon* 75 (1962): 367–82.

Troupeau, Gérard. "Quelle était la *nisba* de Yaḥyā ibn ᶜAdī?" *Arabica* 41 (1994): 416–18.

Urvoy, Dominique. *Les penseurs libres dans l'Islam classique.* Paris: Albin Michel, 1996.

Urvoy, Marie-Thérèse. *Traité d'éthique d'Abû Zakariyyâ᾽ Yahyâ Ibn ᶜAdi: Introduction, texte et traduction.* Études chrétiennes arabes. Paris: Cariscript, 1991.

van Roey, Albert. *Nonnus de Nisibe, Traité apologétique: Étude, texte et traduction.* Bibliothèque du Muséon 21. Louvain: Peeters, 1948.

Walzer, Richard. "Akhlāk." Pages 325–39 in vol. 1 of *The Encyclopaedia of Islam: New Edition.* Edited by H. A. R. Gibb et al. 10 vols. to date. Leiden: Brill, 1960–.

Yousif, Ephrem-Isa. *Les philosophes et traducteurs syriaques: D'Athènes à Bagdad.* Paris: Harmattan, 1997.

Zurayk, Constantine K. *Tahdhīb al-akhlāq li Abi ʿAlī Aḥmad ibn Muḥammad Miskawayh.* Beirut: American University of Beirut, 1966.

———, trans. *Miskawayh, The Refinement of Character.* Beirut: American University of Beirut, 1968.

Index

About the Translator

SIDNEY H. GRIFFITH is Professor of Semitic Languages at The Catholic University of America in Washington, D.C. He received his Licentiate in Theology and Ph.D. from The Catholic University of America, specializing in Syriac and Medieval Arabic. Professor Griffith is past president of both the Byzantine Studies Conference and the North American Patristics Society. He has been a fellow at the Institute for Advanced Studies, the Hebrew University of Jerusalem, and the Dumbarton Oaks Center for Byzantine Studies, and since 1986 has served as a member of the Catholic Delegation to the Eastern Orthodox/Roman Catholic Consultation. Professor Griffith has published widely in the areas of Syriac and Arabic Christianity. He recently served as coeditor of *The Blackwell Dictionary of Eastern Christianity* and is translator of *A Treatise on the Veneration of the Holy Icons by Theodore Abū Qurrah, Bishop of Harrān (c. 755–c. 830 A.D.).*

A Note on the Type

The English text of this book was set in BASKERVILLE, a typeface originally designed by John Baskerville (1706–1775), a British stonecutter, letter designer, typefounder, and printer. The Baskerville type is considered to be one of the first "transitional" faces—a deliberate move away from the "old style" of the Continental humanist printer. Its rounded letterforms presented a greater differentiation of thick and thin strokes, the serifs on the lowercase letters were more nearly horizontal, and the stress was nearer the vertical—all of which would later influence the "modern" style undertaken by Bodoni and Didot in the 1790s. Because of its high readability, particularly in long texts, the type was subsequently copied by all major typefoundries. (The original punches and matrices still survive today at Cambridge University Press.) This adaptation, designed by the Compugraphic Corporation in the 1960s, is a notable departure from other versions of the Baskerville typeface by its overall typographic evenness and lightness in color. To enhance its range, supplemental diacritics and ligatures were created by Jonathan Saltzman in 1997 for the exclusive use of the Institute for the Study and Preservation of Ancient Religious Texts.

About the Series

The literature of Eastern Christianity is a rich and varied resource that is vital to many fields of religious and academic inquiry. Yet scholars and students are often deterred from its study by the lack of accessible and reliable texts and by the remoteness of the source languages. EASTERN CHRISTIAN TEXTS provides specialists and nonspecialists with contemporary English-language translations of seminal works paired with original-language texts. Each volume is produced to meet the highest academic and editorial standards and is elegantly designed to reflect the dignity of the tradition it represents.

EASTERN CHRISTIAN TEXTS is published by Brigham Young University Press and distributed through the University of Chicago Press.

http://meti.byu.edu/

◆